Child Psychotherapy and

Child Psychotherapy and Research brings together some of the most exciting and innovative research activity taking place within psychoanalytic child psychotherapy today.

Drawing on the expertise of an international range of contributors, this book describes work at the cutting edge of research in psychoanalytic child psychotherapy and related areas. It presents many of the emerging findings while also illustrating a whole range of methodologies – both quantitative and qualitative – that have been developed to investigate this field. The book examines the historical and philosophical background of child psychotherapy research and shows how research illuminates different clinical phenomena, the processes of psychotherapy, its evaluation and outcome.

Recent developments in therapeutic work with children, including the increased focus on evidence-based practice, make research a much higher priority in the field than ever before. With this increasing significance, a whole new generation of clinicians are required to become familiar and competent with research methods and research literature. *Child Psychotherapy and Research* will be a vital resource for anyone involved in research and training related to psychotherapy and child mental health, as well as of great interest to a range of mental health professionals.

Nick Midgley is a Child Psychotherapist and a Clinical Tutor at the Anna Freud Centre, London.

Jan Anderson has a lead role for research in Child Psychotherapy for the North Essex Partnership NHS Foundation Trust.

Eve Grainger is a Consultant Child and Adolescent Psychotherapist for the North-East London NHS Foundation Trust.

Tanja Nesic-Vuckovic is a Consultant Child Psychotherapist and Head of Service in South Essex Partnership NHS Trust and clinical director of the Pebbles Therapeutic Community.

Cathy Urwin is a Consultant Child Psychotherapist and Research Fellow at the Tavistock Clinic.

Child Psychotherapy and Research

New approaches, emerging findings

Edited by Nick Midgley,
Jan Anderson, Eve Grainger,
Tanja Nesic-Vuckovic and
Cathy Urwin

Routledge
Taylor & Francis Group

LONDON AND NEW YORK

First published 2009
by Routledge
27 Church Road, Hove, East Sussex BN3 3FA

Simultaneously published in the USA and Canada
by Routledge
270 Madison Avenue, New York NY 10016

*Routledge is an imprint of the Taylor & Francis Group,
an Informa business*

© 2009 selection and editorial matter, Nick Midgley, Jan Anderson,
Eve Grainger, Tanja Nesic-Vuckovic and Cathy Urwin;
individual chapters, the contributors

Reprinted 2010

Typeset in Times by
RefineCatch Limited, Bungay, Suffolk
Printed and bound in Great Britain by
the MPG Books Group, Bodmin and King's Lynn
Paperback cover design by Sandra Heath

This publication has been produced with paper
manufactured to strict environmental standards
and with pulp derived from sustainable forests.

British Library Cataloguing in Publication Data
A catalogue record for this book is available from the British Library

Library of Congress Cataloging-in-Publication Data
Child psychotherapy and research : new approaches, emerging
findings / edited by Nick Midgley . . . [et al.].
    p. cm.
  Includes bibliographical references and index.
  1. Child analysis—Research.   2. Child psychotherapy—
Research.   I. Midgley, Nick, 1968–
  [DNLM: 1. Child.   2. Psychotherapy—methods.   3. Child
Psychiatry—methods.   4. Child Psychology—methods.
  WS 350.2 C53632 2009]
  RJ504.2.C485 2009
  618.92′89140072—dc22   2008027319

ISBN: 978-0-415-42202-4 (hbk)
ISBN: 978-0-415-42203-1 (pbk)

Contents

Contributors

Anne Alvarez PhD, MACP is an Honorary Consultant Child and Adolescent Psychotherapist and a retired co-convener of the Autism Service, Tavistock Clinic. In 2005 she was Visiting Professor, at the San Francisco Psychoanalytic Society. Her publications include *Live Company: Psychotherapy with Autistic, Borderline, Deprived and Abused Children.*

Janet Anderson has a lead role for research in Child Psychotherapy for the North Essex Partnership NHS Foundation Trust. Building on her experience of doctoral research, using grounded theory, she is actively involved in the development of further research projects.

Kay Asquith is Course Tutor for two developmental MSc programmes at the Anna Freud Centre/University College London and has a history of research work with adopted families. She worked on the first phase of the Attachments in Adoption Study at the Centre and has taken part in the development and evaluation of a parenting skills programme for adoptive families.

Mary Boston, now retired, worked as a Consultant Child Psychotherapist at Great Ormond Street Children's Hospital and the Tavistock Clinic. She is the co-editor of two books, *The Child Psychotherapist and Problems of Young People* and *Psychotherapy with Severely Deprived Children.*

Gunnar Carlberg PhD is an Associate Professor and Director of the Erica Foundation in Stockholm, Sweden. A licensed psychologist and psychotherapist, he has published various studies, e.g., in psychodynamic developmental psychology and child psychotherapy research. He is project leader of the Erica Process and Outcome Study (EPOS).

Peter Fonagy PhD, FBA is Freud Memorial Professor of Psychoanalysis and Director of the Sub-Department of Clinical Health Psychology at University College London and Chief Executive of the Anna Freud Centre, London.

Eve Grainger is a Consultant Child and Adolescent Psychotherapist in the

Borough of Barking and Dagenham. She has been Joint London Regional Advisor for child psychotherapy since 1990, and was Lead Clinician for her local CAMHS Service from 2002 until 2005.

Saul Hillman MSc is a Research Psychologist at the Anna Freud Centre involved with the design, data collection, coding and analysis of the adoption research study at the Centre. He is currently coordinating and delivering Story Stem trainings while undertaking a PhD.

Jill Hodges is a Consultant Child Psychotherapist at the Department of Psychological Medicine, Great Ormond Street Hospital, London, and an Honorary Senior Lecturer in the Behavioural Sciences Unit, Institute of Child Health, London. In her research she has studied adoption and the impact of early adversity on later development.

Ilan Joffe is a Consultant Child and Adolescent Psychiatrist based in Hemel Hempstead, Hertfordshire. His areas of research interest include the treatment of depression in children and adolescents, eating disorders in adolescents and ethnicity factors in relation to childhood mental health.

Jeanne Kaniuk has been the Head of the Coram Adoption Service since 1980. Coram specializes in placing older children who have suffered adversity, and the agency has developed programmes to support these families and children in the longer term.

Anthony Lee was formerly a research psychologist in the field of developmental psychopathology. He trained as a Child and Adolescent Psychotherapist at the Tavistock Clinic where he now works as part of the autism service's multidisciplinary team.

Dora Lush, now retired, worked as a Consultant Child Psychotherapist in the Child Guidance Training Centre at the Tavistock Clinic.

Linda C. Mayes is the Arnold Gesell Professor of Child Psychiatry, Pediatrics and Psychology in the Yale Child Study Center, Special Advisor to the Dean in the School of Medicine, and a member of the directorial team of the Anna Freud Centre in London.

Nicholas Midgley is a Child and Adolescent Psychotherapist and Head of Programme for Children and Young People at University College London/ the Anna Freud Centre.

George Moran was a Child and Adult Psychoanalyst and Director of the Anna Freud Centre, London, from 1987 until his early death in 1992.

Tanja Nesic-Vuckovic is a Consultant Child Psychotherapist and Head of Service in South Essex Partnership NHS Trust and clinical director of the Pebbles Therapeutic Community.

Janet Philps is the Senior Child and Adolescent Psychotherapist at the Milton Keynes Specialist CAMHS in the Milton Keynes Primary Care Trust. She was a teacher and supervisor at the Tavistock Clinic for a number of years.

Anna Pruetzel-Thomas completed an MSc in Psychoanalytic Developmental Psychology at the Anna Freud Centre/University College London in 2006. Since then she has worked at the Anna Freud Centre and in the NHS.

Maria Rhode is Professor of Child Psychotherapy at the Tavistock Clinic/University of East London, a member of the Association of Child Psychotherapists and of the Tavistock Society of Psychotherapists, and co-editor of three books on childhood psychosis and autism.

Michael Rustin is Professor of Sociology at the University of East London and Visiting Professor at the Tavistock Clinic. He is an Honorary Affiliate Member of the British Psychoanalytical Society. His books include *The Good Society and the Inner World*.

Abby Schachter is a Clinical Psychologist working in private practice. She received a PhD from University College London in 2005. Research interests include the long-term outcome of childhood psychotherapy, attachment, and attitudes toward seeking psychological help. She is affiliated with the Anna Freud Centre, London, and the Tel-Aviv University Psychology Department, Israel.

Celeste Schneider PhD is a Clinical Psychologist working with children, adolescents and adults in private practice. She is an Associate Professor at Saint Mary's College School of Education in California and a psychoanalytic candidate at the San Francisco Center for Psychoanalysis.

Miriam Steele, formerly of the Anna Freud Centre, London, is currently Associate Professor of Clinical Psychology at the New School for Social Research in New York. Her interests focus on intergenerational patterns of attachment in a range of clinical contexts including adoption, foster care, and family preservation.

Mary Target PhD is a Clinical Psychologist and Psychoanalyst. She does research on the outcomes of child psychotherapies and lifespan development, emphasizing attachment and mentalization. She runs an MSc in psychoanalytic theory at University College London where she holds a Readership, is Professional Director of the Anna Freud Centre and has a half-time psychoanalytic practice.

Prakash K. Thomas MD is a lecturer in child and adolescent psychiatry at the Yale Child Study Center and has a private practice in New Haven, Connecticut.

Judith Trowell is a Child and Adult Psychoanalyst, an Honorary Consultant Psychiatrist at the Tavistock Clinic and the West Midlands NIMHE/CSIP Professor of Child Mental Health. She has done extensive clinical work, training, and research, and also works as an expert witness in the family courts.

Cathy Urwin is a Consultant Child Psychotherapist and Research Fellow at the Tavistock Clinic. She is co-author of *Changing the Subject: Psychology, social regulation and subjectivity* (Methuen 1984, republished Routledge 1998) and the author of numerous articles and papers in developmental psychology and in child psychotherapy.

Figures

Tables

BOX

Preface

There are many reasons to turn to an inspiring, multifaceted book by clinicians who conduct research into child psychotherapy.

To begin with, of course, children's psychological well-being is hugely important. Indeed, it is so important, that many of us are inclined to divert our eyes from the prevalence of misery, distress, unmanageable emotion, and unrewarding behaviour among children, as well as to underestimate the extent of the poverty, deprivation and abuse that many children have to face. Researchers are committed to addressing such matters directly, through measurement and systematic description. In so doing, they make it that much more difficult for any of us to marginalize uncomfortable facts of many children's lives. They help us to face truths we would rather not see.

Then there is the brighter side of the picture. It is not simply that we need to identify the sources and implications of childhood psychological disorder. Thankfully, we have opportunities to intervene to make things better. Research evidence is a vital force in changing social policy, both directly in its input to political decisions that concern public health, and indirectly through its effects on public opinion. When disseminated effectively, it can affect societal attitudes to the upbringing of children, as well as the provision of care for those who are disadvantaged or troubled.

If these rather abstract reflections appear to advocate research to do with children's plight in general, what relevance do they have for child psychotherapy rather than for, say, child psychiatry?

Child psychotherapy has a special place, and a special value, within the broader range of research on the psychopathology and treatment of troubled children. One reason is that child psychotherapists have an unremitting concern with how children experience others, how they experience themselves, and how they experience the world in which they live. Where much (not all) of the practice of child psychiatry is somewhat distanced from intensive, long-term involvement with particular children by the pull toward medical objectivity and nosological clarity (although when it comes to childhood disorders, 'clarity' is perhaps a charitable term), child psychotherapists expose themselves to the full force of children's emotional turmoil.

Child psychotherapy is about creating conditions in which a therapist is able to move toward a child or family (or in the case of group psychotherapy, children) in such a way as to register the emotional impact of disturbing, sometimes alarming, sometimes despairing experiences. The rationale is that to register, contain and understand such experiences – and to convey that understanding in an appropriate form – is to provide something that is not merely humane and deeply valuable in itself, but also a means to promote the children's mental integration and to foster trust and hope. One far-reaching effect is to enhance children's potential for new forms of involvement with others.

It is a special virtue of this book that the central importance of children's experience, and the vital role played in treatment by the emotional availability and interpersonal understanding of child psychotherapists, permeate every chapter. Here are professionals intent on pursuing new ways to capture and study what some scientists would relegate to the 'merely subjective'. What these investigators' work demonstrates is that science may yet tap into realms of interpersonal and intrapsychic functioning that might have seemed too personal (and deep) for its reach. The range of facts that science cannot ignore is being extended, and what counts as science is being transformed in the process.

Of course, there are grounds for scepticism about the potential benefits of child psychotherapy for fostering mental health *in general*. So another role of research is to explore just when, in what circumstances, and for whom, child psychotherapy 'works'. Can it really make troubled children better, in respects that matter? Some of the research presented here is designed to address facets of this deceptively simple question.

Yet research in child psychotherapy entails much more than evaluating the effectiveness of a particular intervention. Yes, there needs to be public, replicable evidence for the benefits of any treatment for vulnerable people, and especially children. In addition, however, there are profound scientific challenges in specifying, measuring and making manifest the developmental processes that are at work to influence emotional development, for good or ill. Child psychotherapy research promises to reveal much, not only about the mechanisms of change in psychotherapy itself, but also about processes that play a pivotal role in the enhancement of resilience and mental growth in contexts of adversity or disability, as well as in the pathogenesis of psychological disorder.

The power of child psychotherapy lies in the disciplined therapeutic attitude and practice that it involves. The practice not merely allows but also demands that the psychotherapist follows and strives to understand the detailed, moment-by-moment, session-by-session movements of feeling and relatedness between child and therapist. This devoted attentiveness affords a unique perspective on the nature of human mental functioning – or more simply expressed, how children tick – and in particular, the relation between what happens (and develops) within a child's mind, and what happens (and develops) within relationships.

Clinical experience, like everyday experience, is that interpersonal understanding and relationships can promote integration and well-being, and lack of understanding and disturbed relationships can promote psychological disintegration and ill-health. What child psychotherapists achieve beyond the insights of everyday experience is a profound analysis of what happens to make this so, and what is needed to harness the therapeutic power of relationships. What research needs to offer – and what this book offers – are creative ways of capturing relevant aspects of the things that child psychotherapists do and observe, and/or what child psychotherapists have discerned to be important in and beyond the consulting room, in such a way as to make these amenable to public awareness and subject to scientific evaluation.

Given that a research design appropriate to examine one issue may be totally inappropriate for another, no wonder that the present book on child psychotherapy research displays a rainbow of methodological approaches. Here we find methods to track changes in individual cases in psychotherapy, approaches to studying the effects of treatment for different groups of troubled children, and strategies to distil simple, tractable indices of complex intrapsychic and relational processes. For this reason (among others), we can be grateful for an excellent introduction and summary overviews of each of the major sections of the book. The diversity of the book's contributions attests to the fact that psychotherapy research does not need to be reductionist in scientific method, nor monolithic in conception. In helping us to understand the potential scope of research into psychoanalytically informed aspects of child development as well as childhood psychopathology, and to be sensitive to the needs of children in general as well to those who are disturbed or disabled, this book has immense value.

Peter Hobson

Introduction

Cathy Urwin, Jan Anderson, Eve Grainger,
Nick Midgley and Tanja Nesic-Vuckovic

What is child psychotherapy?

In 1900 a revolutionary step was taken in the understanding of the mind when Sigmund Freud put forward a model that integrated emotional life and mental processes. This was as relevant to so-called normal people as to those who were more emotionally troubled. In this model the capacity for symbol formation, particularly through the use of verbal language, was crucial. Freud had originally seen the power of putting previously forgotten, socially undesirable or sanctioned thoughts into words in releasing the patient from the grip of disabling states of mind. To what was initially called 'the talking cure' (Breuer & Freud 1893), Freud added an equally important emphasis on the work of dreaming, 'the royal road to the unconscious'. Freud saw dreams both as revealing the workings of the mind and as the means through which the mind represents its motivations and experiences to itself, as conflicts and frustrations are worked through in the relative safety of sleep (Freud 1900).

But how and when do such processes begin? Unlike adults, young children do not report their dreams very much, might lack language and have limited means of expressing themselves verbally. Nevertheless, they use play to express their wishes and preoccupations. In many respects such play functions as a vehicle for working through fantasies, frustrations and reactions to anxiety-provoking situations, comparable to the function of dreaming in adults. Children also express themselves through actions, facial expressions, bodily movement and non-verbal communication, as well as through the effects they induce in other people. Arguably, behavioural disturbance might also be a way in which they draw attention to emotional disturbance or distress.

Child psychotherapy is a specialized treatment for children and young people with emotional, social and/or behavioural difficulties. Its central assumption is that it is possible, and may be helpful, to communicate with internal, emotional and imaginative parts of ourselves that are particularly active in childhood but which remain influential throughout our lives, even if we are not always aware of them. Originating in the interwar years, child psychotherapy's development was catalysed by the social concerns that led to the emergence of the child guidance movement in the United States in the 1920s and by the belief in the value of play influencing education at this time. It drew its theoretical base from the theory and practice of psychoanalysis or dynamic psychology. By the post-war years, psychotherapy with children had rapidly developed as a discipline in its own right. Pioneers of child psychotherapy include the child psychoanalysts Anna Freud, Melanie Klein, and Donald Winnicott, and also the child psychiatrist and paediatrician Margaret Lowenfeld, whose primary influence was not psychoanalysis but dynamic psychology, a movement in psychiatry influenced by Freud's thinking that proved effective in treating shellshock after the First World War.

It was, in fact, Lowenfeld who established the first child psychotherapy training in the 1930s in London (Urwin & Hood-Williams 1986). Her emphasis was primarily on the value of play and processes inherent in the child for working through conflicts and traumatic experiences through the creation of imagery and symbols. Initially, her approach did not stress the role of early social–emotional relationships and how the effects of these might be manifested in the child–therapist relationship. But during the Second World War, groups of child analysts and psychoanalytically informed paediatricians, social workers and educationalists in the UK became concerned about the effects of evacuation on children's emotional well-being, and particularly the effects of separating young children from their parents. Evacuation drew the nation's attention to the health needs of many of its poorest children; it also raised awareness of children's emotional lives and the need for staff training.

Public sympathy with the idea of emotional as well as physical health was one factor that led John Bowlby to argue the need for child psychotherapy within the National Health Service in the UK when it was established in 1948. Initially the number of practising child psychotherapists was relatively small and largely based around London. Nevertheless it was sufficient for the formation of a professional body, the Association of Child Psychotherapy, and for establishing trainings at what became the Tavistock Centre, London, and the Hampstead Child Therapy Clinic (later the Anna Freud Centre), also in London. Whilst a training that Margaret Lowenfeld founded at the Institute of Psychology eventually closed in the early 1970s, new trainings followed, notably the Jungian training at the Society for Analytical Psychology (SAP), where the theoretical ideas of Michael Fordham were particularly important, and at the British Association of Psychotherapy (BAP). More recently, although the trainings at the Anna Freud Centre and the SAP have ceased, there are now trainings in the North of England, Birmingham and Scotland, and further developments are planned. These trainings are regulated by the same professional body and have provided models for trainings in other countries. Although there are differences in theoretical orientation, there is sufficient consensus to establish training requirements and broad agreement about fundamental parameters for working with children therapeutically (Horne & Lanyado 1999).

Central to the child psychotherapist's approach is establishing what is called the 'setting' for child psychotherapy. The psychotherapist aims to provide a consistent and predictable context such that the child feels safe enough to explore difficult or uncomfortable issues as they emerge within the therapeutic relationship, such as fear of abandonment, hostility to parents or siblings, feelings of rejection, disappointment, terror or guilt. To facilitate this, the child is seen by the same therapist at regular times and in the same room, and has his or her own personal set of play equipment and toys. This consistency provides a predictable context, in some respects separable from the outside world, that allows the child to express, test out or discover emotional experiences as they are invoked in the relationship with the therapist. It also allows for the possibility of developing a sense of security and trust, which in some cases may have been absent from the child's experience prior to entering therapy. As Emanuel (2006) has pointed out, many children seen in treatment have had such traumatic experiences that they lack a basic emotional vocabulary and their mental functioning has been overwhelmed or shattered. Such children first have to be able to talk about *what* has happened before they can begin to understand *how* it might have happened. This process can only occur in the context of a relationship with a receptive person. Hopefully, the exploration of the child's experiences, in a largely child-led process, appropriate to the child's level, contributes to a modification of internal relationships, and a processing of emotional experience so that it becomes available for thinking. These internal changes allow relationships in the outside world to become more adaptive and the child to be freer to benefit from learning opportunities.

The contemporary context of child psychotherapy

Since its inception, the province and status of child psychotherapy has grown considerably. An emphasis on team work has always been strong, particularly in the public sector in the UK, where child psychotherapists work as members of a core profession within Child and Adolescent Mental Health Services (CAMHS) in teams with other professionals, such as child psychiatrists, psychologists, social workers, family therapists and nurse specialists. In addition to individual work with children and adolescents, child psychotherapists often undertake parent and family work, group work, and work with mothers and infants (Waggett 2007). They usually provide consultation and supervision for colleagues from other disciplines, and undertake assessments for members of the multidisciplinary team, for Social Services and for the Courts. The basic principles that guide these applications are derived from the discipline's understanding of development and interpersonal dynamics.

However, the need for working familiarity with – and preferably some expertise in – other newly emergent psychological approaches is emphasized.

Children seen in individual psychotherapy may well be amongst the most disturbed children seen within CAMHS (Rance 2003). Family complexity means that several agencies are often involved. Co-morbidity is typically high; that is, the child may be suffering from multiple problems and displaying a range of difficulties. In such cases, good multidisciplinary working and interagency cooperation in which communication lines are well-established is of paramount importance.

But contextual complexity, presenting problems and underlying psychopathology are not the only factors affecting the child psychotherapist's role. Whatever context they may be working in, child psychotherapists will inevitably be affected by changes in policy and legislation surrounding children's welfare. In the UK, particularly important is the National Service Framework for Children, which establishes the importance of consulting with patients and service users and the principle of informed patient choice (Department of Health (DoH) 2004). This itself presupposes that all interventions should be evidence based. Economic considerations also dictate that models of best practice include considerations of value for money. Comparable pressures to ensure vigilance in matters of child protection and welfare and to provide an adequate evidence base are felt internationally. Economic drivers apply in both the public sector, where evidence is used to support funding treatment resources, and in the private sector, where insurance companies require best evidence to justify funding a particular treatment (Leuzinger-Bohleber & Target 2002). Parents themselves increasingly have access to research and other findings about treatment benefits through the internet and clinicians are under pressure to take this into account.

Alongside these changing demands and external pressures, however, child psychotherapists have themselves become increasingly interested in developing ways of investigating their practice more systematically and in developing models of best practice to ensure the optimum use of child psychotherapy as a treatment resource.

The evaluation challenges of child psychotherapy

Until recently, there has been a marked tension between child psychotherapy and mainstream empirical research. Researchers may regard child psychotherapy as subjective and untestable; practitioners may doubt how far the child psychotherapy process can fit with traditional research models, and whether they can capture child psychotherapy's value, both clinically and in enriching understanding of children's emotional development and how the mind develops. However, as Desmarais (2007) has pointed out, historically there have been different models of the relationship between psychoanalysis and science, each of which is underpinned by different epistemological assumptions, or assumptions about truth. From these epistemological assumptions different methodological implications follow.

For psychoanalysis, the methods of traditional experimental science pose particularly severe challenges. Traditional scientific research models generally require techniques that cannot easily be applied to child psychotherapy practice. For example, the randomized controlled trial (RCT) is typically regarded as the 'gold standard' of outcome research, because this method allows one to be most certain about a causal relation between a particular intervention and its effects. This method requires carefully matching populations and assigning individuals randomly to treatment, or to no treatment or to treatment-as-usual groups. Comparisons in rates of change are made between the groups and any difference between them indicates that the change is a result of the treatment rather than other factors. However, like adult psychotherapy, as an intervention child psychotherapy is seldom orientated to tight goals. In addition, traditional experimental research models often presume a homogeneity in the presenting problems of populations receiving treatment that does not fit with the diversity of children, families, presenting problems and circumstances seen in both the private and public sectors (Rustin 2000, Kam & Midgley 2006). Furthermore, the RCT method requires large samples of cases and considerable funding. This is not commensurate with the fact that, given the time-consuming nature of child psychotherapy, an individual psychotherapist in a particular service will be limited in how many treatments can be undertaken at any one time. Funding bodies may therefore be unwilling to invest in such research. This problem is not insurmountable (it can be addressed through multisite research projects, for example). However, it requires ingenuity in research design and contributes to the relative difficulty in creating the conditions for evaluating short and long-term effects of child psychotherapy. Other, more fundamental, criticisms of RCTs point to the difficulty of generalizing appropriately from group results to complex individual cases (Hollway 2001).

These kinds of difficulties may appear to put in question the possibility of scientific rigour within child psychotherapy and to prohibit designing tests of child psychotherapy's effectiveness that are practicable, scientifically rigorous and clinically valid. As Fonagy has pointed out (see Chapter 1), this may lead to the erroneous but too-often-presented argument that such difficulties reflect weaknesses in the psychotherapy method rather than in available research methodologies. Alternatively, proponents point to the richness of child psychotherapy's theoretical base and its capacity to evaluate itself and evolve within the treatment context. As Rustin argues (see Chapter 2), the diversity of cases that child psychotherapists' treat successfully, often after other methods have reached a ceiling on progress, is demonstrably increasing. From this position, the challenge is to provide research methods that do justice to complex developmental processes in ways that will enrich theory and understanding, with implications for practice and technique.

Despite the apparent divide, over the last ten years dialogue between child psychotherapists and mainstream academic researchers has begun to increase. On the one hand, the growing external pressures have encouraged child psychotherapists to be more courageous in offering their work for scrutiny. On the other hand, innovatory steps have been taken by child psychotherapists themselves, contributing to a number of developments in research design. Child psychotherapy trainings, too, have recently been transformed into doctoral programmes, with research dissertations as required outcomes. These changes have themselves been greatly aided by the burgeoning of innovative methodologies and qualitative approaches in the social sciences, which have much to offer research into both psychotherapy process and psychotherapy outcome. To assess the relevance of these approaches it is necessary to explore their conceptual and philosophical underpinnings, after first examining how child psychotherapy traditionally evaluates and consolidates its knowledge base.

The evidence base generated by the child psychotherapy process

Freud's own view of the nature of psychoanalytic evidence can be summarized in his famous insistence on psychoanalysis constituting a special case within science owing to an 'inseparable bond between cure and research'; the patient's progress towards recovery is evidence of the theoretical presupposition that the cure demonstrates (Freud 1927, Midgley 2006a). In psychoanalysis, the regularity and constancy of the setting provides a built-in basis for evaluating and checking the validity of the findings, the consulting room acting as a kind of 'laboratory' (Rustin 2002). According to Freud, if the psychotherapist's interpretations are true, valid or useful, then the patients' responses will confirm this. If the interpretation effectively makes contact with the patient's unconscious, that is, it is what Strachey (1934) called 'mutative', then new material will be revealed, new defences drawn upon, or in other ways the process will be moved forward, ultimately towards reducing the patient's difficulties. It is in this sense that the method and its 'cure' test the truth of the theories on which the method depends.

These principles also apply to children's responsiveness in child psychotherapy. However, where Strachey's account focused on the adult neurotic patient, child psychotherapy may involve very young, preverbal, learning disabled and/or highly traumatized children for whom a major task is to bring them to the position of wanting to engage with or socialize with others, or to where verbal interpretation of processes unavailable to consciousness begins to be possible. This work involves increasing the communicative potential of the child and has become a major component of child psychotherapy. It has been influenced by infant and young child observation, by Anna Freud's theoretical concept of 'developmental help' (Hurry 1998) and by developmental applications of Bion's (1962) theory of communication and containment (Alvarez 1992). Here the validity of the underlying theory will be supported by developmental changes in the patient such as increased capacity for thinking or reflection, for imagination and play.

Although these developments have occurred since Freud's time, even within his own lifetime there were those who challenged Freud's belief that the case history ensures scientific rigor as misplaced (Guntrip 1968). Freud's insistence on the self-reflexive capacity of the discipline to test its fundamental propositions did not satisfy the rigorous demands of the positivist philosophy of the twentieth century, as both Popper (1963) and Grunbaum (1984) argued. Popper went so far as to suggest that true science proceeds on the basis of disconfirming hypotheses rather than through confirming them, which for him meant that psychoanalysis could not be evaluated scientifically. For Popper, psychoanalysis was additionally weakened by its limited ability to generalize its findings outside the consulting room.

By contrast, the social scientist Thomas Kuhn (1962) argued for a notion of scientific 'paradigms' through which working assumptions, theories and methods frame a research tradition, defining appropriate questions and methods; in this view theories are not overturned by disconfirming evidence, but through the development of new theoretical models with greater explanatory power. In the 1970s it became widespread within the philosophy of science to assume that different sciences have their own specific, theoretical, methodological approaches and truth criteria, rather than a unified understanding of what science is, does or should be (Leuzinger-Bohleber & Target 2002).

These developments were particularly evident within sociology, beginning in the United States and paralleled in the European context, by the growth of the hermeneutic tradition concerned with interpretation and meaning and their relation to human interests (see Desmarais 2007). These traditions have in common an emphasis on the rule-governed nature of human behaviour, and on the power of description and its constitutive effects. More recently, the poststructuralist movement has emphasized the need to deconstruct and go beyond the systems of classification and interpretation that regulate human action, emphasizing that the creation of specialized knowledge will inevitably involve relations of power (Foucault 1977). This is a particular version of a wider argument that science is never value free. It highlights how research involving children's mental health and the role of parents must contend with constitutive and potentially alienating effects of promoting particular views of what counts as 'normal'.

There are philosophical and epistemological positions underlying the research traditions outlined above. Crudely speaking, they reflect a contrast between 'realist' positions on the one hand (which hold that reality is 'out there' waiting to be measured) and 'constructivist' and 'hermeneutic' positions (which argue that all reality is in some ways constructed) on the other. They are associated with different kinds of methodologies. The realist position is associated with the hypothetico-deductive methods of natural science, with the aim of balancing explanatory parsimony against reducing the number of possible explanatory variables. By contrast, constructivist and hermeneutic approaches favour qualitative methodologies such as open-ended interviewing, and analytic procedures for uncovering meanings and rule structures. These methods include grounded theory, and discourse, phenomenological, narrative and hermeneutic analyses, all developed in the social sciences over the last thirty years or so (Smith 2003). Crucially, the traditions differ on what constitutes and might be taken as adequate evidence for truth. If the first tradition aims at proof that will close doors that lead to blind allies, the second aims to open them and to increase explanatory power, conviction being based on a different logic of explanation.

Arguably in this debate psychoanalysis can actually be located within each methodological and philosophical tradition, with Freud himself providing evidence through several different trajectories (Midgley 2006b). On the one hand, like the discourse theorists of today, Freud admitted that the effectiveness of his accounts had to do with the 'ring true' quality of a good detective story, thus sharing something fundamental with narrative processes in literature. While Freud could thus be described as a forerunner of hermeneutics, in his famous insistence on 'the inseparable bond between cure and research' he put forward a version of constructivism that accepts that an object of study like the mind can only be known through instruments – with one of the most important of these instruments being the mind itself. On the other hand, Freud insisted on the biological basis of the work, apparently adopting a realist position seen most obviously in his early *Project for a Scientific Psychology* (Freud 1895). Here he put forward a conceptualization for a functional, evolutionary biology in which brain structures and cultural universals would both find a place. Today, psychoanalysts collaborating with neuroscience researchers are actively developing such a trajectory (e.g. Solms & Turnbull 2002).

Commentators often write as if, over his lifetime, Freud consecutively replaced one viewpoint or philosophical position with another, as if he had found the first position wanting. More accurately, Freud's earlier views did not necessarily disappear. Freud repeatedly shifted from one vertex to another, as if to check the validity of one position against other views. Freud assumed – with the realists – the importance of material reality, even if ultimately unknowable, as Bion (1962) argued. Freud's three-cornered approach, or capacity to view his work from contrasting perspectives, enables him to avoid sliding between the dangers of reductionism on the one hand and relativism on the other, associated with the extremes of realism and constructivism respectively.

How does this bear on the evidence base for child psychotherapy? In the current political and economic climate, the term 'evidence-based' practice

often means an exclusive reliance on the findings from outcome research –
and in particular the kind of outcome research, such as the RCT, that is
prioritized by organizations such as the National Institute of Health and
Clinical Excellence (NICE). This special authority is responsible for publishing clinical appraisals of whether particular treatments should be considered
worthwhile by the NHS in England and Wales. Cost-effectiveness is weighted
heavily in this process. Any form of treatment that wishes to remain part
of publicly funded services must clearly respond to this pressure. The enor-
mous challenges in carrying out this kind of outcome research for modalities
such as child psychotherapy would make an increasing recognition of the
need for more pragmatic RCT models reflecting the realities of child patient
populations particularly welcome. Furthermore, the overriding importance
of such research in the public domain does not mean that this is the only true
way in which psychotherapy can engage with research that benefits patients,
improves practice and develops understanding. Desmarais (2007) has pointed
out that accepting any particular view on the relationship between psychoanalysis and science will inevitably bring both gains and limitations, because
the viewpoints tend to define themselves in opposition to each other. More
useful may be the attempt to articulate the strengths and limitations of
each tradition, making way for a pluralistic research programme. This raises
the question: Under what conditions does one decide the relative benefit of
one stance over another? As Midgley (2004) has pointed out, the child psychotherapist's task in identifying do-able research and choosing appropriate
methodology can be like trying to negotiate between Scylla and Charybdis;
plumping for one kind of methodology will inevitably bring restrictions as
well as gains. Midgley advocates defining the purposes of the investigation
and asking to whom the argument will eventually be addressed. Making
a strong case for an expansion of psychotherapy services, for example, may
require quantitative results and research methods designed to produce them.
Research designed to find out more about the psychopathology of a small
number of children in particular circumstances may require qualitative
methodologies that can lead to practical arguments and recommendations
relevant to particular cases.

Summary and outline

The spirit of this book is to support a pluralistic and pragmatic research
agenda. This introduction has aimed to establish a context for research that
encompasses, in particular, thinking about child psychotherapy's effectiveness, its processes and its contribution to knowledge. We have stressed the
ongoing impact of the psychoanalytic tradition on the child psychotherapy
discipline. But we have also highlighted the changing context in which child
psychotherapy is practised. The discipline's multifaceted lineage is crucial to
understanding the complexity of its epistemological base, the pressures that

make an increase in research activity imperative, and the potential gains that this may bring.

We have described how different views of the relationship between psychoanalysis and science contribute to favouring explanations based on causes on the one hand, and on reasons and meanings on the other. These different philosophical and epistemological positions underpin different methodological traditions. This tension is often enacted through a debate over the relative methods of quantitative and qualitative methodologies. Our aim here is not to arbitrate between these positions but to illustrate the scope of different approaches in relation to the different kinds of research questions in the context of different areas of human need. Our general belief is that, as in the psychoanalytic tradition that Freud founded, not only is a variety of approaches necessary to do justice to this complex and evolving field but that moving from one methodological vertex to another may be essential for the intellectual growth of child psychotherapy.

Such a variety of approaches is illustrated by the various chapters of this book, which brings together some of the most exciting and innovative work in the field to illustrate this creative diversity and to provide useful models. The studies described are psychoanalytic and reflect work from a range of backgrounds representing the different major theoretical traditions. We have not included non-psychoanalytic child psychotherapy here because, although it is a growing field, our aim is to highlight the considerations that must be addressed if research is to do justice to the distinctiveness of the psychoanalytic approach. A comprehensive, systematic review of evidence on child psychotherapy outcomes and a thematic review of the full range of child psychotherapy research can be found in Kennedy (2004) and Kennedy and Midgley (2007). Here, the papers are organized into four parts, each with an introduction that provides a context for the chapters that follow.

Part 1 takes further the philosophical, theoretical and political issues that are raised in this introduction. The views expressed in the two chapters highlight how contrasting positions on the relationship between child psychotherapy and scientific endeavour have quite different implications for research priorities and for how research is to be undertaken. Nevertheless, these chapters share a commitment to the importance of research in raising public awareness of child psychotherapy's field of practice, the evidence for its effectiveness and its potential contribution to knowledge.

Respect for the nature of the therapeutic process as it occurs in the consulting room is of central concern in *Part 2*. This presents psychotherapy process research, a research area that includes studies that try to understand how change may come about for a particular child or group of patients. The variety in the kinds of tools that can be used to explore the interaction between therapist and child is illustrated here – from an intricate, thematic analysis of the progress of an individual child to the use of standardized instruments that facilitate across-group comparisons. Different epistemological assumptions underlie these approaches, but each may be valuable in addressing the wider question of *how* child psychotherapy works.

It is increasingly recognized that more understanding of the process of change is an important step in designing larger scale projects for evaluating the clinical effectiveness of child psychotherapy and demonstrating outcomes. *Part 3* concerns evaluation and outcome. It presents examples of different kinds of approaches to the task of examining whether child psychotherapy has produced significant and meaningful changes for the child and for the child-in-the-family. Together, these chapters show the importance of recognizing the different points of view from which questions of the value of child psychotherapy intervention can be addressed.

Finally, *Part 4* illustrates ways in which child psychotherapy research gains from interacting or collaborating with other disciplines or frames of reference, such as developmental psychology, neuroscience and sociology. The productive tension generated through such work on the borders with other disciplines is proving to be generative for child psychotherapists' practice, as well as opening up the relevance of their work to a wider multidisciplinary community. It also reflects the complex, multidisciplinary nature of the knowledge embodied within child psychotherapy as a profession.

Among the many new chapters included in this book, we have also chosen to republish a few classic studies exemplifying pioneering work, as indicated in the section introductions where applicable. By and large, we have focused on research involving children receiving or who have received psychotherapy, or studies exploring the nature of the child psychotherapy process itself, rather than its many applications. Exceptions are a chapter on neuroscience and an account of the use of Story Stems, one of the most widely used standardized methods for gaining information about children's internal worlds. There are many examples of psychotherapy research and the applications of psychotherapy that we have not been able to include, including, for example, work on adolescence, with under-5s and parent–infant psychotherapy (see Kennedy & Midgley, 2007, for a more thorough review). This book represents a selection of pioneering studies that we hope will mark a milestone in establishing a pluralistic research endeavour for child psychotherapy.

References

Alvarez, A. (1992) *Live company*. London: Routledge.

Bion, W. (1962) *Learning from experience*. London: Heinemann.

Breuer, J. & Freud, S. (1893–5) *Studies in hysteria*. Standard edition, vol. 2. London: Hogarth.

Department of Health (DoH) (2004) *National Service Framework for Children, Young People and Maternity Services*. London: DoH.

Desmarais, S. (2007) Hard science, thin air and unexpected guests: A pluralistic model of rationality, knowledge and conjecture in child psychotherapy research. *Journal of Child Psychotherapy, 33*(3), 203–307.

Emanuel, R. (2006) Child and adolescent psychotherapy. In S. Bloch (ed.) *An intro-duction to the psychotherapies* 4th edn. Oxford: Oxford University Press.

Foucault, M. (1977) *Discipline and punish*. London: Allan Lane.

Freud, S. (1895) *Project for a scientific psychology*. Standard edition, vol. 1, p. 175. London: Hogarth.

Freud, S. (1900) *The interpretation of dreams*. Standard edition, vol. 4–5. London: Hogarth.

Freud, S. (1927) *The question of lay analysis*. Standard edition, vol. 20, pp. 179–258. London: Hogarth.

Grunbaum, A. (1984) *The foundations of personality: A philosophical critique*. Berkeley: University of California Press.

Guntrip, H. (1968) *Personality structure and human interaction*. London: Hogarth.

Hollway, W. (2001) The psycho-social subject in 'evidence-based practice'. *Journal of Social Work Practice*, *15*(1), 9–22.

Horne, A., Lanyado, M. (1999) *Handbook of child psychotherapy*. London: Routledge.

Hurry, A. (ed.) (1998) *Psychoanalysis and developmental therapy*. London: Karnac.

Kam, S., Midgley, N. (2006) Exploring 'clinical judgement': How do child and ado-lescent mental health professionals decide whether a young person needs individual psychotherapy? *Clinical Child Psychology and Psychiatry*, *11*(1), 27–44.

Kennedy, E. (2004) *Child and adolescent psychotherapy: A systematic review of psycho-analytic approaches*. London: North Central London Strategic Health Authority.

Kennedy, E., Midgley, N. (2007) *Process and outcome research in child, adolescent and parent-infant psychotherapy: A thematic review*. London: North Central London Strategic Health Authority.

Kuhn, T. (1962) *The structure of scientific revolutions*. Chicago: University of Chicago Press.

Leuzinger-Bohleber, M., Target, M. (eds) (2002) *Outcomes of psychoanalytic treat-ment: Perspectives for therapists and researchers*. London: Whurr.

Midgley, N. (2004) Sailing between Scylla and Charybdis: Incorporating qualitative approaches into child psychotherapy research. *Journal of Child Psychotherapy*, *30*(1), 89–111.

Midgley, N. (2006a) The 'inseparable bond between cure and research': Clinical case study as a method of psychoanalytic inquiry. *Journal of Child Psychotherapy*, *32*(2), 122–147.

Midgley, N. (2006b) Psychoanalysis and qualitative psychology: Complementary or competing paradigms? *Qualitative Research in Psychology*, *3*(3), 213–232.

Popper, K. (1963) *Conjectures and refutations*. London: Routledge.

Rance, S. (2003) Report on the survey of ACP members about the Outcome Study. Part II: Summary of therapist activity and child data. *Bulletin of the Association of Child Psychotherapists*, *133*, 25–32.

Rustin, M.E. (2000) What follows breakdowns? Assessing children who have experi-enced deprivation, trauma and multiple loss. In M.E. Rustin and E. Quagliata (eds) *Assessment in child psychotherapy* (pp. 74–94). London: Duckworth.

Rustin, M. (2002) *Reason and unreason: Psychoanalysis, science and politics*. London: Continuum Books.

Smith, J.A. (ed.) (2003) *Qualitative psychology*. London: Sage.

Solms, M., Turnbull, O. (2002) *The brain and the inner world: An introduction to the neuroscience of subjective experience*. London: Karnac.

Strachey, J. (1934) The nature of the therapeutic action of psychoanalysis. *International Journal of Psychoanalysis, 15*, 127–129.

Urwin, C., Hood-Williams, J. (eds) (1986) *Child psychotherapy, war and the normal child: Selected papers of Margaret Lowenfeld.* London: Free Association Books.

Waggett, N. (2007) *New ways of working.* Leeds: Northern School Publication.

Part I

What is child psychotherapy research?

Introduction

The title of this book, 'Child Psychotherapy and Research', might suggest a fairly straightforward connection between two distinct, but well-defined fields. In fact, this is far from the case. Not only is *child psychotherapy*, even within the psychoanalytic tradition, made up of a range of concepts and clinical practices; but the term *research* also covers a number of quite different activities, each based on quite distinct philosophical and methodological assumptions. Finding an appropriate methodology for research in psychoanalytic child psychotherapy, sustained by cogent theory from the philosophy of science, has been a challenge identified by Mary Boston almost twenty years ago (Boston 1989), and has been the topic of lively debate among child psychotherapists themselves in recent years (e.g. Midgley 2004, 2006, Anderson 2006, Desmarais 2007).

The first part of this book, therefore, aims to highlight some of the complex issues that are raised when we ask 'what do we mean by "child psychotherapy research"?' While the scientific community has often been preoccupied with the question of whether psychoanalytic concepts can be tested in a suitably rigorous and scientific way, clinicians have often been more concerned about whether the approaches taken to investigating psychotherapy can truly capture the complexity of the work, or whether they will distort what is important in the very act of studying it.

But gradually the discussion has become more sophisticated, so we can now talk about a range of approaches to doing psychotherapy research, informed by different models of science and with different scientific and political aims. Desmarais (2007) identifies five broad ways in which the relationship between psychoanalysis and research has been configured, from extreme forms of empiricism to radical hermeneutic approaches. Although Desmarais' paper implies a pluralistic model of child psychotherapy research, tensions and debates about the nature of the research process in child psychotherapy and which approaches are more valid or important remain.

The two chapters in this part of the book present two very different, but influential, views about the nature of research in child psychotherapy. Peter Fonagy, a clinical psychologist and psychoanalyst, argues for the integration of child psychotherapy research with mainstream research methods in psychology. He sees a fault line that runs between experimental psychology and psychoanalysis and calls for more communication across this divide. Fonagy urges the child psychotherapy profession to develop a unified model of the mind and argues that cross-fertilization with other research traditions, such as developmental neuroscience, can help child psychotherapy to put its own findings on a firmer footing.

Michael Rustin, a social scientist with a deep interest in psychoanalysis, puts forward the view, well illustrated by the work of the post-Kleinian schools, that research in child psychotherapy has been taking place since its inception. He argues that this clinical research process, carried out singly or as part of clinical-case workshops, has led to the development of valuable clinical concepts and theories as clinicians struggle, individually and collectively, to find ways of understanding the complex situations that they face in their clinical practice.

Both Peter Fonagy and Michael Rustin are aware of the need to take psychoanalytic findings beyond the consulting room to the wider community, and while they share this aim they offer contrasting views about the best way to do this, each with its own merits and limitations. The development of the understanding of the mind calls on the mental capacity to hold conflicting and contradictory aspects of a situation in view simultaneously. In presenting these two chapters we hope that readers will draw on this capacity in themselves in order to appreciate the value of multiple perspectives in what is a very complex field.

References

Anderson, J. (2006) Well-suited partners: Psychoanalytic research and grounded theory. *Journal of Child Psychotherapy*, *32*(3), 329–348.

Boston, M. (1989) In search of a methodology for evaluating psychoanalytic psychotherapy with children. *Journal of Child Psychotherapy*, *15*(1), 15–46.

Desmarais, S. (2007) Hard science, thin air and unexpected guests: A pluralistic model of rationality, knowledge and conjecture in child psychotherapy research. *Journal of Child Psychotherapy*, *33*(3), 283–307.

Midgley, N. (2004) Sailing between Scylla and Charybdis: Incorporating qualitative approaches into child psychotherapy research, *Journal of Child Psychotherapy*, *30*(1), 89–111.

Midgley, N. (2006) The 'inseparable bond between cure and research': Clinical case study as a method of psychoanalytic inquiry. *Journal of Child Psychotherapy*, *32*(2), 122–147.

Chapter 1

Research in child psychotherapy: Progress, problems and possibilities?

Peter Fonagy

Introduction

This chapter overviews the relationship between research and psychoanalytic child psychotherapy. It notes the complex attitudes that psychoanalysis adopts towards the systematic gathering of data, and will attempt to understand the partial lack of past interest in systematic empirical work related to child therapy in terms of the clinical rootedness of the discipline. This first part of the chapter touches briefly on epistemological issues that affect all professionals practising psychoanalytic psychotherapy or psychoanalysis, and considers various suggestions that have been advanced to address the epistemic problems inherent in psychoanalytic approaches. The second part of the chapter attempts to show how the conceptual challenges of modern psychodynamic thought may be at least partially addressed by extraclinical theory and research. The paper gives an example using evidence gathered from developmental psychopathology, in particular social cognition, which not only provides evidence that is at least consistent with many of the psychoanalytic model's assumptions but also helps to organize psychoanalytic thought in some ways. I point to some key issues regarding the communication of psychoanalytically informed ideas within the wider community. Finally, I turn briefly to the external validation of psychodynamic thought, and point to some difficulties involved in conducting empirical studies of the outcome of psychodynamic child psychotherapy.

The problem of child psychotherapy

Talking about research to psychotherapists can feel like selling deep freezes to Eskimos. Paul Whittle (Whittle 2000) has drawn attention to 'a fault line running down the middle of psychology'. There are two cultures with completely different attitudes to empirical research. On the one side there are those in experimental psychology, cognitive neuroscience, neurobiology, human development and other subspecialties of the 'science of the mind', who have embraced empirical research and benefit from a powerful, reasonably well-funded discipline that has progressed particularly rapidly over the last quarter of a century. This discipline prides itself on having a cumulative knowledge base that is strong enough both to generate a range of technologies and to interface with neighbouring disciplines, and it is generally acclaimed as a relatively successful natural science. On the opposite tectonic plate, Whittle argues, psychotherapists have historically restricted themselves to personal insight; that is, the objective study of subjectivity.

Whether understandings gleaned through psychotherapy can be considered 'true' depends on there being an accepted criterion for truth, but such a criterion has thus far eluded all students of the mind. In terms of personal accounts, most of us who have had substantial psychotherapeutic experiences can readily testify to moments of genuine recognition that have extended our understanding of ourselves, and which we would have little hesitation in labelling as 'truths'. It would be overly simplistic to define the fault-line as the boundary between science and non-science. Whereas psychotherapy is probably not a science, by most definitions of this term, the whole question of what is scientific is so fraught, subjective and ambiguous that entering into it here would only obscure the debate. The issue is not whether psychotherapy can be made scientific by changing our definition of science or the way we carry on our business. Far more important than a mere label, however prestigious, is whether the scope of research work undertaken by psychotherapists can be meaningfully extended without destroying the precious understandings that can be achieved through clinical work.

So, what is the nature of the fault or, perhaps preferably, where is the line between the two traditions in the study of mind? In psychotherapy, communication, whether in writing or clinical discourse, is judged by its *impact*. We accept that something has been understood when the discourse about it evokes a response. Elusiveness and ambiguity are not only permissible in the context of a psychotherapeutic process, they might also be critical to accurately depicting the complexity of a piece of human experience and its evolution. By contrast, the culture of systematic research, particularly that of experimental psychology, is governed by the principle of 'cognitive asceticism', as Whittle has termed it. From this perspective, interpretation and theoretical constructions are temptations to be resisted: a position can justifiably be maintained only if it is demonstrable. Given these constraints, it is not easy for empirical psychologists to account for subjective experience, and they have largely preferred to steer clear of attempting to provide such accounts until quite recently, when functional magnetic resonance imaging (fMRI) has brought subjective experience and demonstrable phenomena (brain activity) into close contact again (e.g. Eisenberger & Lieberman 2004, Pessiglione, Schmidt, Draganski, Kalisch, Lau, Dolan & Frith 2007).

But even here there remain incompatibilities between an approach that is essentially 'first person', concerned with individual subjective experience, and a third-person observation of neuronal states that represents the traditional neuroscience approach (Northoff, Bermpohl, Schoeneich & Boeker 2007). No wonder psychotherapists fear that the introduction of empirical research methods from this barren world risks the destruction of the phenomena they cherish. Cognitive asceticism is of little relevance to the clinician, whose principal task is to help patients create a narrative that fills the gaps in their understanding of themselves and how they have come to be the way they are. Theory has a heuristic value, supporting a clinician's understanding of particular cases. Historically, psychoanalytic theories have not been bound by the constraints of empirical research methodology. They can be seen as acts of imagination about how our minds function, which are judged principally according to how well they are felt to fit our own and our patients' subjective experience. This is not to say that the theories are not true; rather, they are best understood as metaphoric approximations at a subjective level of certain types of deeply unconscious internal experience. We should not accept simplistic critiques of metaphoric thought in psychoanalysis. As Eisenberg (1992), Rothbart (1997) and many others have noted, science uses metaphor in the absence of detailed knowledge of the underlying process. Provided that metaphor is not confused with a full understanding, or, to use Freud's metaphor, provided that the scaffolding is not mistaken for the building (Freud 1900 p. 536), heuristic considerations outweigh any disadvantages of their use.

However, the problem of psychotherapeutic theorizing is precisely one of heuristics (Fonagy 2003c). The very fecundity of clinically rooted concepts is beginning to threaten the clinical enterprise. Psychotherapists appear to take special pride in producing new theories, fresh elaborations based on the same data. There are currently over 500 distinct clinical approaches to psychological therapy for children (Kazdin 2004). It is hard to believe that all are necessary, or indeed that all are working on different and distinct principles. This has led to an (over) abundance of ideas in the field. What we do less well is to test these ideas in meaningful ways that might help eliminate some of these suggestions. Psychotherapists, like all of us, are vulnerable to uncritical acceptance of charismatically presented new ideas, which then come to be pooled in an eclectic purée of clinical strategies and techniques that create increasing problems in the transmission of psychoanalytic knowledge and skills. Conceptual research, as advocated by Dreher (2000), for example, which aims at the systematic clarification of psychoanalytic concepts, could be an answer. But, despite some brilliant attempts, for example, Sandler's (1987) examination of identification, projection and projective identification, I know of no example where a serious conceptual study has led to a generally accepted reconceptualization of any psychoanalytic construct. Sadly, the very complexity of extant theory also makes for a built-in resistance to the systematization of psychoanalytic knowledge, as those whose frame of reference depends on ambiguity and polymorphism can be threatened by scientifically based systematic clinical reasoning. In defence of this overly liberal epistemology, many fall back on the Freudian argument of 'the inseparable bond' between cure and research (Freud 1926 p. 256).

Psychotherapeutic practice, like all clinical endeavour, has well-established limitations as a form of research. The chief problem with using clinical experience as research is the well known one of induction (Wason & Johnson-Laird 1972). In our clinical activity we mostly tend to concentrate on confirming our theory-based expectations from our patient's material, and data is not the plural of anecdote. A physician practising internal medicine learns from clinical observations, but is not under the illusion that he or she is engaged in research. However, we are entitled to expect that the physician's work will be influenced by the results of research, and that his or her reasoning will have been disciplined by scientific training. Of psychoanalytic psychotherapy, it is fair to expect something comparable.

The difference in epistemic approach between psychoanalytic clinician and psychological researcher is largely explained by a distinction in the content of the enquiry. The clinical aims of psychotherapy, and its firm grounding in the context of personal relationships, inevitably push theory towards the deep understanding of mental contents, which can be construed as the key themes that underpin the patient's reported experiences, feelings and ideas. On the other side of the fault-line, the other sciences of mind such as experimental psychology and cognitive neuroscience are more concerned with mental processes, the way that the mind functions, and the machinery that gives rise to feelings and ideas. Each has its preferred focus. There are occasional attempts to stray into the other domain – social psychology often concerns itself with mapping norms and beliefs, whereas ego psychology attempted to generate a general psychology that anticipated cognitive science in many respects (e.g. Rapaport 1950). But the legitimate concern of psychotherapists that our theories should hold meaning not just for our patients and for other psychotherapists, but also for the broader social world, has led us to overlook the need to define the mechanisms of the psychological world/mental processes. Clinical observations cannot be replicated in the laboratory for a host of good reasons, but systematic observations can and should be used to inform us about the psychological processes underpinning clinical phenomena, which we currently use the metaphoric language of metapsychology to approximate.

The argument that psychotherapeutic observations concerning human behaviour are in some sense incommensurate with any other form of observation is untenable. The mind remains the mind whether it is in the consulting room or the laboratory (Fonagy 2003b). However, if integration of findings from other domains with psychotherapeutic observations is undertaken piecemeal, this leads us into the temptation to identify those sets of findings from neighbouring fields that best fit our preconceptions. Conceptual integration, like clinical work, is rarely truly without memory or desire (Bion 1967). Contrary to the suggestion that closer proximity to neighbouring sciences may be damaging to psychotherapy, a strong case can be made (see e.g. Kandel 1998) that the rich insights from psychotherapy can be strengthened by closer integration with biological psychology and psychiatry if this is undertaken in a rigorous and systematic manner. The most powerful domain of relevance is that of neuroscience and recent reviews bear out its value to psychotherapy practice and research (Fonagy 2004). Psychotherapy, as repeatedly pointed out by leaders in the field (e.g. Cooper, Kernberg, Schafer & Viederman 1991, Michels 1994, Cooper 1997, Olds & Cooper 1997), will become extinct if we continue to isolate ourselves from important scientific advances in other fields. Systematic study of the relation of findings from other disciplines with psychotherapeutic insights could achieve a high level of integration and a great deal of increased sophistication in the way that psychotherapists talk about remembering, imagining, speaking, thinking, dreaming and so on. What is required for integrative initiatives is a broader range of methods and an openness to and excitement about new ideas.

The clarification, operationalization and communication of psychoanalytic ideas

In the attempt to integrate findings from other disciplines with psychoanalytic concepts, Mary Target and I have explored the utility of the concept of a 'theory of mind' for the understanding of early (self) development. The theory of mind literature is a prototypical example of how observations of clinical phenomena (the absence or distortion of a capacity or function) can sometimes enlighten us about normal development. This is an epistemic strategy that psychoanalysis shares with the newer discipline of developmental psychopathology, bridging child psychiatry and psychology.

The origin of the theory of mind concept is in philosophy of mind (Brentano 1924, Dennett 1978); it was adopted in comparative psychology (Premack & Woodruff 1978), elaborated in experimental developmental psychology (Wimmer & Perner 1983), then extended to the study of autism (Baron-Cohen, Leslie & Frith 1985), and somewhat later to psychoanalytic approaches to borderline personality disorder (Fonagy & Higgitt 1989). In a particularly generative combination of clinical (Fonagy 1991) and experimental (Fonagy, Steele & Steele 1996) studies, we were able to demonstrate that some individuals with histories of maltreatment appear defensively to inhibit their capacity to think of others (or themselves in relation to others) as intentional beings, as having a mind, and as being motivated not by external circumstances but by feelings, beliefs and desires. We call this capacity to think of others as intentional beings _mentalization_. Our work has given some substance to many clinical observations concerning the experiences of patients with histories of maltreatment, at the same time as being more specific about the kinds of mental processes that may result from certain forms of splitting, attacks on linking, and perhaps even dissociation.

Developments such as these give weight to the interdisciplinary approach and to the cross-fertilization of ideas.

Our model of early development focuses on the emergence of the agentive self, particularly as revealed by the vicissitudes of the unfolding of the capacity to mentalize (Fonagy, Gergely, Jurist & Target 2002a). Our approach is rooted in attachment theory, but it claims a further evolutionary rationale for the human attachment system that goes beyond Bowlby's phylogenetic and ontogenetic claims for proximity to the protective caregiver (Bowlby 1969) and considers the major selective advantage conferred by the opportunity that proximity to concerned adults affords for the development of social intelligence and meaning making (Fonagy 2003a). The capacity to interpret human behaviour requires the 'intentional stance'; that is, 'treating the object whose behaviour you want to predict as a rational agent with beliefs and desires' (Dennett 1987 p. 15). Close proximity in infancy to another human being may be crucial in facilitating the comprehensive development of the biologically based capacity for interpretation in psychological terms, which we have labelled the Interpersonal Interpretive Function (IIF). Thus we claim that the disruption of early affectional bonds not only sets up possibly life-long maladaptive attachment patterns (e.g. Hamilton 2000, Waters, Merrick, Treboux, Crowell & Albersheim 2000), but also that it undermines a range of capabilities vital to the processing of information related to mental states. We claim that the link to attachment (the secure base) is made on the basis of the prediction that individuals who are secure in their early attachment will do better at tasks that call for these capacities.

We suggest that the contingent and congruent responding of the attachment figure in infancy is far more than the provision of reassurance about a protective presence. It is the principal means by which we acquire an understanding of our own internal states, which is an intermediate step in the acquisition of an understanding of others as psychological entities. We have elaborated a complex model of the steps involved and identified a significant body of empirical evidence consistent with it (see Bleiberg 2001, Allen & Fonagy 2002, Fonagy, Target, Gergely, Allen & Bateman 2003, Bateman & Fonagy 2004). Our configuration explicitly rejects the classical Cartesian assumption that emotional and other internal mental states are from the start directly experienced introspectively and will, as a consequence, inevitably give rise to the concept of the emotion in the child's mind. The Cartesian doctrine of the primacy of 'first person' experience has been seriously challenged in current philosophy of mind, cognitive neuroscience and developmental theory on a number of grounds, for example, by Dennett (1991), Gopnik (1993), Damasio (1994), Wegner & Wheatley (1999), Carpendale & Lewis (2004), Fonagy & Higgitt (2007). Instead, we suggest that in the first instance mental states are discovered through contingent mirroring interactions with the caregiver (Gergely & Watson 1996, Target & Fonagy 1996, Gergely & Watson 1999). Babies learn to differentiate the internal patterns of physiological and visceral stimulation that accompany different emotions by observing their caregivers' facial or vocal mirroring responses to these, as Legerstee and Varghese (2001), Meltzoff (1990) and others have indicated.

This model makes the neuroscience developments on mirror neurons, described by Mayes and Thomas (see Chapter 14), particularly interesting. We suggest that the contingent and congruent responding of the attachment figure in infancy is the principal means by which we acquire an understanding of our own internal states, which is an intermediate step in the acquisition of an understanding of others as psychological entities. We have elaborated a complex model of the steps involved and identified a significant body of empirical evidence consistent with it and which can account for non-adaptive or pathological states likely to be associated, via early attachment mechanisms, with early difficulties in relatedness (see Bleiberg 2001, Allen & Fonagy 2002, Fonagy et al. 2003, Bateman & Fonagy 2004). The model is itself being tested and developed in the clinical context (Fonagy & Target 2002). For example, recent work from the Mount Hope Family Center at the University of Rochester, New York, is consistent with the assumption of profound impairment of social cognition associated with maltreatment – characterized by gross impingements and failures in mirroring – and the potential for reducing this impairment through a relationship-focused intervention (Toth, Maughan, Manly, Spagnola & Cicchetti 2002, Cicchetti, Rosgosch & Toth 2006).

Is the model of mentalization and the cognitive deficits that follow from trauma a psychoanalytic model? We would of course wish to argue that it is. Not only does the model lean heavily on psychoanalytic explorations of mentalization by the Parisian psychosomatic school, in the work of Marty and De M'Uzan, and the London tradition of post-Kleinian thinking built around Bion's concept of containment, which is especially evident in the work of Segal, Britton and Steiner, but it is also an Anna Freudian dynamic model, where social cognition in general and mentalization in particular are seen as capacities that the child is capable of voluntarily foreclosing in order to optimize adaptation and minimize psychic pain. The model is not intended to reflect all aspects of the rich (perhaps sometimes excessively rich) psychoanalytic clinical model. It is advanced to highlight one aspect of mental function and to provide a helpful focus for constructing an interpretative psychotherapeutic intervention which is not insight oriented but has the recovery of mentalization in the context of emotional arousal at its core (Bateman & Fonagy 2006, Fearon, Target, Fonagy, Williams, McGregor, Sargent & Bleiberg 2006).

Mentalization is just one construct out of many within cognitive neuroscience that may be of help in understanding disorders, clarifying psychoanalytic constructs and reshaping interventions to be more focused. Triangulating with other disciplines can help identify overlapping ideas within psychoanalytic conceptualization that can be brought together and linked to extraclinical insights. This should enrich neuroscientific ideas as well as clarifying pluralistic thinking within the psychoanalytic field.

The external functions of research

In addition to what we might describe as the 'internal' role of research in refining our models of psychological mechanisms, research has four further 'external' functions linking clinical practice to the outside world: communication, theoretical validation, clinical validation, and the creation of an integrated science of the mind.

Concerning the communication function of research, I would simply wish to point to a thus-far largely unexploited potential. Research, by adopting a language that, by necessity, mental health specialists hold in common, could act as the major channel for communicating psychoanalytic ideas to other disciplines. This is to some degree beginning to happen, at least in the adult field. For example, by a simple operationalization of the concept of counter-transference, Drew Westen and colleagues managed to introduce therapists of varying orientations to a relatively rich conceptualization of this complex phenomenon originally identified by psychoanalysts (Betan, Heim, Zittel Conklin & Westen 2005). In general, if we translate our ideas into a language that is less dependent on the personal experience of psychotherapy, we find that those who are not normally exposed to it appreciate, understand and benefit from ideas first distilled in the cauldron of the analytic encounter. If these observations are important they will be discovered anyway by others and described and claimed in their own terms. We need only think about how modern cognitive behavioural therapy (CBT) is rediscovering psychoanalytic object relations theory and the formative influence of early attachment experiences (e.g. Young 1990). When we undertake extraclinical research we borrow research methods from other disciplines; as a by-product, we establish lines of communication with them, giving them access to our thoughts and speculations.

The clinical validation of psychodynamic child psychotherapy is a far more burning issue. The 'outcomes' enterprise at the moment is technique rather than theory based. Most treatments are multicomponent, with few connections between the mechanism of causation and the specific techniques for intervention (Weersing & Weisz 2002). For example, showing CBT to be effective does not validate social cognitive theory because of the loose coupling of the two. Yet, as mental health practitioners, we clearly have social responsibilities. Society expects a mental health treatment to show marked reduction in the patients' symptoms and conscious distress. Our patients understandably share this expectation. Furthermore, those on the opposite side of the fault-line need to find evidence that clinicians are seriously committed to the validation endeavour.

Before turning to the research on outcome that has been carried out, we should first consider the alternative to empirical validation by stepping outside the constraints that society imposes on health practitioners. We could abandon the idea of offering 'treatment' in favour of providing a particular form of intense subjective experience that deepens self-awareness. Thus we would evade the ogre of evidence-based practice, but exchange empirical studies for even more fickle and ambiguous social criteria for satisfactory professional performance (something akin to what playwrights, directors and actors experience in relation to theatre critics). This is not an unreasonable approach, and it in fact has significant currency in work with adults in francophone countries, where the influence of evidence-based medicine has not yet influenced the provision of mental health care in a major way (Perron 1999). It is also consistent with the ideas of some relational psychoanalytic thinkers. But this is not the best solution. It would cut psychotherapy adrift from other professionals involved in mental health service delivery. In most parts of the world the practices of adult and child psychotherapy depend not only on concerned adult 'patients' or parents of children where there is a belief in an underlying disorder, but also on attracting new recruits to the profession who would already hold to this commitment.

Finally, but perhaps most importantly, the study of human subjectivity will become increasingly essential to the biological sciences as the mystery of the human genome unfolds. This development was anticipated by Robert Emde twenty years ago (Emde 1988a, 1988b), when he suggested that the complexity of behavioural genetic findings would rekindle an interest in subjectivity on the part of our biological psychiatric colleagues. Accumulating evidence over the past decade from molecular biological research has made clear that the development of psychopathology involves a gene-environment interaction. Empirically, however, this interaction has proved hard to find. Some quantitative behaviour genetic studies strongly suggest interactive processes whereby a genetic vulnerability is triggered by environmental exposure. For example, the classic Finnish adoptive family study of schizophrenia suggested that children with a schizophrenic biological parent were more likely to develop a range of psychiatric problems if, and only if, they were adopted into dysfunctional families (Tienari, Wynne, Moring, Lahti & Naarala 1994).

One might legitimately ask why, if this is such a pervasive process, the quantitative behaviour genetic evidence is so sparse? Psychotherapists, of course, have a ready answer: the environment that triggers the expression of a gene is not objective; it is the child's experience of the environment that counts, and this is a function of appraisal. The manner in which the environment is experienced will act as a filter in the expression of genotype into phenotype. And here we touch on the pivotal role of psychoanalysis for genetic research. The primary concern of psychoanalysis, as we have seen, is with the subjective, the interaction of multiple layers of representations in generating developmental outcomes. Data from genetics call for exactly such sophistication in understanding the way genes may or may not be expressed in particular individuals. Studies in this area will perhaps provide a key role for psychotherapy in its second century. But, to fulfil its destiny as the science of subjectivity and to interface with microbiology and the other neurosciences, psychotherapy must at least establish a base camp on the other side of the fault-line. To what extent can outcome research help to bring this about?

The empirical basis of psychodynamic child psychotherapy

There are few comprehensive reviews of outcome studies of psychodynamic approaches to child and adolescent mental health difficulties. Surveys tend to focus on the treatment of children with mental health problems in general (Fonagy, Target, Cottrell, Phillips & Kurtz 2002b, Kazdin 2004, Target & Fonagy 2005), or on psychosocial interventions limited to 'evidence-based treatments' (Hibbs 2004, Weisz 2004). The most comprehensive survey of outcome studies specifically concerned with psychodynamic treatment was undertaken by Kennedy (2004), who undertook a systematic review of child and adolescent psychotherapy outcome research on behalf of the North Central London Strategic Health Authority. This was followed by a thematic review undertaken by Kennedy and Midgley (2007) to examine both outcome and process research and assessment, and evaluation tools in greater depth. On the basis of the studies reviewed by Kennedy, one might be tempted to conclude that the evidence base for child psychotherapy is quite poor, a conclusion related to methodological limitations. For example, as raised in a later section in this book, for a number of reasons it has proved very difficult to establish really good RCTs of psychodynamic psychotherapy with children. The few controlled trials are underpowered and suffer from other methodological limitations. All but one of those trials contrasted individual child psychotherapy with another active treatment. These designs make it hard to demonstrate reliable differences between the effectiveness of different treatments.

While the strength of the evidence itself does vary, and in some cases is insufficient to arrive at firm conclusions, a number of studies suggest that psychodynamic psychotherapy may be useful in the treatment of a variety of disorders commonly observed in children. It also indicates that a 'one size fits all' attitude, or the idea that everyone benefits from psychodynamic psychotherapy, is probably not justified, and that a more subtle approach to matching patients to treatments using diagnostic indicators might be helpful (Fonagy et al. 2002b, Target & Fonagy 2004, Wolpert et al. 2006).

There is increasing recognition of the problems with using DSM IV, the psychiatric system most commonly used in the UK, to define groups receiving intervention, particularly given that co-morbidity (around 75% is typically found in clinical populations) makes studies claiming diagnosis-specific outcomes hard to interpret. It is likely that future diagnostic systems will be less atheoretical and more focused on disease mechanisms and processes, and that treatment implications will therefore be easier to draw out from intervention research.

In the meantime, what we have are a significant number of studies showing that therapy improves various aspects of mental health problems associated with specific diagnostic conditions. Clinical problems or diagnostic categories given particular attention, and with examples of illustrative studies, include: anxiety disorders (Target & Fonagy 1994a); childhood depression (Target & Fonagy 1994b, Trowell, Joffe, Campbell, Clemente, Almqvist, Soininen et al. 2007); disruptive disorders (Fonagy & Target 1994, Baruch 1995); specific learning difficulties (Heinicke 1965, Heinicke & Ramsey-Klee 1986); pervasive developmental disorders (Fonagy & Target 1996, Reid, Alvarez & Lee 2001, Alonim 2003, Wieder & Greenspan 2003, Target & Fonagy 2004); chronic illness (Moran, Fonagy, Kutz, Bolton & Brook, 1991); eating disorders (Robin, Siegel & Moye 1995a) and the effects of trauma (Lush, Boston, Morgan & Kolvin 1998, Trowell, Kolvin, Weeramanthi, Sadowski, Berelowitz, Glaser et al. 2002).

Those who argue (correctly in my view) for continued investment in psychoanalytic psychotherapy point to the limitations of the evidence base supporting other approaches such as CBT (e.g. Westen, Novotny & Thompson-Brenner 2004) or pharmacological approaches (e.g. Whittington, Kendall, Fonagy, Cottrell, Cotgrove & Boddington 2004). Notwithstanding the general weakness of the evidence base of mental health treatments for children, ultimately such a negative case cannot persuade policy makers and funders. Without intense research on the effectiveness of the method deeply rooted in and shaped by psychological models of pathology, the long-term survival of this orientation is not assured (Gabbard, Gunderson & Fonagy 2002). This is not to say that the techniques that have evolved as part of this approach will not survive; they are effective and clinicians, being pragmatic people, will continue to discover and use them. But they will be increasingly absorbed into alternative models, and the unique approach pioneered by Freud and developed by Anna Freud, Klein, Winnicott and others might then be discontinued.

Conclusion

We need to look to research in child psychotherapy to elaborate our model of underlying mental processes and to systematize our knowledge base so that integration with the new sciences of the mind will become a possibility. We also need to communicate with other scientists about our discoveries, as well as show that our treatment works. But research is not for everyone. Researchers in child psychotherapy must be willing to work in a professional no-man's land, their motives regarded as suspect or even treacherous both by clinicians, who regard attempts to establish an evidence base as misguided, and by workers in experimental psychology. They will have to work harder than most, like children trying to prove their loyalty to two separated parents, and must bear feeling incompetent in both of their professions, where necessary surviving on a thin diet of conviction. It is my belief, however, that in time, the value of this enterprise will be recognized on both sides of the fault-line. And at that moment there will be rejoicing in both these lands.

References

Allen, J. G., Fonagy, P. (2002) The development of mentalizing and its role in psychopathology and psychotherapy. Technical Report No. 02–0048. Topeka, KS: The Menninger Clinic, Research Department.

Alonim, H. (2003) The Mifne Method – ISRAEL: Early intervention in the treatment of autism/PDD: A therapeutic programme for the nuclear family and their child. *Journal of Child and Adolescent Mental Health, 16,* 39–43.

Baron-Cohen, S., Leslie, A. M., Frith, U. (1985) Does the autistic child have a 'theory of mind'? *Cognition, 21,* 37–46.

Baruch, G. (1995) Evaluating the outcome of a community-based psychoanalytic psychotherapy service for young people between 12 and 25 years old: Work in progress. *Psychoanalytic Psychotherapy, 9*(3), 243–267.

Bateman, A. W., Fonagy, P. (2004) *Psychotherapy for borderline personality disorder: Mentalization based treatment.* Oxford: Oxford University Press.

Bateman, A. W., Fonagy, P. (2006) *Mentalization based treatment for borderline personality disorder: A practical guide.* Oxford: Oxford University Press.

Betan, E., Heim, A. K., Zittel Conklin, C., Westen, D. (2005) Countertransference phenomena and personality pathology in clinical practice: an empirical investigation. *American Journal of Psychiatry, 162,* 890–898.

Bion, W. R. (1967) Notes on memory and desire. *Psychoanalytic Forum, 2,* 272–273; 279–280.

Bleiberg, E. (2001) *Treating personality disorders in children and adolescents: A relational approach.* New York: Guilford Press.

Bowlby, J. (1969) *Attachment and loss. Vol. 1: Attachment.* London: Hogarth Press and the Institute of Psycho-Analysis.

Brentano, F. (1924) *Psychologie vom empirischen standpunkt.* Leipzig: O. Kraus.

Carpendale, J. I. M., Lewis, C. (2004) Constructing an understanding of mind: The development of children's social understanding within social interaction. *Behavioral and Brain Sciences, 27,* 79–151.

Cicchetti, D., Rogosch, F. A., Toth, S. L. (2006) Fostering secure attachment in infants in maltreating families through preventive interventions. *Developmental Psychopathology, 18,* 623–649.

Cooper, A. M. (1997) *Psychoanalytic education: Past, present and future.* New York: Association for Psychoanalytic Medicine.

Cooper, A. M., Kernberg, O. F., Schafer, R., Viederman, M. (1991) Report of the curriculum review committee. New York: The Columbia Center for Psychoanalytic Training and Research.

Damasio, A. R. (1994) Descartes' error and the future of human life. *Scientific American, 271,* 144.

Dennett, D. (1987) *The intentional stance.* Cambridge, MA: MIT Press.

Dennett, D. C. (1978) *Brainstorms: Philosophical essays on mind and psychology.* Montgomery, VT: Bradford.

Dennett, D. C. (1991) *Consciousness explained.* Boston: Little Brown.

Dreher, A.U. (2000) *Foundations for conceptual research in psychoanalysis*. London: Karnac Books.

Eisenberg, A. (1992) Metaphor in the language of science. *Scientific American, 266*(5), 144.

Eisenberger, N. I., Lieberman, M. D. (2004) Why rejection hurts: A common neural alarm system for physical and social pain. *Trends in Cognitive Sciences, 8*, 294–300.

Emde, R. N. (1988a) Development terminable and interminable II. Recent psychoanalytic theory and therapeutic considerations. *International Journal of Psycho-Analysis, 69*, 283–286.

Emde, R. N. (1988b) Development terminable and interminable. I. Innate and motivational factors from infancy. *International Journal of Psycho-Analysis, 69*, 23–42.

Fearon, P., Target, M., Fonagy, P., Williams, L., Mcgregor, J., Sargent, J., Bleiberg, E. (2006) Short-term mentalization and relational therapy (SMART): An integrative family therapy for children and adolescents. In J. Allen, & P. Fonagy, (eds.) *Handbook of mentalisation based treatments*. London: John Wiley.

Fonagy, P. (1991) Thinking about thinking: Some clinical and theoretical considerations in the treatment of a borderline patient. *International Journal of Psycho-Analysis, 72*, 1–18.

Fonagy, P. (2003a) The development of psychopathology from infancy to adulthood: The mysterious unfolding of disturbance in time. *Infant Mental Health Journal, 24*, 212–239.

Fonagy, P. (2003b) Genetics, developmental psychopathology and psychoanalytic theory: The case for ending our (not so) splendid isolation. *Psychoanalytic Inquiry, 23*, 218–247.

Fonagy, P. (2003c) Some complexities in the relationship of psychoanalytic theory to technique. *Psychoanalytic Quarterly, 72*, 13–48.

Fonagy, P. (2004) Psychotherapy meets neuroscience: A more focused future for psychotherapy research. *Psychiatric Bulletin, 28*, 357–359.

Fonagy, P., Gergely, G., Jurist, E., Target, M. (2002a) *Affect regulation, mentalization and the development of the self*. New York: Other Press.

Fonagy, P., Higgitt, A. (1989) A developmental perspective on borderline personality disorder. *Revue Internationale de Psychopathologie, 1*, 125–159.

Fonagy, P., Higgitt, A. (2007) The early social and emotional determinants of inequalities in health. In G. Baruch, P. Fonagy, & D. Robins, (eds.) *Reaching the hard to reach: Evidence-based funding priorities for intervention and research*. Chichester, UK: Wiley.

Fonagy, P., Steele, H., Steele, M. (1996) Associations among attachment classifications of mothers, fathers, and their infants: Evidence for a relationship-specific perspective. *Child Development, 67*, 541–555.

Fonagy, P., Target, M. (1994). The efficacy of psychoanalysis for children with disruptive disorders. *Journal of the American Academy of Child and Adolescent Psychiatry, 33*, 45–55.

Fonagy, P., Target, M. (1996) Predictors of outcome in child psychoanalysis: A retrospective study of 763 cases at the Anna Freud Centre. *Journal of the American Psychoanalytic Association, 44*, 27–77.

Fonagy, P., Target, M. (2002) Early intervention and the development of self-regulation. *Psychoanalytic Inquiry, 22*(3), 307–335.

Fonagy, P., Target, M. (2004) Relationships to bad objects: Repetition or current self-disorganization? *Psychoanalytic Dialogues, 14*(6), 733–742.

Fonagy, P., Target, M., Cottrell, D., Phillips, J., Kurtz, Z. (2002b) *What works for whom? A critical review of treatments for children and adolescents*. New York: Guilford.

Fonagy, P., Target, M., Gergely, G., Allen, J. G., Bateman, A. (2003) The developmental roots of borderline personality disorder in early attachment relationships: A theory and some evidence. *Psychoanalytic Inquiry, 23*, 412–459.

Freud, S. (1900) The interpretation of dreams. In J. Strachey (Ed.) *The standard edition of the complete psychological works of Sigmund Freud*. London: Hogarth Press.

Freud, S. (1926) The question of lay analysis. In J. Strachey (Ed.) *The standard edition of the complete psychological works of Sigmund Freud*. London: Hogarth Press.

Gabbard, G. O., Gunderson, J. G., Fonagy, P. (2002) The place of psychoanalytic treatments within psychiatry. *Archives of General Psychiatry, 59*, 505–510.

Gergely, G., Watson, J. (1996) The social biofeedback model of parental affect-mirroring. *International Journal of Psycho-Analysis, 77*, 1181–1212.

Gergely, G., Watson, J. (1999) Early social-emotional development: Contingency perception and the social biofeedback model. In P. Rochat, (Ed.) *Early social cognition: Understanding others in the first months of life*. Hillsdale, NJ: Lawrence Erlbaum Associates.

Gopnik, A. (1993) How we know our minds: The illusion of first-person knowledge of intentionality. *Behavioral and Brain Sciences, 16*, 1–14; 29–113.

Hamilton, C. E. (2000) Continuity and discontinuity of attachment from infancy through adolescence. *Child Development, 71*, 690–694.

Heinicke, C. M. (1965) Frequency of psychotherapeutic session as a factor affecting the child's developmental status. *The Psychoanalytic Study of the Child, 20*, 42–98.

Heinicke, C. M., Ramsey-Klee, D. M. (1986) Outcome of child psychotherapy as a function of frequency of sessions. *Journal of the American Academy of Child Psychiatry, 25*, 247–253.

Hibbs, E. D. (Ed.) (2004) *Psychosocial treatments for child and adolescent disorders: Empirically based strategies for clinical practice* (2nd edn). Washington, DC: American Psychological Association.

Kandel, E. R. (1998) A new intellectual framework for psychiatry. *American Journal of Psychiatry, 155*, 457–469.

Kazdin, A. E. (2004) Psychotherapy for children and adolescents. In M. Lambert, (Ed.) *Bergin and Garfield's handbook of psychotherapy and behavior change* (5th edn). New York: Wiley.

Kennedy, E. (2004) *Child and adolescent psychotherapy: A systematic review of psychoanalytic approaches*. London: North Central London Strategic Health Authority.

Kennedy, E., Midgley, N. (eds.) (2007) *Process and outcome research in child, adolescent and parent-infant psychotherapy: A thematic review*. London: NHS London.

Legerstee, M., Varghese, J. (2001) The role of maternal affect mirroring on social expectancies in 2–3 month-old infants. *Child Development, 72*, 1301–1313.

Lush, D., Boston, M., Morgan, J., Kolvin, I. (1998) Psychoanalytic psychotherapy with disturbed adopted and foster children: a single case follow-up study. *Clinical Child Psychology and Psychiatry, 3*(1), 51–69.

Meltzoff, A.N. (1990) Foundations for developing a concept of self: The role of imitation in relating self to other and the value of social mirroring, social modeling and self practice in infancy. In Cicchetti D. & Beeghly M. (eds), *The self in transition: Infancy to childhood* (pp. 139–164). Chicago: University of Chicago Press.

Michels, R. (1994) Psychoanalysis enters its second century. *Annual of Psychoanalysis*, *22*, 37–45.

Moran, G., Fonagy, P., Kurtz, A., Bolton, A., Brook, C. (1991) A controlled study of the psychoanalytic treatment of brittle diabetes. *Journal of the American Academy of Child and Adolescent Psychiatry*, *30*, 926–935.

Northoff, G., Bermpohl, F., Schoeneich, F., Boeker, H. (2007) How does our brain constitute defense mechanisms? First-person neuroscience and psychoanalysis. *Psychotherapy and Psychosomatics*, *76*, 141–53.

Olds, D., Cooper, A. M. (1997) Dialogue with other sciences: Opportunities for mutual gain. Guest Editorial. *The International Journal of Psycho-Analysis*, *78*, 219–226.

Perron, R. (1999) Reflection on psychoanalytic research problems – the French-speaking view. In P. Fonagy, H. Kachele, R. Krause, E. Jones, R. Perron, & L. Lopez, (eds.) *An open door review of outcome studies in psychoanalysis*. London: International Psychoanalytical Association.

Pessiglione, M., Schmidt, L., Draganski, B., Kalisch, R., Lau, H., Dolan, R. J., Frith, C. D. (2007) How the brain translates money into force: A neuroimaging study of subliminal motivation. *Science*, 316, 904–906.

Premack, D., Woodruff, G. (1978) Does the chimpanzee have a 'theory of mind'? *Behavioural and Brain Sciences*, *1*, 515–526.

Rapaport, D. (1950) On the psychoanalytic theory of thinking. *International Journal of Psycho-Analysis*, *31*, 161–170.

Reid, S., Alvarez, A., Lee, A. (2001) The Tavistock autism workshop approach. In: Richer J., Coates S. (eds), *Autism – the search for coherence* (pp. 182–192). London: Jessica Kingsley.

Robin, A. L., Siegel, P. T., Moye, A. (1995a) Family versus individual therapy for anorexia: Impact on family conflict. *International Journal of Eating Disorders*, *17*, 313–322.

Rothbart, D. (1997) *Explaining the growth of scientific knowledge: Metaphors, models, and meanings*. Lewiston, NY: E. Mellen Press.

Sandler, J. (1987) The concept of projective identification. In Sandler J. (ed.), *Projection, identification, projection identification* (pp. 13–26). Madison, CT: International Universities Press.

Target, M., Fonagy, P. (1994a) The efficacy of psychoanalysis for children with emotional disorders. *Journal of the American Academy of Child and Adolescent Psychiatry*, *33*, 361–371.

Target, M., Fonagy, P. (1994b) The efficacy of psychoanalysis for children: Developmental considerations. *Journal of the American Academy of Child and Adolescent Psychiatry*, *33*, 1134–1144.

Target, M., Fonagy, P. (1996) Playing with reality II: The development of psychic reality from a theoretical perspective. *International Journal of Psycho-Analysis*, *77*, 459–479.

Target, M., Fonagy, P. (2004) The psychological treatment of child and adolescent psychiatric disorders. In A. Roth, & P. Fonagy, (eds.) *What works for whom? A critical review of psychotherapy research*. New York: Guilford.

Target, M., Fonagy, P. (2005) The psychological treatment of child and adolescent psychological disorders. In A. Roth, & P. Fonagy, (eds.) *What works for whom? A critical review of psychotherapy research* (2nd edn). New York: Guilford Press.

Tienari, P., Wynne, L. C., Moring, J., Lahti, I., Naarala, M. (1994) The Finnish adoptive family study of schizophrenia: Implications for family research. *British Journal of Psychiatry*, *23*, 20–26.

Toth, S. L., Maughan, A., Manly, J. T., Spagnola, M., Cicchetti, D. (2002) The relative efficacy of two interventions in altering maltreated preschool children's representational models: Implications for attachment theory. *Developmental Psychopathology*, 14, 877–908.

Trowell, J., Joffe, I., Campbell, J., Clemente, C, Almqvist, F., Soininen, M., et al. (2007) Childhood depression: A place for psychotherapy. An outcome study comparing individual psychodynamic psychotherapy and family therapy. *European Child and Adolescent Psychiatry*, *16*(3): 157–167.

Trowell, J., Kolvin, I., Weeramanthri, T., Sadowski, H., Berelowitz, M., Glaser, D., et al. (2002) Psychotherapy for sexually abused girls: psychopathological outcome findings and patterns of change. *British Journal of Psychiatry*, *180*, 234–247.

Wason, P. C., Johnson-Laird, P. N. (1972) *Psychology of reasoning: Structure and content*. Cambridge, MA: Harvard University Press.

Waters, E., Merrick, S. K., Treboux, D., Crowell, J., Albersheim, L. (2000) Attachment security from infancy to early adulthood: A 20 year longitudinal study. *Child Development*, *71*, 684–689.

Weersing, V. R., Weisz, J. R. (2002) Mechanisms of action in youth psychotherapy. *Journal of Child Psychology and Psychiatry*, 43, 3–29.

Wegner, D. M., Wheatley, T. (1999) Apparent mental causation: Sources of the experience of will. *American Psychologist*, *54*, 480–492.

Weisz, J. R. (2004) *Psychotherapy for children and adolescents: Evidence-based treatments and case examples*. Cambridge: Cambridge University Press.

Westen, D., Novotny, C. M., Thompson-Brenner, H. (2004) The empirical status of empirically supported psychotherapies: Assumptions, findings, and reporting in controlled clinical trials. *Psychological Bulletin*, *130*, 631–633.

Whittington, C. J., Kendall, T., Fonagy, P., Cottrell, D., Cotgrove, A., Boddington, E. (2004) Selective serotonin reuptake inhibitors in childhood depression: Systematic review of published versus unpublished data. *Lancet*, *363*, 1341–1345.

Whittle, P. (2000) Experimental psychology and psychoanalysis: What we can learn from a century of misunderstanding. *Neuro-psychoanalysis*, *1*, 233–245.

Wieder, S., Greenspan, S. I. (2003) Climbing the symbolic ladder in the DIR model through floor time/interactive play. *Autism*, *7*(4), 425–435.

Wimmer, H., Perner, J. (1983) Beliefs about beliefs: Representation and constraining function of wrong beliefs in young children's understanding of deception. *Cognition*, *13*, 103–128.

Wolpert, M., Fuggle, P., Cottrell, D., Fonagy, P., Phillips, J., Pilling, S., Stein, S., Target, M. (2006) *Drawing on the evidence: Advice for mental health professionals working with children and adolescents (2nd edn)*. London: CAMHS Publications.

Young, J. E. (1990) *Cognitive therapy for personality disorders: A schema-focused approach*. Sarasota, FL: Professional Resource Exchange.

Chapter 2

What do child psychotherapists know?

Michael Rustin

In the decades after the death of Freud in 1939, the psychoanalytic tradition in Britain was substantially shaped by child analysis. Melanie Klein's discoveries emerged from psychoanalytic practice with children, which was based on her 'play technique'. Some of Donald Winnicott's most important ideas were developed through work with children, and through study of the relationships of mothers and babies. There are also notable parallels between Esther Bick's understanding of the acute anxieties of infancy (the fear of 'falling to pieces') and Bion's understanding of the fragmented states of mind occurring in psychotic patients. Anna Freud was as dedicated as Melanie Klein to the analysis of children, and many of her principal contributions to psychoanalysis were based on this. Thus the theoretical advances of the 1940s and 1950s in the British psychoanalytic tradition could not have occurred without the priority given to the psychoanalysis of children, and the corpus of ideas and techniques with which British analysts now work can scarcely be imagined without that contribution.

This should hardly be a surprise. Psychoanalysis is a theory of development, explaining the psychic pain and malfunctions that are its clinical concern through understandings of what happens, internally and externally, in the early life of children. Most psychoanalysts believe that they have access, through the psychoanalysis of adults to the 'child in the adult'. Freud thought of psychoanalysis in part by analogy with archaeology, as the excavation of buried layers of consciousness. The psychoanalysis of children gave new and direct access to these early formations of mind.

In the past few decades, the new profession of psychoanalytic child psychotherapy has grown up. Child psychotherapy remains closely linked to the mainstream psychoanalytic tradition in Britain, but the migration of child analysis to child psychotherapy, largely being undertaken within public mental health services for children and families,[1] means that if we want to

1 In the NHS, child psychotherapists mostly see patients on a once-weekly basis, although intensive cases provide a major element of their training. It often proves possible to do transference-based psychoanalytic work in this situation.

understand the generation of new knowledge in child analysis in Britain today, it is to child psychotherapy we must look.

The generation of knowledge in psychoanalysis

In this chapter, I review some major achievements of the clinical research programme of child psychotherapy, and then go on to consider the encounter between psychoanalysis and 'mainstream' social scientific research methods. But before doing this, it is necessary to say something about scientific methods more broadly.

Since its invention as a new paradigm by Sigmund Freud, psychoanalysis has evolved as a productive research programme. Its primary research method has been clinical, its main laboratory has been the consulting room. Its theories and classifications (of developmental patterns, psychic structures, psychopathologies) have continued to develop, as psychoanalysts take account of new clinical evidence. The main purpose of this gathering of knowledge has been to inform clinicians in their practice.

It is normal in the history of the sciences for techniques of investigation to evolve in response to the nature of particular objects of research. Consider, for example, the differences between:

- The mathematical sciences, which study 'virtual objects'.
- Physics, whose commitment is to discovering uniform and universal laws about the elementary properties of nature.
- The biological sciences, much of whose agenda has until recent years been the description and classification of the diversity of species, unified by the theory of natural selection, which is most informative in its application to particular species and ecosystems.
- The human sciences, which have to take account not only of the diversity of human kind, but also of the self-understanding and self-transformative properties of human subjects. The human sciences for these latter reasons have had to acknowledge limitations to the empirical scope of the theories they devise – they continually track a moving target. A further complication of the human sciences is that their perspectives are shaped by commitments of value, which sustain different research agendas, as human scientists seek to understand the conditions of possibility of imaginable worlds. It is not only the 'immaturity' of the human sciences (including psychoanalysis) that have led to their disunity, but the differences of moral viewpoint that continue to inform and divide them.

There is thus not one science, but many (Galison & Stump 1996). Psychoanalysis has too often been negatively judged by criteria deriving from a philosophy of science whose ideal typical model was the physical science of the early twentieth century,[2] and from a positivist psychological tradition which reduced the complexity of its human subjects in order to follow its preferred methods of experiment and measurement.

In psychoanalysis and child psychotherapy, knowledge has been advanced through the juxtaposition of new clinical findings, with established classifications, and theories. Newly recognized phenomena have been designated by new concepts (M.J. Rustin 2001, 2007, Hughes 2004). Taxonomies (for example of psychopathologies) have evolved to become more differentiated and fine-grained in response to clinical experience. Kuhn (2000) in *The Road Since Structure*, described the proliferation of ideas within a paradigm that accompanied the 'puzzle solving' of normal science as a kind of 'speciation', comparing this with the evolution of living species. This is a useful metaphor for understanding the proliferation of concepts and theories in psychoanalysis.

There is a tension in psychoanalysis between the wish to understand particular experiences and persons, and the goal of discovering uniformities and laws governing all psychic phenomena. If one is too taken up with individuals, there will be no concepts or theories to confer meaning. But if one is too committed to abstractions, one loses sight of individual persons, making descriptions lifeless and without meaning to patients themselves. When Bion urged that analysts 'eschew memory and desire', and be open to an experience of 'unknowing', he was emphasizing the dangers that the dead hand of theory and preconception could bring to the analytic encounter. But he remained deeply committed to theoretical notations, and attempted their systematic classification in the formulation of his 'grid'. Like complexity theorists who have defined 'the edge of chaos' as the primary location of creativity and innovation, Bion insisted that psychoanalysts need to expose themselves to the disorientation that inevitably follows experiences of the particular, but also remain attentive to the explanatory power that psychoanalytic thinking embodies.

One can think of psychoanalytic concepts as constituting a 'virtual library' of resources for naming and explaining clinical phenomena. The clinical task is to decide on the most useful correspondences between new clinical phenomena, and the pre-existing ideas which can give them meaning, either by 'vertical' deduction from more abstract principles (e.g. the Oedipus complex) or by 'horizontal' analogy with other known cases.

The practice of 'normal science' or 'puzzle solving' in psychoanalysis involves at a basic level understanding individual patients. It is because of this

---

2 David Stove (1982) suggested that Popper's model of 'falsifiability', which rejects the inductive principle that positive empirical evidence provides good reasons for belief in a theory, and thus proposes a rigorous scepticism, was a response to the upheaval to Newtonian science brought about by Einstein. Popper wished to ensure that no one would ever again be deceived by certainty. Permanent scientific revolution would henceforth rule. One can see how Kuhn's theory of scientific revolutions gave this programme a historical perspective.

commitment to the complexity of its individual subjects that its findings have been best represented in case studies and monographs rather than in the codified style of a textbook or manual.

However, under pressure of difficulties in understanding recalcitrant clinical phenomena, analysts sometimes reflect on the adequacy of the concepts available to them, and propose new conceptions. The development of theories, taxonomies and techniques in psychoanalysis takes place in response to encounters with recalcitrant facts; emergent theories then being subjected to later clinical test and trial. The history of psychoanalytic theory is thus the record of a continuing clinical research programme; imaginative conjecture and deductive brilliance have had a major place. But theories have usually been barren in this field unless they have rapidly found a clinical referent or some other application to experience.

This development has usually proceeded according to criteria that have been given little explicit specification. Psychoanalysis has been a field of 'tacit knowledge', in Michael Polanyi's (1958) terms, of 'craft practices' and intellectual sensibilities, fine-honed and shared within the knowledge-community of the profession, but subject to little formal clarification at 'meta-levels' of justification. The length and intensity of training of psychoanalytic training and the meticulous routines (observation, supervision, personal analysis) of which its learning processes are made up, are designed to achieve a consistent quality of practice, internalized as professional 'second nature' (M.J. Rustin 2003).

This situation has begun to change, under two opposite pressures. On the one hand, implicit claims to professional competence do not fare well in the culture of 'evidence-based medicine' – psychotherapists are placed under pressure to provide empirical justification of their knowledge and practice. On the other hand, former orthodoxies in the philosophy of science have been challenged and there is greater understanding of the actual diversity of scientific methods. Psychoanalysts are coming to see that their procedures can be made more accountable without compromising the essence of psychoanalytic practice.

One lesson that can be learned from the recent history and sociology of science, for example in the work of Kuhn (1962, 2000) and Latour (1983, 1987), is that descriptive questions concerning what scientists do, and how they do it, are more illuminating than prescriptive judgements that seek to demarcate 'good' from 'bad' scientific practice. Thus, the best starting point for considering the role of research in child psychotherapy is to review the contributions to knowledge that have been achieved by this discipline since its inception in 1948. I will give some examples.

Clinical research in child psychotherapy

Consider, first, what has been learned over the past thirty years about psychoanalytic work with severely deprived children since the publication of

Gianna Williams' seminal 1974 paper, *Doubly Deprived* (Williams 1974). Here was a population of children earlier thought untreatable by psycho-analytic methods. The embryo profession of child psychotherapy, embedded as it was in community mental health services, began to respond to the needs of patients drawn from families who had experienced often catastrophic breakdowns. These children might, by the time of referral, be in children's homes, or later in foster- or adoptive-placements, which often proved to be difficult for all concerned.

Gianna Williams recognized that 'deprivation' in the lives of such children was not merely 'external', as in a child's loss of its birth parents, but also had another dimension, in the damage to a child's 'internal parents' effected by traumatic experiences or abandonment. Unless this internal damage was addressed it was likely that attempts to achieve external reparation through providing a new family for a child would encounter great difficulties. Children in such placements were often found to test their new foster-carers to the point of despair, as they lived out the damaged object-relationships of their internal worlds in the vulnerable settings of their new homes.

The child psychotherapists' method of investigating this situation was primarily clinical. Psychotherapists tried to work therapeutically with such patients, adapting their technique accordingly. They developed ideas that enabled them to understand their clinical experience. They practised a cooperative method of work, 'the practitioners' workshop' (M.E. Rustin 1991) as a way of thinking together, and supporting each other in coping with the extreme stress of this work. Mary Boston and Rolene Szur's edited collection, *Psychotherapy with Severely Deprived Children* (1983) was the outcome of such a workshop. Informally, clinical workshops like this enable practitioners to explore and test out ideas with many similar cases, and make possible a measure of generalization.[3]

The most significant clinical evidence arose from the severity of the impact of these patients on their therapists. The patients' hostility, desperation and rejection was often overwhelming. Theoretically essential was attention to the countertransference, and to what Betty Joseph described as the 'total trans-ference situation' (Joseph 1989). Only if what was being experienced by the therapist was understood at least in part as a projection by the child patient of his or her own unbearable states of mind, and as communication to the therapist of what it felt like to be such a child, did the situation become comprehensible, and one with which analytic work became possible.

Bion's concept of the container-contained relation was also central to this exploration. Therapists came to understand that the origin of the patients' difficulty often lay in failures of containment during their earlier history. Gianna Williams (1997) elaborated her understanding of the

---

3 The Anna Freud Centre also established clinical workshops at an early stage, which gave rise to some important papers, for example Rosenfeld and Sprince (1963).

container-contained relation, to take account of its different possible modalities. In contrast to the form of facilitating containment delineated by Bion's
'alpha function' (the 'metabolization' of psychic experience, in particular
unconscious anxiety, through 'reverie'), she evolved the concept of 'omega
function' to characterize its opposite, namely the intrusive or toxic projection
into others of states of anxiety found unbearable by parental figures.

Williams extended the relevance of this reversal of containment to the field
of eating disorders in children and adolescents (Williams 1997, Williams et al.
2004). In another clinical workshop, she and her colleagues developed an
understanding of the rejection of food, and of other life-giving intakes, as
unconscious responses to early experiences in which feeding was felt to be
emotionally toxic. The clinical evidence for this hypothesis also came from
the dynamics of the transference and the countertransference.

The psychoanalytic understanding of severely deprived children has been
considerably developed since the publication of Williams' original paper and
Boston's and Szur's book. Some writers (M.E. Rustin 2001, Kenrick 2005)
have explored issues of technique, describing the violent attacks on therapist
and setting made by patients, and techniques that they have adopted to cope
with these. This writing has enabled clinicians to feel less overburdened by a
sense of failure, and to anticipate difficult situations. Different behaviours
and states of mind of such patients have been elaborated in significant contributions, for example by Canham (1999, 2004) and Hopkins (2000). This
literature is essentially psychoanalytic in its exploration of the children's
inner worlds.

A field of 'clinical research' of this kind evolves as a 'branching tree' of
classifications. Here we can add the particularity of sexual abuse and sexual
enactment as an aspect of deprivation, and its possible impact in the clinical
situation (Lanyado 1991, Ironside 1995) and the significance of the experience of the Oedipus complex (Anderson 2003, Bartram 2003, Canham
2003) It has more recently become recognized that the management, or mismanagement, of children with difficulties within the care system is the source
of additional problems of its own – a kind of iatrogenic mental illness – and
child psychotherapists have investigated the experiences of transition, in
which a care system seems to lose capacity to hold the children in mind
(Hindle 2000, Hunter 2001, Philps 2003). Margaret Rustin (2005) explored this
situation in her commentary on the difficulties of the care system in responding
to the situation of Victoria Climbié, difficulties that led to her death.

A second major example is from the field of autism and its associated
disorders. Here, a succession of clinical and theoretical studies has been
undertaken by child psychotherapists (Alvarez 1992, Tustin 1992, Rhode
1994, Alvarez & Reid 1999) alongside work by Meltzer, Bremner, Hoxter,
Weddell and Wittenberg (1975), Haag (2000) and Houzel (2004), and in dialogue with experimental psychologists working in child study labs, who have
mapped out aspects of behaviour previously inaccessible to study. Clinical

investigators of autistic phenomena have made extensive use of the methods of psychoanalytic infant observation, which were developed initially by Esther Bick as a preclinical foundation of child psychotherapy training. Child psychotherapists have sought to understand the origin and meaning of these disorders by means of the close observation of the 'state of being' of autistic patients, in their relation to their own bodies, to physical objects and sensations, and to the body and person of their therapists.

Links between the understanding of autism, and the psychoanalytic theory of early development, were very clearly set out in what Frances Tustin (1994) announced as her last published article. In this she described the view of the origin of narcissism she had reached as a consequence of her studies of autism; this contrasted with her earlier view. In her 1994 paper, Tustin rejected the idea that narcissism was, as Freud had written, an original condition from which individuals later emerged. She wrote that narcissism – the delusion of a self-sufficient self, the denial of relationship with an object – is a defence against a separation from mother, which is experienced as traumatic and terrifying. In normal development, the baby is from the beginning in a reciprocal relationship with the breast, and mother. It is this sense of relatedness and safe dependence – containment has become a usual term for it – that sustains the baby's sense of himself or herself, as capable of surviving even when not in close contact with its mother.

The focus within the psychoanalytic study of autism on those very early states of mind that are concerned with basic bodily and psychic integration have brought some progress in understanding early development from a psychoanalytic perspective. The fear of 'falling to pieces', or liquifying, described by Esther Bick (1968) and Sydney Klein (1980) is more primitive than the anxieties about 'objects' posited by the theory of the paranoid-schizoid position. Until some sense of coherence of the self is achieved, there is no possibility of distinguishing self from other, the loved from the hated object. Autism is a defence against the anxiety of disintegration and fragmentation that follows upon the failure of the primary object to support the self in its earliest experiences of separation. This might be the outcome not of actual deficit in the capacity of the primary object, but the consequence of the initial fragility and vulnerability of the infant, perhaps of genetic origin, or a consequence of prematurity or illness in mother or infant. But subjectively, this fragile infant's experience is that any separation is unbearable and is experienced as catastrophic.

The observational and clinical research programme of investigators of autism has been exploring many of the different sensory modalities of the infant's earliest experiences, to see the part each of these has in the development of autistic defences. In Europe, Suzanne Maiello (1995) has studied the primary experience of 'the sound object', tracing this back to prenatal experience and examining its role as an element in the relationship of infant and mother. Genevieve Haag (2000) has developed an understanding of the normal experience of the body as possessing a backbone, and a symmetrical organization of left and right sides, noting the disturbance of this symmetrical unity in autistic development. These observers of autistic children have noted their extreme preoccupation with bodily surfaces and orifices, surfaces providing a kind of contact with or relation to the world in the absence of a sense of that world as three-dimensional, and of recognition that persons and things have interiors and exteriors. Maria Rhode (2004) has explored the infant's experience of the mouth in a situation where there is no tolerance of separation from mother.

These ideas have had consequences for clinical technique. As autistic children's primary form of contact with the world, and with others, may be through adhesion to or exploration of such physical surfaces, it has been found necessary to attend closely to children's physical engagement with the therapist and the setting, seeking out kinds of responsiveness to them that enhances their sense of trust and agency, as the precondition for more complex communications. Anne Alvarez (1992) has described her active technique of 'reclamation', with its aim of enhancing her patient's expressive and communicative repertoire in order to get a live relationship started.

A substantial programme of clinical and observational study of autistic children has given rise to theoretical formulations, setting out the implications of these findings for the understanding of psychic development. One useful theorization of this kind has been set out by Thomas Ogden (1989), in his concept of the 'contiguous–autistic position', which he holds to be a normal stage of development prior to the onset of the paranoid-schizoid and depressive positions theorized by Melanie Klein.

These are examples of fields in child psychotherapy where substantial new knowledge has been generated in the consulting room. One could add many others. For instance, the study of autism has led on to the investigation of Asperger's syndrome (Rhode & Klauber 2004) and of more florid psychotic states (M.E. Rustin, Rhode, Dubinsky & Dubinsky 1997).

The close attention to the anxieties attached to early infancy has led to investigation of the experiences of infants born prematurely, or looked after in neonatal units, throwing light on the traumatic nature of their underprotected situation, and suggesting ways in which the quality of care could be improved.[4] A related field of investigation is 'parent–infant work', in which difficulties in the early relationships between mothers and babies are attended to by creating a therapeutic space in which mothers are able to share some of their fears, and learn that they can understand what is happening to them and their baby. Once mothers' extreme anxieties are relieved, and they become more free to observe and reflect, babies also become less anxious.

---

4 See also Pamela Sorensen's (2000) paper on 'transition-facilitating behaviour', arising from her work in a neonatal unit and, related to this, Didier Houzel's (1995) concept of 'precipitation anxiety'.

Questions of method

My contention is that the established tradition of clinical research in child psychotherapy has been very productive in generating new knowledge. It has enhanced our understanding of child development and its various difficulties and disorders, and has evolved new clinical techniques in response to these. It is the links made between psychoanalytic concepts and theories, and phenomena encountered in clinical practice, which have enabled this knowledge-base to be established.

However, some argue that this is insufficient, and that psychoanalysts and psychotherapists have to move closer to the scientific mainstream if their findings are to have wider credibility. Responding to this, Nicholas Midgley (2004, 2006) has proposed that qualitative research methods developed in sociology and psychology might be useful in clinical research, and can lead to improvements in many of its procedures, in both the gathering and processing of data. He has rightly pointed out that child psychotherapists undertaking doctoral research projects are now making use of systematic qualitative methods, such as 'grounded theory', and the independent rating and interpretation of findings, to set their work on firmer ground. Some substantial projects, such as the Adolescent Depression Study undertaken in London, Helsinki and Athens, have gone further in the formalization of research methods, as is described elsewhere in this book.

Such developments are to be welcomed. Research into the outcomes and effectiveness of treatment is particularly urgent, because in today's 'evidence-based' culture of health care, commissioners demand data to substantiate claims for the value of psychotherapy, and are sometimes unwilling to accept professional advice unsupported by statistical evidence. Outcome studies are one form of research in which systematic quantitative techniques are essential.

But the implied suggestion that psychotherapists have been methodologically naive, compared with the researchers from other human science disciplines, is not well founded. One of Nicholas Midgley's (2004, 2006) two contributions to this debate, 'Sailing between Scylla and Charybis: Incorporating qualitative approaches into child psychotherapy research', cited a three-phase chronology of psychoanalytic research proposed by John McLeod (2001). In the first of these, up to the 1950s, 'the main emphasis was on description and discovery, and the primary means of research was the single case-study'. In the second phase, from the 1950s onwards, 'consolidation and routinisation' gradually became dominant. The aim supposedly shifted from 'discovery to verification, with the aim of establishing a firm professional basis to our work'. In the third and current phase, which Midgley sees as a time of 'uncertainty and opportunity', there are pressures to develop an evidence base using 'scientific' empirical measures, but there are also new opportunities to bring sophisticated qualitative methods to bear on psychoanalytic questions.

Although it is true that the turn to qualitative methods in the social sciences is beneficial for psychoanalysis, McLeod's historical underpinning of this argument is quite misleading. The reality is that psychoanalysts have continued to make major discoveries, using clinical case-study methods, throughout the decades from the 1950s to the present. These years saw major publications by analysts such as Segal, Bion, Rosenfeld, Joseph, O'Shaughnessy, Britton, Sandler, Steiner, Ogden and Bollas, as well as those of the child psychotherapists referred to above. The lexicon of ideas, which is employed by most child psychotherapists today, would not exist without this record of clinical research. For example, one of the crucial ideas now being operationalized in a quantitative empirical form by Peter Fonagy, that of mentalization, seems to have as one of its main origins Bion's theory of the mind.

What also goes unnoticed in the undervaluation of the clinical psycho-analytic tradition are the substantive reflections made by analysts and child psychotherapists on their own methods of research. Bion's investigation of psychotic states of mind required him to recognize as 'data' phenomena that had been hitherto unintelligible to psychoanalysts. His own discussion of the 'selected fact' and the mode of seeing coherence in these phenomena drew on the mathematical ideas of Poincaré, and anticipated the subsequent devel-opment of complexity theory (M.J. Rustin 2002). In a similar way, Betty Joseph's understanding of the 'total transference situation' (Joseph 1989, 1998) required her to reconsider the meaning of the facts of the psycho-analytic encounter, enhancing the level of detail in which clinical phenomena were perceived. It was as if a new instrument had been discovered, which could find meaning in sequence, timing, interactions and silences in clinical interactions. The fundamental idea of projective identification (Sandler 1988) required psychotherapists to think of patients' communications as actions or enactments, rather than merely as signifiers with hidden levels of meaning. Developments in the philosophy of language, which had led to the acknow-ledgement of the 'performative' aspects of 'speech acts' thus had their equiva-lent in psychoanalytic practice, probably not from the direct influence of the philosophers, but as a parallel discovery. Meltzer's commitment to a 'hermeneutic' and vehemently 'non-causal' view of psychoanalytic theory, in his account of the Freud-Klein-Bion tradition, also echoed the 'interpret-ative turn' that was taking place in the 1970s in philosophy and the social sciences. Countertransference is a methodological as well as a clinical resource, because it identifies a new source of information. It is clear that the discoveries of child psychotherapists described above have depended on new ways of perceiving and understanding clinical phenomena, whether through the countertransference or through fine-grained observation of the links between body and mind.

Criticism of psychoanalysis for blurring the boundaries between facts and theoretical inferences drawn from them was anticipated in psychoanalytic and child psychotherapy practice before it became an issue for research methodologists. The tradition of psychoanalytic infant observation was founded in the 1940s on the discipline of detailed, literal, descriptive report, precisely to instil an empirical habit of mind among trainee psychotherapists. *Closely Observed Infants* (Miller, Rustin, Rustin & Shuttleworth 1989), the first book to systematically set out this method, made a commitment to the distinction between data and theory absolutely plain, as did Meltzer (1967). What proved decisive in 'the controversial discussions' in the early 1940s, in gaining support for some of Melanie Klein's ideas, was the evidence provided by her new method of child analysis. It was primarily a new kind of clinical fact that convinced the uncommitted members of the psychoanalytic community.

The fact is that discovery in psychoanalysis has always depended on a self-critical attitude to clinical data. Psychoanalytic theories assign meaning and connectedness to specified kinds of facts; without attention to the nature of these facts and how they are apprehended, there could be no valid or useful theories. The seventy-fifth Anniversary Special Issue (1994) of the *International Journal of Psychoanalysis* on clinical facts was an important milestone in engagement with these issues (Tuckett 1994a, 1994b). Psychoanalysts who began their work in other disciplines, such as Elizabeth Spillius, David Tuckett, Susan Budd and Peter Fonagy, have brought disciplinary cross-fertilization (Fonagy 2001). Glaser and Strauss's grounded theory, which came from sociology but which has been found valuable by psychoanalytic researchers, consists of a method of moving inductively between qualitative data and concepts that is very close to the way in which in clinical practice and supervision meaning is expected to emerge from close study of the material, while holding theoretical preconceptions at a distance.

This is not to question the relevance to child psychotherapy of the range of qualitative methods that has developed in recent years in what has been in fact a veritable 'methodological boom' in the social sciences. Child psychotherapists often feel anxious about their own lack of expertise of research methods, and they find that psychoanalytic ideas are attacked as 'unscientific'. Although they need to respect their own tradition, and understand its contributions to knowledge, it is good that they can now use more systematic and transparent research methods.

Two major complications need to be kept in mind. The first of these is that an 'object' of investigation is usually related to its method of inquiry in quite definite and determinate ways. Ontologies – conceptions of what is – are usually associated in a logical way to epistemologies – conceptions of how one knows something. Research methods are not all-purpose tools, to be bolted-on to any field of study. One would expect that psychoanalysis, with its particular object of knowledge, namely unconscious mental process, would come to have particular methods of research designed specifically for the understanding of this object and its qualities. This is indeed the case.

A related point is that forms of relevant knowledge are specific to their audiences or users, as well as to their objects. Mental health commissioners quite reasonably need to know about the effectiveness of treatments that can be delivered in relatively standard and predictable ways. How else can they make rational judgements about how best to use scarce resources? Particular kinds of knowledge need to be gathered to inform such decision making. But clinicians, expecting to work with individual patients, although they should know about significant research on different categories of patient and their treatment outcomes, need a more particular kind of knowledge as well. This takes the form of a virtual library of relevant conceptions, theories and cases, so that when the 'unknown' appears, they have to hand the discriminations with which they can think about it. Such primary knowledge has a level of delicacy and specificity that managers and policy makers can justifiably leave to practitioners to master.

The fact is that most of the understanding produced hitherto in the practice of psychoanalysis has so far been of a kind relevant to or for clinicians. The 'speciation' of concepts, theories, classifications and techniques has been evolved by them, in response to patients' presenting problems.

It follows that whereas exploration of the range of research methodologies now so evidently on the market should be pursued vigorously by child psychotherapists, the best research outcomes are unlikely to be achieved by treating research methods merely as tool-kits, required as remedies for endemic psychoanalytic backwardness. What is required is the interrogation of available methods to see how far they can provide answers to new research questions, and how far they need development. The subtleties of the psychoanalytic tradition of inquiry, described above, and its rich resources of theory, need to be brought into dialogue with research techniques developed in other contexts. Innovation usually has a methodological as well as a substantive dimension. Such hybridization has already been taking place in the use of 'grounded theory' by psychoanalytic researchers. They, contrary to Glaser and Strauss's original prescription of an initially theory-free inductive approach, have usually chosen to work within a psychoanalytic frame of reference from the start, while remaining open to new conjectures or 'grounded theories' that are informed by it.[5]

There are interesting questions to be addressed in these exchanges. For example, can the procedures adopted to carry out 'outcome studies' not only measure treatment effectiveness, but also throw light on the underlying psychological conditions of patients, and on optimal techniques of treatment? Or will traditional psychoanalytic methods, albeit somewhat up-scaled through multiple and comparative case studies, and made more accountable in their analysis of data, retain their comparative advantage as the best ways of learning about unconscious mental life and the therapeutic process?

5 On the uses of grounded theory in psychoanalysis, see Anderson (2006).

There is much to be learned from the participation of psychoanalysts and child psychotherapists in this growing debate about methods of research.

References

Alvarez, A. (1992) *Live company: Psychoanalytic psychotherapy with autistic, border-line deprived and abused children*. London: Routledge.

Alvarez, A., Reid, S. (1999) *Autism and personality: Findings from the Tavistock Autism Workshop*. London: Routledge.

Anderson, J. (2003) The mythic significance of risk-taking, dangerous behaviour. *Journal of Child Psychotherapy*, *29*(1), 75–92.

Anderson, J. (2006) Well-suited partners: Psychoanalytic research and grounded theory. *Journal of Child Psychotherapy*, *32*(3), 329–348.

Bartram, B. (2003) Some Oedipal problems in work with adopted children and their parents. *Journal of Child Psychotherapy*, *29*(1), 21–36.

Bick, E. (1968) The experience of the skin in early object relations. *International Journal of Psychoanalysis*, *49*, 484–486.

Boston, M., Szur, R. (eds) (1983) *Psychotherapy with severely deprived children*. London: Routledge.

Canham, H. (1999) The development of the concept of time in fostered and adoptive children. *Psychoanalytic Inquiry*, *19*(2), 160–171.

Canham, H. (2003) The relevance of the Oedipus myth to fostered and adopted children. *Journal of Child Psychotherapy*, 29(1), 5–20.

Canham H. (2004) Spitting, kicking and stripping: Technical difficulties encountered in the treatment of deprived children. *Journal of Child Psychotherapy*, *30*(2), 143–154.

Fonagy, P. (2001) *Attachment theory and psychoanalysis*. New York: Other Press.

Galison, P., Stump, D.J. (eds) (1996) *The disunity of science*. Stanford, CA: Stanford University Press.

Haag, G. (2000) In the footsteps of Frances Tustin: Further reflections in the construction of the body ego. *International Journal of Infant Observation*, *3*(3), 7–22.

Hindle, D. (2000) Assessing children's perspectives on sibling placements in foster or adoptive homes. *Clinical Child Psychology and Psychiatry*, *5*(4), 613–625.

Hopkins, J. (2000) Overcoming a child's resistance to late adoption: How one new attachment can facilitate another. *Journal of Child Psychotherapy*, *26*(3): 335–347.

Houzel, D. (1995) Precipitation anxiety. *Journal of Child Psychotherapy*, *21*(1): 65–78.

Houzel, D. (2004) The psychoanalysis of infantile autism. *Journal of Child Psychotherapy*, *30*(2), 225–237.

Hughes, J.M. (2004) *From obstacle to ally: The making of psychoanalytic practice*. Hove, UK: Brunner-Routledge.

Hunter, M. (2001) *Psychotherapy with young people in care: Lost and found*. London: Brunner-Routledge.

Ironside, L. (1995) Beyond the boundaries: A patient, a therapist and an accusation of sexual abuse. *Journal of Child Psychotherapy*, *21*(2), 183–206.

Joseph, B. (1989) *Psychic equilibrium and psychic change: Selected papers of Betty Joseph*. London: Routledge/Institute of Psychoanalysis.

Joseph, B. (1998) Thinking about a playroom. *Journal of Child Psychotherapy*, *24*(3), 359–366.

Kenrick, J. (2005) Where we live: Some dilemmas and technical issues for the child psychotherapist in interpretative work with looked-after and adopted children. *Journal of Child Psychotherapy*, *31*(1), 24–39.

Klein, S. (1980) Autistic phenomena in neurotic states. *International Journal of Psycho-Analysis*, 61, 395–402.

Kuhn, T.S. (1962) *The structure of scientific revolutions*. Chicago: Chicago University Press.

Kuhn, T.S. (2000) *The road since structure: Philosophical essays 1970–1990 with an autobiographical interview*. Conant J., Haugeland J. (eds). London: University of Chicago.

Lanyado, M. (1991) Putting theory into practice: Struggling with perversion and chaos in the analytic process. *Journal of Child Psychotherapy*, *17*(1), 25–40.

Latour, B. (1983) Give me a laboratory and I will raise the world. In K. Knorr-Cetina & M. Mulkay (eds) *Science observed*. London: Sage.

Latour, B. (1987) *Science in action: How to follow scientists and engineers through society*. Buckingham, UK: Open University Press.

Maiello, S. (1995) The sound-object: A hypothesis about pre-natal auditory experience and memory. *Journal of Child Psychotherapy*, *21*(2): 23–42.

McLeod, J. (2001) *Qualitative research in psychotherapy and counselling*. London: Sage.

Meltzer, D. (1967) *The psycho-analytical process*. London: Heinemann.

Meltzer, D., Bremner, D., Hoxter S., Weddell D., Wittenberg I. (1975) *Explorations in autism: A psychoanalytical study*. Perthshire: Clunie Press.

Midgley, N. (2004) Sailing between Scylla and Charybdis; incorporating qualitative approaches into child psychotherapy research. *Journal of Child Psychotherapy*, *30*(1), 89–111.

Midgley, N. (2006) The inseparable bond between cure and research: Clinical case study as a method of psychoanalytic inquiry. *Journal of Child Psychotherapy*, *32*(2), 122–147.

Miller, L., Rustin. M.E., Rustin. M.J., Shuttleworth. J. (eds) (1989) *Closely observed infants*. London: Duckworth.

Ogden, T. (1989) *The primitive edge of experience*. New York: Jason Aronson.

Philps, J. (2003) *Applications of child psychotherapy to work with children in temporary foster care*. D. Psych. Thesis, University of East London.

Polanyi, M. (1958) *Personal knowledge: Towards a post-critical philosophy*. London: Routledge and Kegan Paul.

Rhode, M. (1994) Autistic breathing. *Journal of Child Psychotherapy*, *20*(1), 25–42.

Rhode, M. (2004) Different responses to trauma in two children with autistic spectrum disorder: The mouth as crossroads for the sense of self. *Journal of Child Psychotherapy*, *30*(1), 3–20.

Rhode, M., Klauber, T. (eds) (2004) *The many faces of Asperger's syndrome*. London: Karnac.

Rosenfeld, S.K., Sprince, M.P. (1963) An attempt to formulate the meaning of the concept 'borderline'. *Psychoanalytic Study of the Child*, *18*, 603–635.

Rustin, M.E. (1991) The strengths of a practitioner's workshop as a new model in clinical research. In S. Miller & R. Szur (eds) *Extending Horizons*. London: Karnac.

Rustin, M.E. (2001) The therapist with her back against the wall. *Journal of Child Psychotherapy, 27*(3), 273–285.

Rustin, M.E. (2005) Conceptual analysis of critical moments in Victoria Climbié's life. *Child & Family Social Work, 10*(1), 11–19.

Rustin, M.E., Rhode, M., Dubinsky, A., Dubinsky, H. (eds) (1997) *Psychotic States in Children.* London: Karnac.

Rustin, M.J. (1997/2001) Give me a consulting room . . . The generation of psycho-analytic knowledge. *British Journal of Psychotherapy, 13*(4), 527–541, July (1997). Revised in 2001 *Reason and unreason: Psychoanalysis, science, politics.* London: Continuum Books.

Rustin, M.J. (2002) Looking in the right place: Complexity theory, psychoanalysis and infant observation. *The International Journal of Infant Observation, 5*(1), 122–144.

Rustin, M.J. (2003) Learning about emotions: The Tavistock Approach. *European Journal of Psychotherapy, Counselling and Health, 6*(3), 187–208.

Rustin, M.J. (2007) How do pychoanalysts know what they know? In L. Braddock & M. Lacewing (eds) *The academic face of psychoanalysis.* London: Routledge.

Sandler, J. (1988) The concept of projective identification. In Sandler, J. (ed) *Projection, identification and projective identification.* New York: International Universities Press.

Sorensen, P. (2000) Observations of transition facilitating behaviour – development and theoretical implications. *International Journal of Infant Observation, 3*(2), 46–54.

Stove, D. (1982) *Popper and after: Four modern irrationalists.* Oxford: Pergamon Press.

Tuckett, D. (1994a) Developing a grounded hypothesis to understand a clinical process: The role of conceptualisation in validation. *International Journal of Psychoanalysis, 75*(5/6), 1159–1180.

Tuckett, D. (ed.) (1994b) Anniversary issue of *International Journal of Psychoanalysis on Clinical Facts, 75*(5/6).

Tustin, F. (1992) *Autistic states in children* (revised ed.). London: Routledge.

Tustin, F. (1994) The perpetuation of an error. *Journal of Child Psychotherapy, 20*(1), 3–24.

Williams, G. (previously Henry, G.) (1974) Doubly deprived. *Journal of Child Psychotherapy, 3*(4), 15–28.

Williams, G. (1997) *Internal landscapes and foreign bodies: Eating disorders and other pathologies.* London: Duckworth.

Williams, G., Williams, P., Desmarais, J., Ravenscroft, K. (eds) (2004) The generosity of acceptance. *Vol. 2 Exploring feeding difficulties in adolescents.* London: Karnac.

Part II

Studying the process of child psychotherapy

Introduction

Since the first psychoanalytic psychotherapists began to work with children, clinicians have been fascinated by trying to better understand the nature of the work they are doing. How does the *psychoanalytic process* evolve over time? Why does play seem to be so central to therapy with children? How can we think about the complex emotional interactions between therapist and child? And what aspects of the therapeutic encounter are most important in promoting change?

'Process research' is the empirical study of *what* actually takes place in a psychotherapy treatment. It is also the means by which we systematically explore *why* and *how* change takes place as the consequence of a therapeutic intervention. When faced with a range of understandings of the clinical process, empirical research offers one way of investigating different hypotheses, and can confirm or challenge some of the ways in which we understand child psychotherapy.

But whereas each of the chapters in this section would, broadly speaking, share these aims, there are many debates about how best to undertake such research. Should such research make use of therapists' own reports of the therapy process, or be based on audio- or video-recordings? Should we study one or two therapies in depth, or do we need to study large numbers of treatments to make sure our findings are generalizable? And do we need to develop quantitative measures of what is going on in therapy, so that statistical analyses can take place, or will that lead to a failure to appreciate the true complexity of the therapeutic setting?

Each of the contributions in this part of the book engages with these methodological issues and takes a slightly different stance on how best to represent the most valid understanding of the child psychotherapy process, while at the same time making the study of this process transparent and meaningful.

Philps, a child psychotherapist whose research emerged out of her own work with children in the care system, describes her attempts to map the clinical process in a way that is both systematic but also clinically enlightening. Rather than presenting a single method for studying the process of psychotherapy, Philps illustrates her own research journey, as she re-visits the same clinical material in several ways, each time trying to find the most meaningful way to capture the complexity of the interaction between child and clinician in the therapeutic setting.

By contrast, Schneider, Pruetzel-Thomas and Midgley make use of a quantitative tool (the Child Psychotherapy Q-Set) to try and develop a reliable and valid measure of what takes place in psychoanalytic child psychotherapy, which allows for the possibility of quantification, statistical analysis and comparison with other forms of treatment. Fully aware of the complexities of reducing such a complex set of interactions to any kind of rating scale, these authors nevertheless argue for the value of such an attempt, and its potential value in clinical research.

Moran and Fonagy's chapter, which is included in this book despite having been first published 20 years ago, is still considered one of the most innovative examples of systematic process research done in this field, making use, as it does, of statistical analyses to explore the relationship between certain therapeutic processes and key therapeutic outcomes. The study is an interesting mix of highly sophisticated empirical methods and clinically relevant and theoretically informed data analysis.

Carlberg's chapter takes a somewhat different approach to the other studies in this section. Rather than using records of the clinical session itself as his primary data, Carlberg focuses on a particular theoretical model of the change process – the concept of 'turning points' – and examines it through questionnaires and interviews with practising child psychotherapists, offering a different perspective on the question of how psychotherapy works.

The chapters in this part are just four examples of a burgeoning area of child psychotherapy research. Interesting pieces of research in themselves, they have been chosen here because they illustrate the range of approaches to studying the therapeutic process that are now in use. (For a full overview of process research in this field, see Kennedy and Midgley 2007.) When successful, such empirical study is of value to clinicians who wish to systematically examine the nature of psychoanalytic work with children with the aim of clarifying and improving clinical practice and developing theory. It is also of value to those interested in studying the effectiveness of psychotherapy, as it can help to identify the underlying mechanisms that may contribute to therapeutic change. For that reason, such research is now considered to be 'probably the best short-term and long-term investment for improving clinical practice and patient care' (Kazdin & Nock 2003 p. 1117).

References

Kazdin, A. E., Nock, M. K. (2003) Delineating mechanisms of change in child and adolescent therapy: Methodological issues and research recommendations. *Journal of Child Psychology & Psychiatry*, *44*(8), 1116–1129.

Kennedy, E., Midgley, N. (eds) (2007) *Process and outcome research in child, adolescent and parent-infant psychotherapy: A thematic review.* London: NHS London. Available as a free download at www.acp.uk.net

Mapping process in child psychotherapy: Steps towards drafting a new method for evaluating psychoanalytic case studies

Janet Philps

Introduction

This chapter describes some of the dilemmas experienced in an exploratory research project looking at the application of child psychotherapy to work with children in temporary foster care (Philps 2003). As part of a doctoral research study, I attempted to apply the principles of psychoanalysis as an 'interpretative science' (Emde 1994) to two psychoanalytic cases studies, subsequently evaluating them using other externally and operationally grounded approaches.

In what follows, I describe the way in which quantitative and qualitative research methods were selected, explored and applied to these particular case studies. The particular progressive choice and development of these methods came from a wish to reveal for external scrutiny more of the content and process of therapy itself. I hope to show the way in which such a use of 'mixed methods' can increase shared understanding across disciplines, providing more transparency, impartiality and clarity in the evaluation of psychoanalytic 'clinical facts'.

Among the several consequences of the challenges involved was the drafting of a method for mapping transference, countertransference and outcome episodes in process recordings of child psychotherapy sessions. The research experience leading to this particular method is described. In developing my particular mapping method, my aim was to contribute to a general framework within which to begin to systematically represent such dynamic experiences.

The case studies and their evaluation

In the two case studies presented here, I made use of my own selection of 'clinical facts' from my process recordings of the two children's therapy sessions, and notes of my professional discussion meetings with carers and social workers. My evaluation of the case studies was also based on process recordings of the children's sessions. The data involved throughout was therefore doubly subjective. First, I was both therapist and researcher, and second, my process recordings and my selection of clinical facts from them were based on my representations of others' representations of their experience, as well as my own.

The two children involved – a boy, John, and a girl, Kate (all names have been changed to preserve confidentiality) – were both around ten years old at initial assessment. Both were living in temporary foster care at the time of their therapy, having suffered abuse and neglect in their original families. They went through several different placements before settling permanently. The case study of John was based on an initial assessment and then the first twenty-six months of psychotherapy. That of Kate involved an initial assessment for psychotherapy, but soon after this, therapy was declined. After a gap of twenty months, by which time the placement had broken down, Kate received a second assessment. The two assessments and nearly two years of therapy following the second assessment formed the basis of the second case study. Table 3.1 gives a summary of the methods used to study these two cases.

Through the chronological accounts of the case studies a working hypothesis evolved, concerning the dynamic interplay between some borderline-type features (Rey 1994) in the 'subjective environment' of carers and social workers involved in temporary foster care on the one hand, and developments in the internal worlds of children in such placements on the other. With the intervention of psychotherapy for the children in these settings, progressively less borderline and more consistently depressive types of functioning appeared to develop in both children.

Both children in this study initially presented with a range of difficulties. John showed several borderline features in his assessment, which continued for some time. For example, he presented as highly controlling in concrete enactments and thinking; he demonstrated a sparse sense of 'self' and a confused merging of love and hate. Through his behaviour he showed both his present trauma about placement uncertainty and conflict, as well as the legacy of his past trauma and abuse in his original family. During the course of treatment, a gradual development was expressed in the transference, and in his thinking about his other relationships, past and present, indicating the beginnings of a depressive state of mind (see, for example, Hinshelwood 1991 pp. 138–154) in which he could tolerate and express more concern for others. In this process he appeared to develop away from borderline states towards a more depressive internal integration of good and bad, differentiation of self from other and an internalization of a good parental object with whom he could identify; he also showed more reflective thinking.

The case of Kate was chosen as a relevant contrast to that of John, which promised some clarification of the processes of therapeutic change that were under investigation. Although initially very confused and apparently very mixed in her feelings, Kate presented more depressive than borderline material at the point of initial assessment. For example, her concern, sorrow and pining for her life with her mother and father was poignant; she

Table 3.1 Summary of methods

Method	Material	Selection samples
1. Two single psychoanalytically based case studies	i. Process recordings of children's assessment and therapy sessions ii. Clinical records of meetings and telephone calls with carers and social workers	i. Researcher's selection of 'clinical facts' from representative samples of 26 and 23 process recordings respectively ii. Researcher's summaries of all clinical records of the meetings and phone calls noted during period of study
2. One single inter-disciplinary based case study	iii. Summaries of psychodynamic process of child's assessment iv. Clinical records of meetings with carers and social workers v. Independent researcher's verbatim transcripts of two systemic interviews (Fausset 1996)	iii. Total number of sessions = 2 iv. Researcher's summaries of all clinical records of meetings noted during period of study v. Four representative passages of interview dialogue from 2 interviews
3. Personal Relatedness Profile Rating Scales (Hobson, Patrick & Valentine 1998)	vi. Process recordings of children's assessment and therapy sessions	vi. *Pilot study*: one representative sample of 3 sessions vii. *Main study*: two representative samples of 8 sessions each
4. Content analysis by frequency counts of Borderline (based on Rey 1994) and Depressive (based on Hinshelwood 1991) characteristics	vii. Process recordings of children's assessments and therapy sessions	viii. Two representative samples of 24 and 25 sessions, respectively
5. Mapping psychodynamic process of assessment and therapy sessions (based on Emde 1994)	viii. Process recordings of children's assessments and therapy sessions	ix. Two representative samples of 17 sessions each

expressed guilt over her ambivalent feelings towards her mother; she was afraid for her mother's health, and her reparative feelings towards her were expressed. She showed strong capacities to grieve for her loss, to feel concern for others and to seek to re-establish good object relations in the present and future. This continued throughout her therapy, except around her second assessment after the twenty month gap between assessments, when considerably more borderline material, very similar to John's, appeared. In particular, she presented as being in projective identification with her damaged and helpless maternal object. Her carers at the time also expressed some borderline-type thinking throughout this period and it gradually emerged that such features in the subject environment of her placement might have been influencing 'schizoid' or borderline types of very painful and uneasy splits in Kate's thinking and feelings, which were not so apparent in her way of speaking about her family of origin or in the transference. Subsequently, she came to describe a difference between these three contexts, in terms of how much she felt herself to be believed in, which appeared to make all the difference to her sense of self-efficacy. Gradually, she appeared more able to live with what seemed like a potentially borderline split in herself. She appeared to be able to feel more herself in therapy sessions and in her original family (however traumatic and abusive she portrayed her family to be at times) and not herself in her life in foster care, which she considered 'second rate'. It appeared to me that Kate's increased capacity to integrate her thinking about her experiences, through therapy, enabled her to understand this split and to manage it, rather than acting it out defensively.

As with the case of John, it felt to me that, overall, the work with Kate illustrated the potential benefits of child psychotherapy in the context of extreme states of uncertainty and conflict in which children live in temporary placements in care. At times, the children's carers and social workers also described, in my clinical meetings with them, positive developments in the children's behaviour at home and at school. This went some way in supporting my view, but not always consistently so, as at other times they focused on their own feelings of pressure and stress and the dilemmas experienced in their work.

But can such a personal conviction of the significance of therapeutic work be made more available to public scrutiny? To subsequently evaluate my perception of the children's apparent developments in therapy given in my case studies, I went beyond the methods of evaluation commonly used within the psychoanalytic field, using three different methods (Table 3.1).

Evaluating the children's emotional development with therapy: measuring progress, what happened to process?

In the first stage of evaluating the case material, I used a quantitative measure, the Personal Relatedness Profile (PRP), which Hobson, Patrick and Valentine

(1998) developed to establish the possibility of objective and reliable psycho-analytic judgements about adult subjects' psychological functioning. The Profile has thirty items in three scales of ten items each, representing paranoid–schizoid and depressive states of mind regarding 'personal related-ness', 'characteristics of people (objects)' and 'predominant affective state'. Each subject is rated on each item on a five-point scale and an overall single score is obtained. A higher score indicates a greater degree of depressive rather than paranoid–schizoid functioning. In their initial study, the authors found that borderline and dysthymic groups were significantly distinguished by the PRP.

Although generated with video-taped assessment interviews with adult sub-jects, rather than process recordings of children's sessions, the PRP appeared relevant to the theoretical framework of the case studies, in particular where I suggested therapeutic developments in John and Kate in terms of border-line and depressive states of mind. However, the applicability of the PRP to children's process recordings was uncharted and required some exploration.

In a pilot study, the feasibility of applying the PRP to evaluate process recordings of children's therapy sessions was established on the basis of independent ratings of the Profile on three representative sessions, carried out by a total of five experienced child psychotherapists, and compared with my own ratings. Following this, representative samples of the children's sessions occurring at four fixed time points over a thirty-two month period (at assess-ment, and at twelve, twenty-four and thirty-two months from first assess-ment) were rated on the PRP by two further independent raters (both child psychotherapists) and again compared with my own ratings. In total, eight sessions for each child were included in the study, two from each time point.

Figure 3.1a illustrates the mean scores obtained for John at each time point, from my own ratings (J) and those of two independent raters (L and R). Figure 3.1b illustrates the mean scores obtained for Kate.

In Figure 3.1a, the interrater reliability appears poor for John's assessment sessions, but improves after that. Nevertheless, the trend of the scores by all three raters appears generally consistent in direction. All show a more marked increase in depressive scores by the end of the first year of therapy. Following the first year, depressive functioning appears either to have been more or less maintained at the higher level, or to have increased more slowly.

Figure 3.1b shows the agreement between all three raters over the marked decrease in Kate's scores on the PRP between the first and second assessments, reflecting my case-study description of her change to more borderline func-tioning after the gap without therapy between her two assessments. Her scores then all show some gradual retrieval of higher depressive scores after that.

These measures of borderline/depressive functioning on the PRP appear to support the suggestion in the descriptive case studies that the children's depressive functioning developed positively with therapy, while their border-line functioning diminished. Also highlighted in the second study was the

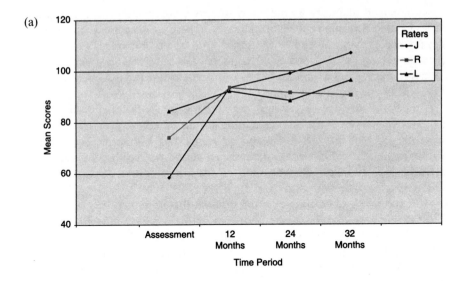

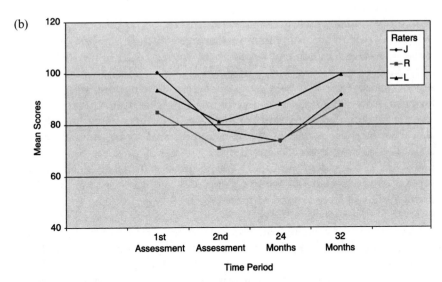

Figure 3.1 (a) PRP scales: John's ratings. (b) PRP scales: Kate's ratings.

implication that, during the gap in therapy, Kate's depressive functioning deteriorated in the foster-care environment, and recovered somewhat once therapy began.

However, I remained curious about the single score indicating level of paranoid–schizoid/depressive functioning (PS-D) obtained by the PRP method, because these two types of functioning are not regarded in the psychoanalytic literature as mutually exclusive, and overlap occurs particularly in the definition of their defences. There is usually a stable predominance of more of one or the other state in any individual's awareness, presentation and actions over time, but there seem to be no conceptual reasons for assuming PS-D fluctuations to be along a single dimension as presented, for example, by the statistically generated factor analysis of the PRP.

Concerned that the use of a single measure of PS-D functioning might encourage a foreclosing on the nature of the complexity of the psychodynamic interrelationship between depressive and borderline functioning within the individual in theory and in the children in my study, I subsequently attempted to 'unpack' the meaning of the single scores obtained, using different sources of definition from the PRP.

As a second stage in the evaluation process, therefore, I carried out, in two separate content analyses, some frequency counts of, first, fifteen borderline (Rey 1994) and, second, twenty-one depressive characteristics (Hinshelwood 1991). Such a content analysis approach is regarded in statistical terms as a 'nominal scale' measure, not least because the characteristics counted were no longer assumed to relate to each other along a single quantified continuum, as with the PRP, but rather to be distinct categories that are not necessarily mutually exclusive.

For this part of the evaluation, further representative samples of process recordings were selected, and added to the samples used in the PRP study. The additions represented highly transitional points and apparently mutative sessions during the first two years of therapy. Twenty-four sessions were included from John's therapy, and twenty-five from Kate's. Presence and absence of both depressive and paranoid–schizoid functioning in each process recording was counted. Where there appeared to be some ambiguity about the status of any characteristic in the material, presence was counted, but a 'query' was also indicated. The proportional incidence of the two types of characteristics, shown in Figures 3.2a and 3.2b for John and Kate, respectively, can be compared with each other.

These figures show that the borderline characteristics decreased with therapy over time for both children. The increase for Kate between the first and second assessments, following the gap in therapy, again shows up. These results apparently support those from the PRP in a fairly straightforward way.

Turning to the depressive characteristics, it appears that initial depressive functioning in Kate's case was more or less maintained at a higher level throughout the period studied, whereas in John's case the level appears to oscillate more markedly. A closer examination of the 'queries' mentioned above revealed that the level of depressive functioning might have been inflated in John's assessment sessions, suggesting that this fluctuation might have been shallower than shown in Figure 3.2a between assessment and the first year of therapy, whereas the increase in his level of depressive functioning after that is somewhat more marked.

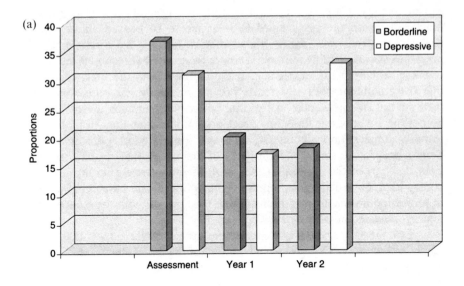

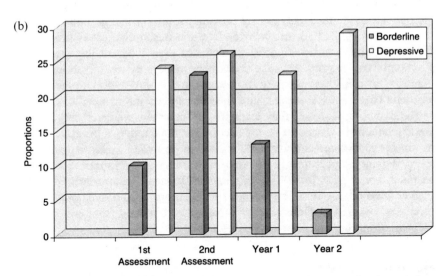

Figure 3.2 (a) John's proportions of borderline/depressive characteristics (rounded-up percentages). (b) Kate's proportions of borderline/depressive characteristics (rounded-up percentages).

A further examination suggested that whereas the depressive character-istics overall perhaps fluctuated, but then seemed to increase in John's case, albeit with considerable defensiveness, they were more or less maintained throughout in the case of Kate. This maintenance also appeared to be mark-edly more defensive by the time of her second assessment, at the end of the gap in therapy. Kate's gradual retrieval of her general level of depressive functioning with therapy seemed to continue to be hedged about with a defensiveness that was slightly higher than at her original assessment, but nevertheless considerably reduced in comparison with her second assessment.

These developments supplemented the findings from the PRP, clarifying that these children both apparently became markedly less borderline with therapy. But this new stage of the study indicated that such a reduction in borderline functioning does not necessarily imply that they both became commensurately more depressive, although some modest gains may have been in progress during the second year of therapy. Rather, it was suggested from this part of the evaluation that, with therapy in these settings of temporary care, both children's depressive functioning may have become freer from borderline constraints, even though for both of them depressive functioning remained notably defensive.

In turn, the PRP and the content analyses offered some support (PRP) and refinement (content analyses) to the findings of the initial clinical studies, and this suggested that they both lent some credibility to the case-study method itself.

However, this phase of my evaluation process highlighted a dilemma. On the one hand, the measures clearly provided some clarification and support to the initial clinical picture provided by the descriptive case studies. On the other hand, there was a cost in terms of their inherent limitations for psychoanalytic enquiry. Because these measures are by nature static, rather than dynamic, in their capacity to describe and compare developments, my accounts based upon these measures necessarily became stripped of the 'life' of the dynamic processes they evaluated, which were rendered mute, or at least sidelined. In this context, my account of the children's progress shown by changes in scores could not be shown to be linked systematically with relevant dynamic processes in therapy. Only inferences and suggestions could be made about such links. For this reason, it seemed important to find a further method for revealing systematically more of the dynamics of the processes involved in these cases than could be obtained from either measurement alone, or from the case studies alone.

Mapping process

In the next stage of evaluation, my aim was therefore to discover whether further representative subsamples of process recordings could be systematically mapped or charted, displaying the psychodynamics of the process, and whether descriptions and conclusions based on them would corroborate, or vary in any significant sense from, those obtained in the case studies.

In considering how to do this, I found Emde's (1994) thinking helpful. Discussing and developing the contributions of Sandler (1994) and Stern (1994) with regard to the definition of what they all term 'psychoanalytically meaningful units of experience', Emde describes 'identified reliable measures of central relationship patterns' such as Luborsky and Crits-Christoph's (1989) Core Conflictual Relationship Theme measure (CCRT).

Emde suggests, first, that in the basic dynamic unit of psychoanalysis 'the dynamic sequence is not only within the individual (intrapsychic) but between individuals (interpersonal) . . . I would prefer to call them interpersonal dynamic configurations' (Emde 1994 p. 44). Second, Emde suggests that a new level of 'interpersonal context' results from the interactions involved in the 'wish of the self, the response of the other, and response of the self (A B A′):

> The new level of context created within the dynamic sequence reflects a new level of organisation, co-construction and imaginative perspective (A B A′ → C). The resultant represents shared meaning . . . which becomes a basis for further development.
>
> Emde (1994 p. 45)

This kind of thinking formed a general framework on which to begin to base my particular attempt to map process. The process recordings of sessions could be divided into a series of episodes, which appeared to be psychoanalytically meaningful in that each one contained 'transference' (or the child's apparent internal object relations, or 'wish of the self'), 'countertransference' (or 'the response of the other') and 'outcome' (or 'new level of context') components.

To illustrate this, I will present a summary of the process recording of the first four episodes of John's first individual session, followed by my mapping of these episodes. This session was divided into a total of thirteen episodes altogether. (The more detailed process recording on which my mapping was originally based has been summarized here for reasons of confidentiality.)

Episode I

In the waiting room John is sitting besides his escort, reading. When I call his name he looks up expectantly, replaces the book and comes forward looking at me with an open pleasant expression. The escort comes too and says he'll pick up John and they part company. John goes ahead of me down the corridor, working out which doors to go through and which direction, looking back now and again for clarification and confirmation.

Once in the therapy room he stands and turns, scanning the room and drawing in breath and letting out a sigh of satisfaction, and looking both apprehensive and pleased. He looks at me as he sits down in the vacant armchair and I take up my place. His stance seems nervously pressured as he struggles to somehow both settle himself and poise himself to react at the same time.

I comment that this is our second out of three sessions and that it's the first time he's come in on his own.

Episode 2

John waits no longer to tell me, with a surge of feeling, that he wants to tell me about something that makes him feel so very angry. At my slightest nod, he explains in emphatic outraged tones about confronting a woman for having treated him badly, and how he thought this confrontation had been a very severe punishment for the person, who could not deny what he had said.

'Punished by you?'

'Yes!'

My mind was reeling from John's angry, revengeful outpouring; from not having caught on to who exactly he had confronted, why they had met, and when. These confusions were quickly cleared when I commented, in the form of a question, on him telling me about getting revenge and how angry he was with the person for what they had done to him.

'Yes!'

I asked who the person was.

Episode 3

He tells me the details of his relationship to the woman, his other relatives and of parental splits. He goes on to tell me about his father losing his job, being in a fight and getting injured, and now not having anywhere to live.

It all feels extremely intense.

Episode 4

John tells me graphic details of the situation between himself and his family before coming into care permanently. For example, his brother would do things he shouldn't while John watched. When their parents discovered what was wrong, his brother would deny it was him and John would be very severely punished for lying. He says he doesn't know why he had to go into care. He goes back to explaining angrily that he had been 'ready' for the woman when he had the opportunity to confront her, and repeated that she knew it was the truth.

I say that seeing the person again after such a long time brought up all those things again that still make him so angry.

'Yes.'

I wondered if he had been able to tell other people about these things and feelings before.

'No nobody!'

I wondered if John had somehow felt 'ready' for me also this morning then – he'd really let me know the truth at last about his angry tempers.

Mapping the episodes from John's sessions

Figure 3.3 charts the way in which each episode can both be understood in its own terms and becomes the basis for the following episode(s). In Episode 1, John's transference to the whole setting appeared as apprehensive pleasure at being 'inside'. My response was based on the countertransference of John needing information about 'outside' reality at this early stage of therapy. The outcome (which refers on to Episode 2) is summarized as John evacuating excitedly about the maternal object's abuse and his own vengeful feelings towards her.

In Episode 2, John's transference is represented as his punishing feelings towards the abusive maternal object. My countertransference feelings of confusion, and of being swamped by John's outpouring, were the basis for my questions for clarification about his feelings and motives, and who exactly they were aimed at. The outcome (referring to Episode 3) is summarized as John moving on to evacuate anxiety about his lost mother and damaged father.

In Episode 3, John responds by clarifying his relatives' identities. In the transference he expressed intensely evacuated anxiety about his parental objects being lost, damaged and deprived. In the countertransference, I felt the intensity of his desperate feelings of uncontainable anxiety, anger, revenge and grief. The outcome (referring to Episode 4) is represented as John moving on to intensely and excitedly evacuate his experience of past parental abuse and his assumption of his own innocence.

In Episode 4, in the transference John evacuated the abuse experienced, and possibly projected guilt onto the parental couple. My response from the countertransference aimed to contain John's intense rage in the form of an interpretation about our relationship and John being 'ready for me' (just as he had been 'ready' to confront his relative). The outcome (referring to Episode 5, which is not included in this example) summarizes John calming and becoming thoughtful, while I consider his sense of loss of his family.

As this example shows, my summary descriptions of the outcome of each episode were usually in terms of the child's material. At the same time, what is taken in as shared in a particular episode might be inferred as 'context' in Emde's sense for the development in the following episode(s), and so on, throughout the process recording for each session. Thus an episode in the middle of a session may be considered to contain both, 'outcome' or 'context', depending on whether one is looking forward to the next and subsequent episode(s), or backwards to the previous episode(s) in the process. In any event, my 'outcome' is similar to Emde's 'new level of context'.

The above example can begin to give some idea of how this form of

<table>
<tr><th colspan="3">John's Assessment</th><th>1st Individual Session</th><th colspan="6">Technique</th><th colspan="3">Focus</th></tr>
<tr><th>Session No</th><th>Episode No</th><th>TR /CT</th><th>Description</th><th>Reflecting/ Mirroring O=Observing</th><th>Linking</th><th>Actively Support-ing Defence</th><th>Explaining External Reality/ Setting</th><th>Questioning</th><th>Interpreting</th><th>Present</th><th>Past</th><th>Combination</th></tr>
<tr><td>2</td><td>1</td><td>TR
CT</td><td>Apprehensive Pleasure at being 'inside'?
John needs information re reality of setting
OUTCOME: J evacuates excitedly re maternal abuse and John's vengeful feelings</td><td>✓</td><td></td><td></td><td></td><td></td><td>✓</td><td></td><td></td><td></td></tr>
<tr><td>2</td><td>2</td><td>TR
CT</td><td>Punishing towards abusive maternal object
Clarifying Fantasy; confusion swamped by outpouring from John
OUTCOME: J moves on to evacuate anxiety re lost mother and damaged father.</td><td>✓</td><td></td><td></td><td></td><td>✓</td><td></td><td></td><td></td><td>✓</td></tr>
<tr><td>2</td><td>3</td><td>TR
CT</td><td>Anxiety re parental objects being lost/damaged/deprived intensely evacuated
Intense/desperate feelings of uncontainable anxiety, anger, revenge, grief in John
OUTCOME: J moves on to past abuse with his own innocence – intensely evacuated with excitement re both parents</td><td>O</td><td></td><td></td><td></td><td></td><td></td><td></td><td></td><td>✓</td></tr>
<tr><td>2</td><td>4</td><td>TR
CT</td><td>Evacuating abuse and ? projected guilt onto parental couple.
Contain J's rage with interpretation re our relationship "ready for me"
OUTCOME: J Calms and becomes thoughtful; therapist considers J's loss of family</td><td>✓</td><td>✓</td><td></td><td></td><td></td><td></td><td>✓</td><td></td><td>✓</td></tr>
</table>

Figure 3.3 Example of mapping the first four episodes of a session.

organizing the content of a process recording provides a possibility of a systematic map or chart representing the dynamic process of the whole session more intact. With this approach, the kind of therapeutic dynamics described in the case studies were enriched and opened up to outside scrutiny, thus creating the possibility of a more operationally grounded description, even though it essentially remains a highly subjective one.

In Figure 3.3, alongside each episode, the following kinds of therapeutic techniques evident during the episode were indicated by ticks:

Observation only (O), reflecting, mirroring
Linking
Actively supporting defence
Explaining external reality/setting
Questioning
Partially interpreting (ticked with a P) and
Fully interpreting

Finally, the focus of the content of each episode was also indicated in terms of the children's past experience in their family of origin; their present experience in their placement, or in the transference only; or a combination of both past and present.

My particular purpose with these indicators of technique and focus was to provide the possibility of evaluating my impressions in the initial case studies regarding the pattern of use of interpretation and non-interpretative techniques during the therapeutic process. This was especially relevant to considering therapy with individuals in uncertain placement settings in care.

For example, early in the therapy, non-interpretive techniques and some sparse and partial interpretations appeared more prevalent, especially in sessions taking place at acutely transitional points either of the therapy, or of the placement settings; while full interpretations seemed more consistently forthcoming during relatively settled periods. However, the full charts (in Philps 2003) show how, later in the therapy, this distinction dwindled as the transference relationship developed and deepened, so that full transference interpretations tended to occur more consistently over sessions, whether at acutely transitional points, or in more settled periods.

With these two indicators, the description of the fluctuating relationships between technique and focus, between episodes within sessions, and between sessions as a whole, could also be operationally grounded in a way that linked them specifically to the episodes of the process in which they occurred.

For both children, representative sessions (see Table 3.1) were then considered in temporal sequence in a narrative, and the development of the children's object relations, the transference/countertransference relationship, the fluctuations between focus on present and past experience, and the therapist's fluctuations in the use of technique in tune with them, were described in terms of the charted process, which could then be used to monitor my case-study narratives. With the systematic representation of the transference/ countertransference/outcome process, it seems that the inferences made about process could thereby be grounded, shared with and evaluated by others.

With the mapping of the processes of the children's object relations, the descriptions in the two initial case studies were further enriched. Further details were evident of the ways in which both children appeared to become more able to mourn the loss of their original family life, to work through some of the abuse and neglect they had experienced in the past, as well as work through some of the impingements they felt from their current 'subjective environments'. It showed more clearly that while Kate's therapy appeared to involve her in an existential struggle of adjustment in her sense of self and identity following the loss of her original family, John's seemed more involved with his partial recovery from an earlier, more catastrophic and almost total loss of his sense of identity and self.

It became more apparent that, as the therapy proceeded, work in the transference developed consistently towards the beginning of the second year of the periods studied, in spite of the continuing sense of impingements upon the children from their 'subjective environments'. Earlier in the therapy this had seemed to have rendered transference interpretation mute or inappropriate, which may have slowed down such developments compared to therapy with children in more settled homes. But in the context of the therapist's willingness to focus and attune to the meaning of such felt current environmental impingements when brought into sessions by the children, a sense of trust in the continuity of her understanding of their predicaments appeared to have accumulated, strengthening the transference relationship.

Summary and conclusion

This chapter has described the evolution of a clinical research study that attempted to make the clinical process of therapy with children in foster care available to external scrutiny without losing the richness and complexity of the psychodynamic process. My successive choices of methods reflect specific dilemmas in a struggle to find an appropriate methodology for the study of the process of psychoanalytic child psychotherapy. In the initial case studies, I wanted to preserve as far as possible the internal consistency and principles of the psychoanalytic method as an interpretive science of the meaning of experiences. In their subsequent evaluation, I wanted to explore links with other systematic and operationally grounded approaches, drawing on a combination of empirical measurement and psychoanalytically grounded methods.

Using statistical measures of object relations gave some support and refinement to my case-study descriptions of the children's therapeutic developments over time. But because of the static nature of these methods, the psychoanalytic processes involved seemed lost from sight. This compelled me to draft a qualitative method that would bring process out into the open for external and systematic scrutiny in a way that was not offered by either the original case studies or the statistical approaches alone.

Paradoxically, such an additional approach to structuring the material of a psychoanalytic session while preserving its process through mapping also provides an option to measure both content and process. It also offers the possibility to systematically locate selected clinical facts more precisely than before within the whole process of a session, within systematic samples of sessions, or within the whole process of therapy.

References

Emde, R.N. (1994) Developing psychoanalytic representations of experience. *Infant Mental Health Journal, 15*(1), 42–49.

Fausset, A. (1996) *Fostering identities*. MSc dissertation. Kensington Consultation Centre/University of Luton.

Hinshelwood, R.D. (1991) *A dictionary of Kleinian thought*. London: Free Association Books.

Hobson, R.P., Patrick, M.P.H., Valentine, J.D. (1998) Objectivity in psychoanalytic judgements. *British Journal of Psychiatry, 173*, 172–177.

Luborsky, L., Crits-Christoph, P. (1989) A relationship pattern measure: The core conflictual relationship theme. *Psychiatry, 52*, 250–259.

Philps, J.F. (2003) Applications of child psychotherapy to work with children in temporary foster care. Doctoral Thesis, University of East London/Tavistock Clinic.

Rey, H. (1994) *Universals of psychoanalysis in the treatment of psychotic and borderline states*. J. Magagna (ed.). London: Free Association Books.

Sandler, J. (1994) Fantasy, defence and the representational world. *Infant Mental Health Journal, 15*(1), 26–35.

Stern, D. (1994) One way to build a clinically relevant baby. *Infant Mental Health Journal, 15*(1), 9–25.

Chapter 4

Discovering new ways of seeing and speaking about psychotherapy process: The Child Psychotherapy Q-Set

Celeste Schneider, Anna Pruetzel-Thomas and Nick Midgley

> The only true voyage of discovery ... would not be to visit strange lands but to possess other eyes, to behold the universe through the eyes of another, of a hundred others, to behold the hundred universes that each of them beholds, that each of them is.
>
> Marcel Proust (1941) *Remembrance of Things Past*

Can psychotherapy research illuminate and offer clinicians insight about this complex and unique way people meet that we call psychotherapy? Transformative meaning can be derived through history, feeling, words, silence, intuition, play, gesture, gaze; the poetry and poignancy of experience, and can take various shapes and form in the imaginative lives of therapist and child. Yet, in the minds of many clinicians, the concept of 'psychotherapy research' is likely to conjure associations to scientific evidence-based models emphasizing randomized clinical trials, replication, controlled setting, randomly assigned client population, and manualization of treatment; very different bases for evidence of clinically significant experience.

Michael Rustin (2001) highlights the way in which clinicians reflexively discount the work they do as research, reminding us of alternative ways of considering what features we deem 'evidence', and by implication the research designs we then construct. Speaking about the field of psychotherapy research, Alan Kazdin (2003) points out that despite the considerable progress made in psychotherapy outcome research with children, we are faced with significant gaps in our understanding:

> Despite the progress fundamental questions remain about therapy and its effects ... a great deal of concern in contemporary research focuses on the extent to which treatment effects obtained in research generalize to practice. Because we do not understand why or how most treatments

work, we do not know which facets of treatment are particularly important to clinical practice.

(Kazdin 2003 p. 17)

Because of the pressure to 'prove' the effectiveness of treatments by means of
outcome studies, researchers have been led to answer assumed questions
regarding 'what works for whom' (Paul 1967), before sufficiently understanding the pathways to those conclusions. This *consequentialist* (Fonagy, Target,
Phillips & Kurtz 2002) trend has resulted in validation and comparison of
'brand-name' therapies (Shirk & Russell 1996), leading us far from the experiences in many consulting rooms, especially those of clinicians practising child
psychotherapy and psychoanalysis, and so creating serious gaps between the
efforts, experience and discoveries of clinicians and researchers.

It appears that a critical reading of this predominant and influential
'evidence-based' paradigm is called for within the context of psychotherapy
research, and for psychotherapists and psychotherapy researchers to gather
various kinds of evidence, and methods that move beyond a constricted
version of the scientific method (Midgley 2004). Empirical methodologies
employed in outcome research may bolster our conceptual landscape by generating shared discourse, systematic inquiry and the recognition of patterns
otherwise neglected, but they are often lacking means to make room for the
creative and intuitive dimensions of our work. Worse, they may unknowingly
constrict intuition at the very core of its epistemology. If we are to strive for
methodological rigour and generalizability we must retain the subtleties
and appreciation of the *unknowable*, and the *patience* needed to truly learn
from, rather than about, experience. The Child Psychotherapy Q-Set (CPQ),
described in this chapter, is a methodology and an instrument developed
with the above proposition in mind.

History of Q-methodology

Q-methodology is a general scaling technique used to provide convenient ways
of organizing data in terms of their representativeness of a particular construct, person, or situation being described. Q-technique refers to the research
instrument developed for Q-methodology. William Stephenson (1935, 1953)
is recognized as the person who did most to develop Q-methodology. Originally trained as a quantum physicist, Stephenson forged his way through the
tensions between classical Newtonian physics, based on sense perception and
observables, and quantum theory, which is based on the behaviour of sub-
atomic particles and involves complex structures and systems of states not
amenable to direct observation (Goldman 1999). Stephenson applied these
interests to the field of experimental psychology while under the mentorship
of Charles Spearman at University College London, a period during which
he was also nominated by Ernest Jones for psychoanalysis with Melanie

Klein (Brown 1991). Central to his theory is that factor theory in psychology and quantum theory in physics have parallel mathematical and statistical foundations.

Jack Block (1961, Block & Haan 1971), a personality psychologist known for his extensive elaborations and applications of Q-methodology, elaborated Stephenson's techniques and principles. He developed observer-rating procedures utilizing Q-methodology, the California Q-Set, and the California Child Q-Set (Block 1969). Block's work facilitated communication among research psychologists about how commonly used psychological terms, labels and constructs are understood and what they mean to the individuals using them.

Enrico Jones, a psychoanalyst and psychotherapy researcher dedicated to encouraging discourse between these two fields, further extended Q-methodology in developing the Psychotherapy Process Q-Set (Jones 1985, 2000). The PQS offers us a language and a rating procedure to draw out and describe the unique and guiding dynamics of the interplay between therapist and child. Raters undertake an evaluation of videotapes and transcripts of actual clinical experience in a Q-Sorting procedure that both identifies salient observable themes, and gathers underlying organizing principles of a session. Theoretical terminology is kept to a minimum, allowing for theoretically 'un-saturated' portraits of therapist–patient interaction. Such description allows for comparison of process across various theoretical orientations and offers a closer look at what clinicians and researchers mean when referring to particular theoretical dynamics and constructs (for example, see Jones & Price 1998).

The PQS has been recognized for its effectiveness in capturing the complexity of psychotherapy process in adult treatments and has contributed valuable information about adult psychotherapy process and its relationship to outcome. The work of Jones and colleagues has challenged accepted notions about various treatment modalities, revitalized the use of single-case research design in psychotherapy research, and promoted the study of long-term psychotherapy and psychoanalysis (e.g. Jones, Cumming & Horowitz 1988, Jones & Windholz 1989, Jones, Hall & Parke 1991, Jones & Pulos 1993, Ablon & Jones 1998, 1999, 2002). One example is the work of Jones and Pulos (1993), who applied the PQS to compare process in psychodynamic and cognitive behavioural treatments. These researchers discovered that *both* CBT and psychodynamic treatments were more likely to have a successful outcome when the therapist was making greater use of *psychodynamic* factors.

Such findings illustrate how outcome studies focused on 'brand-name' treatments may fail to tell us about the significant process factors that are essential to therapeutic change and the importance of case-based research (Midgley 2006). The Child Psychotherapy Q-Set carries on the tradition of research set forth by Jones in the context of child psychotherapy.

The Child Psychotherapy Q-Set

The Child Psychotherapy Q-Set (CPQ; Schneider & Jones 2004) is designed for work with children ages 3–13. To allow for greater reliability, a coding manual provides clear definitions and examples of each item reflecting features that can be assessed using video-tapes of child psychotherapy sessions – always seeking a delicate balance between that which is observable and that which has to be inferred.

The instrument consists of 100 cards with statements that represent a selection from a pool of items culled from an extensive review of child psychotherapy literature (including empirically validated treatment methods, as well as psychoanalytic approaches), existing process instruments and adaptations from the adult PQS. The instrument development project spanned four years and involved a recursive process of item construction, piloting for clinical validity and item reconstruction. Each of the CPQ development studies mutually informed the other and modifications to the items and the manual were made after consideration of the results along the way. The initial items, culled from an extensive review of child psychotherapy literature, were reviewed by experienced clinicians representing various theoretical viewpoints (including CBT, psychoanalytic and psychodynamic), who provided feedback on item clarity, redundancy, coverage and representativeness. To establish item validity across different children in various modes of psychotherapy, members of the Berkeley Psychotherapy Research Group used the revised CPQ to describe process in twenty video-tapes of child therapy representing cognitive behavioural, psychodynamic and psychoanalytic treatments. An item correlation matrix of these ratings identified items that demonstrated little variance across cases (that is failed to differentiate across subjects) and that were redundant with other items.

As a full set, the items of the CPQ represent a broad range of child and therapist characteristics as shown in Table 4.1.

The rating procedure is relatively straightforward. After studying video-tapes of child therapy and arriving at some formulation of the material,

Table 4.1 Examples from the Child Psychotherapy Q-Set

Description	Example
i. Items describing child's attitudes, feelings, behaviour or experience	CPQ Item 29: the quality of child's play is fluid, absorbed vs. fragmented or sporadic
ii. Items reflecting the therapist's actions and attitudes	CPQ Item 12: therapist models unspoken or unelaborated emotions
iii. Items attempting to capture the nature of the interaction of the dyad or the atmosphere of the encounter	CPQ Item 45: therapist tolerates child's strong affect or impulses

Note: CPQ, Child Psychotherapy Q-Set.

raters sort the 100 CPQ cards into one of nine categories, placing at one end those cards believed to be most characteristic or salient of the material, and at the other end cards believed to be most saliently uncharacteristic. A fixed number of items are placed in each category, with more items placed centrally, reflecting less or undecriptive items than at the tails of the distribution.

Raters engage in a meta-analytic process that moves between intuition, conceptualization and objective cues within the session. It is the rater's necessary movement between formulation and observation that offers a description of process beyond the mere identification of behaviour. As the rater emphasizes and de-emphasizes specific items of the CPQ to describe a session, a mosaic of therapeutic patterns begins to emerge. This mosaic will help depict the interactive process between therapist and child in ways that may not have been *consciously* in the mind or formulation of the therapist or the rater.

Whereas the CPQ can be used to provide a 'snapshot' of therapeutic processes, a more dynamic portrait of therapeutic work would entail tracing factors, item clusters or *interaction structures* (Jones 2000) that emerge in CPQ ratings over time using factor analytic techniques, as evidenced in research carried out by Jones and colleagues (Jones, Ghannam, Nigg & Dyer 1993, O'Crowley 1999, Jones 2000, Coombs, Coleman & Jones 2002, Duncan 2006, Schneider & Midgley 2007). Even when used in these sophisticated ways, there are myriad dynamics and nuances within sessions that Q-ratings cannot capture. However, as another stream of clinical inference, the Q-ratings may contribute to the complex dialogue that every case evokes and may help us towards a systematic investigation of clinical practice as illustrated by the following example of research conducted at the Anna Freud Centre, London.

The Child Psychotherapy Process Outcome Study (CPPOS) at the Anna Freud Centre

The Anna Freud Centre has a long history of research in the field of child therapy, including a major retrospective outcome study and a long-term follow up (Schacter & Target 2007, and see Chapter 9). As part of this on-going work, the Centre has built up a unique database – much of it yet to be analysed – providing a mass of material related to treatment, including video-tapes of clinical sessions and regular and systematic assessment data. Drawing on this gold-mine of material, the Child Psychotherapy Process Outcome Study (CPPOS) aims to explore in depth the nature of the therapy process and its relation to outcome.[1]

1 We are grateful to the organizers of the original study – Peter Fonagy, Mary Target and Karin Ensink – for permission to use this data, as well as the therapists and families who took part in the research. This project received financial support from the Tavistock Institute of Medical Research and the International Psychoanalytical Association Research Advisory Board.

The CPPOS project aims to apply a range of research methodologies – mostly developed in the field of adult psychotherapy research – to clinical work with children in order to progress towards identifying key mechanisms involved in therapeutic change. The primary data used in this study are the video-recording and therapist process notes of a small number of psycho-therapy treatments, alongside a battery of standardized measures used before, during and after the end of each treatment, which had been collected as part of a pilot project for a prospective outcome study of child analysis and psychotherapy.

As a first step in this on-going project, a selection of sessions from a number of therapies – both psychodynamic and cognitive behavioural – were coded using the CPQ. Videos of four psychodynamic treatments (two intensive, two non-intensive) and two cognitive behavioural treatments, all with children between eight and twelve who were referred because of anxiety and/or depression, were available for use.

This stage of the study aimed to address the following questions:

1   What similarities or differences are there across different psychodynamic treatments, either involving the same or different therapists?
2   Is there a measurable difference between what goes on in psychodynamic child psychotherapy and CBT?
3   How does what takes place in psychodynamic child psychotherapy sessions relate to the 'prototype' of what expert clinicians believe should take place?

I. What similarities or differences are there across different psychodynamic treatments, either involving the same or different therapists?

To begin with, we were curious to know to what degree a certain therapist–child dyad had a consistent pattern of engagement during the 'middle period' of treatment, a stage at which one would expect the analytic process to be fully engaged. After establishing interrater reliability with an experienced child psychotherapist in the use of the CPQ, three sessions from the middle period of each of the four psychodynamic treatments were rated by one of the authors (A.P.T.) and correlations were measured between the three sessions *within* each of the treatments. (The relatively small amount of data used must be borne in mind when considering what follows.) As one might have expected, highly statistically significant positive correlations were found between the three sessions within each of the treatments studied. It therefore appears that, once therapy has been on-going for a certain period of time, there is some degree of consistency in the style of interaction within each child–therapist dyad.

When each of the four psychodynamic child treatments was compared to each other, however, the findings were somewhat different. Although the same therapist worked with two of the children, the overall correlation between these two treatments was fairly weak, suggesting that there was more difference than similarity between the patterns of interaction in these two treatments, despite the therapist being the same person. This might suggest that the range of techniques and patterns of engagement used by a child psychotherapist are a response to a particular therapist–child dyad, rather than being a 'set' style, characteristic of that particular therapist, which is then used across all cases.

In contrast, a highly significant, strong association existed across all 100 Q-items between the treatments of two other children, although they were treated by *different* therapists. Wanting to understand this finding better, we looked in more detail at different aspects of the CPQ. When the 'child' items of the CPQ were separated out for examination, a highly significant positive correlation was found between the behaviour of these two children, both of whom displayed phobic behaviour and used highly affect-laden communications. In addition, both children demonstrated ready understanding of the therapist's comments, and were highly responsive to these. Perhaps responding to the way in which these two children engaged in therapy, there was a significant similarity in how the respective therapists engaged with these two children, and the interactive patterns that emerged within each of these dyads had marked similarities. This finding might suggest that a particular type of behaviour on a child's part elicits a certain kind of technique from the therapist, creating greater similarity in style and technique between two *different* therapists working with 'similar' children than between treatments in which the *same* therapist is working with two children who engage in therapy in very different ways.

2. Is there a measurable difference between what goes on in psychodynamic child psychotherapy and CBT?

A further question that this study explored was whether the CPQ could capture the difference between what goes on in a psychodynamic child psychotherapy treatment compared with cognitive behavioural therapy. Both by looking at the descriptive statistics and by examining correlations, the results would suggest that this is indeed the case.

Interestingly, a highly significant positive correlation was found between the *child* items for the two types of treatment, suggesting that the way in which the children presented in the two different types of treatment was quite similar. This may be due to the fact that they were matched in terms of their ages and their level and type of disturbance in the original study. However, a significant (although not strong) *negative* correlation across the therapist items suggests that techniques that feature highly in psychodynamic treatment were noticeably absent in the CBT treatment, and vice versa.

These findings were echoed (and elaborated) by the descriptive statistics, which indicate that a number of items that received low ratings across psychodynamic psychotherapy treatments rated among the highest in the CBT treatments (see Tables 4.2 and 4.3).

The portrait that emerged from these findings is a psychodynamic child psychotherapy in which the therapist encourages further elaboration from the child in a sensitive manner, and attempts to verbalize the child's feelings, including interpretations of unconscious or warded off thoughts and feelings, but does not necessarily 'help' the child to manage difficult feelings. Neither does the therapist behave in a didactic manner, nor attempt to teach the child to behave in a particular way; but certain areas are rarely discussed, including early developmental phases and the reason why the child is in treatment. Interestingly, the transference relationship and its interpretation does not appear to be a central feature of the work.

In the cognitive behavioural psychotherapy, there is a much greater emphasis on the child's current life situation, and the therapist is far more

Table 4.2 Items with the highest and lowest mean ratings in psychodynamic child psychotherapy

Item number	Item type	Item title	Mean rating
Highest			
50	Therapist	Therapist draws attention to feelings regarded by the child as unacceptable (e.g. anger, envy, or excitement)	7.83
97	Therapist	Therapist emphasizes verbalization of internal states and affects	7.33
77	Therapist	Therapist's interaction with child is sensitive to the child's level of development	7.17
67	Therapist	Therapist interprets warded-off or unconscious wishes, feelings or ideas	7.08
7	Child	Child is anxious and tense (vs. calm and relaxed)	6.75
73	Child	Child expresses fear or displays phobic behaviour	6.67
6	Therapist	Therapist is sensitive to child's feelings	6.67
31	Therapist	Therapist asks for more information or elaboration	6.58
Lowest			
40	Child	Child communicates without affect	2.42
37	Therapist	Therapist behaves in a teacher-like didactic manner	2.83
4	Dyad/ general	There is discussion of why child is in therapy	3.00
55	Therapist	Therapist directly rewards desirable behaviours	3.00
56	Child	Child is distant from his or her feelings	3.08
63	Dyad/ general	Child explores relationships with significant others	3.25
89	Therapist	Therapist acts to strengthen defences	3.33
82	Therapist	Therapist helps child manage feelings	3.42

Table 4.3 Items with the highest and lowest mean ratings in cognitive behavioural therapy

Item number	Item type	Item title	Mean rating
Highest			
69	Dyad/general	Child's current or recent life situation is emphasized	9.0
65	Therapist	Therapist clarifies, restates or rephrases child's communication	8.5
17	Therapist	Therapist actively exerts control over the interaction (e.g. structuring, introducing new topics)	8.5
37	Therapist	Therapist behaves in a teacher-like didactic manner	8.5
48	Therapist	Therapist sets limits	8.0
23	Dyad/general	Therapy session has a specific focus or theme	8.0
4	Dyad/general	There is discussion of why child is in therapy	8.0
Lowest			
98	Dyad/general	The therapy relationship is discussed	1.0
93	Therapist	Therapist is neutral	1.5
100	Therapist	Therapist draws connections between the therapeutic relationship and other relationships	2.0
12	Therapist	Therapist models unspoken or unelaborated emotions	2.0
45	Therapist	Therapist tolerates child's strong affect or impulses	2.0
46	Therapist	Therapist interprets the meaning of the child's play	2.0
77	Therapist	Therapist's interaction with child is sensitive to the child's level of development	2.0

controlling of the session, setting limits, helping the child to plan behaviour outside the session, modifying distortions in the child's thinking and directly rewarding desirable behaviours. Like the psychodynamic therapist, the therapist encourages further elaboration of the child's thoughts and feelings, but the focus is not on the therapeutic relationship, nor does the therapist attempt to interpret the child's play.

At face value, these descriptions of what was actually taking place in the two types of treatment show clear differences from each other, but also seem to be recognizable to clinicians working with these respective models. But in order to explore to what degree the treatments actually reflected psychodynamic and cognitive behavioural models of what *should* take place, we decided to take our study one stage further.

3. How does what takes place in psychodynamic child psychotherapy sessions relate to the 'prototype' of what expert clinicians believe should take place?

Prior to our work on the Anna Freud Centre data, Schneider (2004) invited an international sample of thirty senior clinicians, representing cognitive behavioural and psychodynamic orientations, to rate the 100 CPQ items in terms of the extent to which they appeared characteristic (or uncharacteristic) of their 'ideal' practice with children.

In that study, two distinct factors emerged to exemplify an 'ideal' representation of psychodynamic and cognitive behavioural therapies, respectively. According to these experts, the work of the psychodynamic child therapist is best captured by items on the CPQ that describe working with powerful feelings and affects, looking for recurrent themes and interpreting warded-off experiences; they felt that behaviours such as direct reassurance, helping the child plan behaviour outside the session or rewarding desirable behaviours was not part of their approach. By contrast, the cognitive behavioural child therapists saw their role as involving precisely those features that were not deemed relevant by the psychodynamic therapists (rewarding desirable behaviours and offering reassurance, self-disclosing, exerting control over the interaction, etc.), and items that emphasize working directly with the therapeutic relationship or offering interpretations were seen as least relevant to a CBT approach.

Curious to know how far these 'ideal' prototypes reflect the way that psychodynamic and cognitive behavioural therapists work in practice, a further stage of analysis was carried out by two of the authors (A.P.T. and N.M.). This involved a comparison of the profile of psychodynamic and cognitive behavioural child psychotherapy that emerged from the Anna Freud Centre study with the 'ideal prototypes' of treatment described above.[2] However, when comparisons were made, not a single significant correlation, positive or negative, was found between any of the experts' ratings and the data collected in the study by the Anna Freud Centre. This would seem to imply that there is no clear association between the 'ideal type' of these two kinds of treatment, as described by expert clinicians, and the actual practice, as observed in the video-tapes of real treatments.

When the descriptive statistics were examined more closely to see what CPQ items occurred in both the 'ideal' treatment and the actual treatment sessions, it appeared that the profile of CBT, as observed on the video-taped sessions, adhered rather better to the ideal prototype than did the psychodynamic psychotherapy data. For the latter, while there were some similarities between the most salient items, as observed in the video-taped treatments and the psychodynamic 'ideal prototype' (e.g. the therapist drawing attention to, and interpreting, unacceptable or warded-off feelings, whilst taking a non-didactic, non-judgemental attitude), an inverse relation between 'actual'

---

2 Because the experts' ratings did not follow the forced normal distribution, usually applied to Q-Sort ratings, these were recoded and correlational comparisons used Spearman's Rank Correlation Coefficient. Means for each of the treatment orientations were calculated and correlated with the mean ratings for the psychoanalytic psychotherapy and CBT treatments, from this study.

sessions and 'ideal' sessions was found for certain items. For example, experts considered it to be characteristic of an 'ideal' session that the child and therapist explore an earlier developmental phase – this was found to rarely take place in practice.

Although there were some similarities in the experts' views on what should take place in a session, overall, an absence of any significant association was more striking. One possible explanation for this lies in the fact that many of the expert clinicians who were asked to describe their 'ideal' prototype of treatment commented that they found this exercise at an angle to their familiar modes of conceptualizing cases. In describing their 'ideal', clinicians were asked to generalize *across* cases in their clinical experience using Likert methodology. But it may be that 'ideal' prototypes are like a painter's palette, offering a range of colours with which the artist may work, but without life until the act of creation begins. Perhaps it is only once work with a *particular* child begins that one can discover what aspects of the technical 'palette' will be drawn upon, or how they will be mixed? Certainly, on-going research at the Anna Freud Centre, which we hope to publish soon, using the CPQ to describe the evolution of patterns of interaction across the course of a single treatment, indicates the unique way in which the process of psychodynamic psychotherapy evolves, and the potential of the CPQ to capture some aspect of this act of creation (Duncan 2006, Schneider & Midgley 2007).

Concluding thoughts

In sum, the Child Psychotherapy Q-Set is designed to offer a language and research vantage point on psychotherapy process. It can be used in a variety of settings and across theoretical orientation. As we hope to have demonstrated in this chapter, the Q-Set appears able to describe some clinically relevant aspects of the clinical encounter, and to differentiate between different forms of treatment, within the context of a validated, empirically based measure.

The potential contribution of psychotherapy process research using the CPQ lies not simply in its applicability across theoretical terrains, but also in its capacity to draw out the unique, guiding dynamics that cross boundaries of theory and practice. The hope is that the CPQ may contribute to the on-going discussion of how to reach and help children in therapy. Between familiarity and discovery, spontaneity and constraint, lies the on-going tapestry of clinical work. To recall Proust, psychotherapy process research employing the CPQ has the potential to offer a 'different set of eyes', thus taking us on a true voyage of discovery, one in which we can find another way to observe and to learn from the work and play of children and their therapists.

References

Ablon, J.S., Jones, E.E (2002) Validity of controlled clinical trials of psychotherapy: Findings from the NIMH treatment of depression collaborative research program. *The American Journal of Psychiatry*, *159*, 775–783.

Ablon, J.S., Jones, E.E. (1999) Psychotherapy process in the national institute of mental health treatment of depression collaborative research program. *Journal of Consulting and Clinical Psychology*, *67*, 64–75.

Ablon, J.S., Jones, E.E. (1998) How expert clinicians' prototypes of an ideal treatment correlate with outcome in psychodynamic and cognitive-behavioral therapy. *Psychotherapy Research*, *8*(1), 71–83.

Block, J., Haan, N. (1971) *Lives through time*. Berkeley, CA: Bancroft Books.

Block, J. (1969) *The California Q-Set*. Berkeley, CA: Department of Psychology, University of California at Berkeley.

Block, J. (1961) *The Q-sort method in personality assessment and research*. Springfield, IL: Charles C. Thomas.

Brown, S. (1991) Obituaries: William Stephenson (1902–1989). *American Psychologist*, *46*(3), 244.

Coombs, M., Coleman, D., Jones, E.E. (2002) Working with feelings: The importance of emotion in both cognitive-behavioral and interpersonal therapy in the NIMH treatment of depression collaborative research program. *Psychotherapy*, *39*, 233–244.

Duncan, A. (2006) *A developmental line for child psychotherapy*. MSc dissertation, University College London.

Fonagy, P., Target, M., Phillips, J., Kurtz, Z. (2002) *What works for whom? A critical review of treatments for children and adolescents*. London: Guilford Press.

Goldman, I. (1999) Q-methodology as process and context in interpretive, communication, and psychoanalytic psychotherapy research. *The Psychological Record*, *49*, 589–604.

Jones, E. E. (2000) *Therapeutic action, a guide to psychoanalytic therapy*. Northvale, NJ: Jason Aronson.

Jones, E. E., Price, P. (1998) Examining the alliance using the psychotherapy process Q-set. *Psychotherapy*, *35*, 392–404.

Jones, E.E., Ghannam, J., Nigg, J.T., Dyer, J.F.P. (1993) A paradigm for single case research: The time series study of a long-term psychotherapy for depression. *Journal of Consulting and Clinical Psychology*, *61*, 381–394.

Jones, E.E., Pulos, S.M. (1993) Comparing process in psychodynamic and cognitive behavioral therapies. *Journal of Consulting and Clinical Psychology*, *61*, 306–316.

Jones, E.E., Hall, S., Parke, L.A. (1991) The process of change: The Berkeley psychotherapy research group. In L. Beutler & M. Crageo (eds) *Psychotherapy research: An international review of programmatic studies* (pp. 98–107). Washington, DC: American Psychological Association.

Jones, E.E., Windholz, M. (1989) The psychoanalytic case study: Toward a method for systematic inquiry. *Journal of the American Psychoanalytic Association*, *38*, 985–1015.

Jones, E.E. Cumming, J.D. & Horowitz, M. (1988) Another look at the non-specific hypothesis of therapeutic effectiveness. *Journal of Consulting and Clinical Psychology*, *56*, 48–55.

Jones, E.E. (1985) Manual for the psychotherapy process Q-set. Unpublished manuscript, University of California, Berkeley.

Kazdin, A. E. (2003) Psychotherapy for children and adolescents. *Annual Review of Psychology*, *54*, 253–276.

Midgley, N. (2006) The 'inseparable bond between cure and research': Clinical case study as a method of psychoanalytic inquiry. *Journal of Child Psychotherapy*, *32*(2), 122–147.

Midgley, N. (2004) Sailing between Scylla and Charybdis: Incorporating qualitative approaches into child psychotherapy research. *Journal of Child Psychotherapy*, *30*(1), 89–111.

O'Crowley, A. (1999) *The analysis of the transference*. Ann Arbor, MI: Dissertation Abstracts.

Paul, G. (1967) Strategy of outcome research in psychotherapy. *Journal of Consulting Psychology*, *31*, 109–118.

Proust, M. (1941) *Remembrance of things past. The captive* (vol. 2,559). New York: Random House.

Rustin, M. (2001) *Reason and unreason: Psychoanalysis, science, and politics*. London: Continuum.

Schacter, A. and Target, M. (2009) The adult outcome of child psychoanalysis: The Anna Freud Centre long-term follow-up study. In Midgley, N., Anderson, J., Grainger, E., Nesic-Vuckovic, T., Urwin, C. (eds) *Child psychotherapy and research: New approaches, emerging findings*. London: Routledge.

Schneider, C., Midgley, N. (2007) Concept and intuition in psychotherapy research. Paper presented at the Joseph Sandler Conference, London, March 2007.

Schneider, C. (2004) The development and first trial application of the child psychotherapy Q-set. Web publication of the International Psychoanalytical Association: http://www.ipa.org.uk/research/schneider.asp

Schneider, C., Jones, E. E. (2004) *Child Psychotherapy Q-Set coding manual*. Unpublished manuscript, University of California, Berkeley.

Shirk, S., Russell, R. (1996) *Change process in child psychotherapy: Revitalizing treatment and research*. New York: Guilford Press.

Stephenson, W. (1953) *The study of behavior: Q-technique and its methodology*. Chicago: University of Chicago Press.

Stephenson, W. (1935) Technique of factor analysis. *Nature*, CXXXVI, 297.

Chapter 5

Psychoanalysis and diabetic control: A single-case study *

George Moran and Peter Fonagy

Introduction

The relationship of hypothesis and evidence in psychoanalytic case reports has never satisfied the canons of eliminative inductivism. Grünbaum's (1984) critique of the epistemology of psychoanalysis aimed to show that the clinical data of psychoanalysis were irretrievably contaminated by persuasive suggestions to a patient in a vulnerable regressed state under the influence of strong positive transference. Many, including some psychoanalysts, have accepted that the psychoanalytic situation is not capable of providing evidential support for psychoanlytic hypotheses according to the generally accepted criteria of modern science and have abandoned Freud's claim for psychoanalysis to have a legitimate place in the domain of natural sciences (Fonagy 1982).

A number of psychoanalysts, however, have decided to take up Grünbaum's challenge (e.g. Edelson 1986, Wallerstein 1986). These authors claim that psychoanalytic hypotheses can be, and in the case of many hypotheses can only be, tested within the methodological requirements of eliminative inductivism. Edelson's suggestions include the use of quasi-experimental designs derived from single-subject research, the use of causal modelling and statisical controls, suggestion-resistant measures of the analysand's response, the use of explicit operational criteria for the classification of the analysand's material and the use of reliable rating scales that permit the assessment of the probable presence of specific clinical themes. The present paper aims to take an initial step towards applying these recommendations to the investigation of the relationship between insight derived from psychoanlalytic treatment and symptomatic improvement.

The hypothesis under investigation concerns the value of insight into unconscious conflict for the alleviation of neurotic symptomatology. Past systematic investigations have failed to provide support for the assumption that symptomatic improvement in psychoanalysis is commensurate with

* This chapter is reproduced with permission from the *British Journal of Medical Pychology* (1987), **60**, 357–372. Printed in Great Britain © 1987 The British Psychological Society.

insight obtained. Wallerstein (1985), for example, reports on the therapeutic outcome of forty-two patients in psychoanalytic and psychotherapeutic treatment within the Menninger Psychotherapy Research Project. Improvement in these patients, whether in psychoanalysis or psychotherapy, was apparently independent of the extent or depth of the insights they obtained in either form of treatment. This and similar studies, however, used between-subject quasi-experimental designs to test the hypothesis that patients who showed the most marked improvement were those who gained most in terms of self-understanding. In evaluating the results of such studies, it is important to bear in mind Gottman's (1973) cautionary note concerning the potentially misleading results that follow from averaging data across individuals in psychotherapy outcome research. For example, the extra therapeutic attention directed towards patients inherently resistant to improvement may lead them to manifest greater insight but little or no therapeutic change. Confounding factors such as this make comparisons across individuals difficult to interpret.

We think that evidential support for the notion of insight-based symptomatic improvement is more likely to be gained from the detailed systematic study of the individual case. Thus, we aimed to test the hypothesis that there is a relationship between insight into unconscious conflict and the amelioration of neurotic symptoms over the course of a psychoanalytic treatment employing a single-case design. Using a probabilistic framework, we predicted that improvements in symptoms would occur in temporal association with psychoanalytically derived insight. Furthermore, psychoanalytic theory required that conflict resolution could be demonstrated to precede symptomatic improvement.

The psychological treatment of individuals with poorly regulated diabetes mellitus provides a useful opportunity for the investigation of the relationship between the resolution of neurotic conflict through psychoanalysis and symptomatic improvement. Insulin-dependent diabetes mellitus is a chronic metabolic disease that results in the diabetic patient's inability to metabolize carbohydrates. The treatment regimen aims to re-establish the delicate balance between carbohydrate intake and the insulin required to convert sugar into cell energy. The diet must be precisely regulated and timed in conjunction with injections of insulin. In order to achieve blood glucose control, levels of blood sugar and energy output (physical exercise) must be carefully monitored. The patient is thought to be in good diabetic control when levels of blood glucose approximate the normal range for non-diabetics.

A small group of diabetic patients have very serious problems regulating their blood glucose levels (brittle diabetes). Their lives are constantly disrupted by episodes of hypoglycaemia and/or hyperglycaemia (Tattersall 1985). These patients often have a history of repeated admission to hospital for treatment of life-threatening episodes of severe metabolic derangement, i.e. hypoglycaemic coma and/or hyperglycaemia leading to diabetic ketoacidosis.

Diabetologists are in agreement that the aetiology of brittle diabetes is psychological rather than organic (Schade, Drumm, Duckworth & Eaton 1985).

The psychological mechanisms that bring about the life-threatening conditions associated with brittle diabetes require clarification. We propose a psychoanalytic model of this disorder, which the present single-case study aims to validate. Two fundamental assumptions underlie the model we propose. The first is that psychological variables are causally related to fluctuations of diabetic control and the second is that these fluctuations are brought about by the conscious and unconscious performance of acts inconsistent with successful management of the disease. We understand such gross transgressions of the diabetic regimen that underlie certain cases of brittle diabetes to be a neurotic response to the anxiety and guilt aroused by unconscious conflict. Thus, it is the child's adaptation to conflict through mismanagement of the diabetic treatment regimen that causes brittle diabetes. It follows from these assumptions that interventions at the level of psychological antecedents may bring about favourable changes in the quality of the management and control of the disease. The intervention that we recommend addresses the preconscious sources of the child's anxieties: the child's conflicts are verbalized and the way in which diabetic mismanagement expresses or serves to divert a child's attention away from repudiated wishes is interpreted. For example, a diabetic child may unconsciously perceive the symptoms of poor diabetic regulation as a punishment for repudiated wishes. Therapeutically derived insight enables the child to identify the conflictual unconscious wishes that bring about the need for self-punishment via deliberately induced diabetic imbalance. More generally, through psychoanalysis the child may gain insight into the functions which diabetic regulation subserves, or the needs which it represents (Moran 1984).

We think that evidential support for the notion of insight-based syptomatic improvement is more likely to be gained from the detailed systematic study of the individual case. Thus, we aimed to test the hypothesis that there is a relationship between insight into unconscious conflict and the amelioration of neurotic symptoms over the course of a psychoanalytic treatment employing a single-case design. Using a probabalistic framework, we predicted that improvements in symptoms would occur in temporal association with psychoanalytically derived insight. Furthermore, psychoanalytic theory required that conflict resolution could be demonstrated to precede symptomatic improvement.

The present chapter is an attempt to validate this model in a systematic single-case study of the relationship between diabetic control and the patterns of conflicts and symptoms over the 3½-year course of five-times-weekly psychoanalysis of a diabetic teenager.

Case history

Diagnosed diabetic at age eight, Sally was referred for psychoanalysis at the age of thirteen because of long-standing physical and emotional problems that had failed to respond to psychiatric and medical treatment over the previous five years. She was consciously and profoundly dissatisfied with being a girl and had a difficult and 'enmeshed' relationship with her mother. One of her most prominent difficulties, her fear of attending school, preceded the onset of the diabetes by two years. Her anxieties were, however, aggravated by frequent admissions to hospital with hypoglycaemia and hyperglycaemia. In the five years preceding the analysis, Sally was admitted to hospital, most often with diabetic ketoacidosis, between two and five times per year. She was a highly intelligent (WISC-R full scale IQ = 130) resourceful girl. She was in child psychoanalysis five times a week for three years.

Aims of the study

The study aimed to examine the association between diabetic control and the variation in the themes of the psychoanalysis. Diabetic control throughout was estimated on the basis of twice-daily urine testing. The content of the psychoanalysis was assessed by independent ratings of the analyst's weekly reports. During the course of the analysis, Sally rarely talked of the results of tests for monitoring her diabetic balance. The analyst thus had only sporadic and inaccurate information concerning Sally's diabetic control.

Time-series analysis (Box & Jenkins 1976) was used to examine the relationship between diabetic control and psychological conflict. This procedure permits the drawing of causal inferences by statistically describing the fluctuations, cycles and trends of two processes: the psychoanalytic themes on the one hand and the measure of diabetic control on the other. If the two processes are uncorrelated, it is unlikely that they are causally connected. Concomitant variation, however, would imply causation if fluctuations in one process are predicted by fluctuations in another. We may then legitimately make a relatively weak causal inference compared to the more robust causal inferences that can be made on the basis of experimental designs.

Content analysis and ratings of the treatment

The progress of Sally's analysis was detailed in weekly reports. The reports contained a summary of the major themes of the week and illustrations of the patient's difficulties and anxieties, the therapist's mode of intervention, and the patient's responses. The weekly reports were themselves based on daily reports written after each session. The latter contained verbatim reports of the patient's presentation of herself in treatment, and an account of how the material was clarified, interpreted or simply registered by the analyst. The prominent themes of the daily reports, which were judged to be most relevant to the patient's experiences and the therapist's understanding and technique, were then summarized by the therapist in weekly reports of approximately 1000 words.

The 148 weekly reports were condensed in a clinical paper and this report was then studied with a view to extracting the major analytic themes of the case. Analytic themes were identified, which could be judged as present or absent in any particular weekly report over the course of the analysis. An original list of eighteen clinical dimensions was drawn up and operational definition of these was attempted. Although we were successful in devising operational definitions in the case of ten analytic themes, crucial aspects of Sally's psychopathology and the analytic process defied our attempts at systematic definition and categorization.

Five of the analytic themes were categorized on the basis of the clinical report to be part of the pathological structures (intrapsychic conflicts) underlying diabetic mismanagement. These conflicts concerned Sally's feeling unloved by her father and angry with him for his lack of responsiveness, and her associated frustration of the wish to be loved, admired and valued by him; her rivalry with her mother for her father's love and attention; her ambivalence towards her mother deriving from the experience of her mother's psychiatric illness when she was aged six; her anxiety and guilt feelings over her death wishes towards her parents and other family members, in whom she felt disappointed; and, finally, her conflicts concerning the threats associated with diabetes, both reality-based and as distorted by defensive processes. A second set of analytic themes of comparable prominence in the treatment referred to material taken up by discussions of Sally's symptoms. These included Sally's imitation of boys and related fantasies, her phobic anxiety in connection with attending school, her imagined or actual intention to punish herself, fantasies concerning a view of herself as being physically damaged, and manifestations of resistance to therapeutic progress in the analysis. Operational definitions were formulated for each of the categories to facilitate the rating of the presence or absence of each theme in each weekly report. An example of the operational definitions of two of the analytic themes, one related to intrapsychic conflict and the other to symptoms, is presented in Table 5.1.

The independent raters of the weekly reports were instructed to read the summary report describing the analysis as a whole before rating the separate weekly reports. This was thought to be necessary in order to familiarize the raters with the therapist's overall understanding of the case, the details of the patient's worries and the metaphors she used to express herself. The two independent raters, both of whom were child analysts, were then asked to rate a random selection of five weekly reports. Ratings were performed on a five-point scale: 'definitely present', 'probably present', 'possible present', 'probably absent' and 'definitely not present'. The ratings were compared with the therapist's ratings and agreements and disagreements were discussed. This aspect of the procedure was then repeated on a second random group of five weekly reports.

The independent raters' and the therapist's ratings of the ten clinical dimensions for each of the 148 weeks were obtained. The correlations between the three raters were computed using Pearson's product moment correlation coefficients. The interrater correlations were moderate to high,

Table 5.1   Clinical dimensions: Operational definitions and examples

Clinical dimension	Operational definition	Examples
Diabetes as an expression of psychic conflict	The patient's experience of diabetes, including the diabetic regimen, fluctuations in diabetic control, worries about the future effects of the illness and the encroachment of such concerns on the capacity psychically to represent conflicts and feelings	
	Diabetic identity	• Interpretation of patient's conflict about wearing 'Medic Alert' necklace • Interpretation of patient's fear of blindness
	Diabetic control	• Report of worry about hypoglycaemia • Verbalization or interpretation of worry about long-term effects of hyperglycaemia (e.g. cardiovascular complications of the disease)
	Diabetic regimen	• Report on verbalization of resentment of injections
	Diabetes as a metaphor for psychic conflict	• Interpretation of worry about being 'low', i.e. hypoglycaemic, to defend against depressive affect or disappointment

Deliberate self-punishment	Patient's conscious or unconscious intention to hurt, punish or damage herself in response to the experience of succeeding or fantasies that entail desired achievements	
	Instances of self-defeating behaviour	• Report of wilful refusal to write correct answers on school exams • Memories and reports of goading mother to restrict patient's activities by arousing mother's anxiety about diabetic control
	Acts perpetrated on the body	• Report of inducing hypoglycaemia • Report of wilful carelessness while cooking
	Anxiety in response to success	• Report of anxiety following success in school examinations

with more than 60 per cent of correlations above 0.65. Three of the analytic themes (conflicts over murderous wishes, the symptoms of a damaged self-representation and resistance to the analysis) had mean interrater coefficients of less than 0.6 and were excluded from further analysis. The average inter-rater correlations for the seven remaining themes ranged from 0.78 to 0.62 with a mean of 0.70.

Time-series analysis requires a continuous series of observations. Ratings of the analytic themes during brief interruptions of the analysis (up to two weeks) were estimated using an autocorrelational technique that utilizes the immediately preceding observations to predict missing values. This procedure is generally regarded as appropriate when missing values occur in a regular sequence (Thrall & Engleman 1981). (Altogether, 19 weeks or 11 per cent of the series were estimated following this procedure.) There were no missing observations for urine glucose.

Diabetic control was assessed in terms of weekly urine glucose content over the 148 weeks of Sally's analytic treatment and the two preceding years. Although home urine testing is regarded as an inaccurate index of blood glucose control with substantial inherent limitations, its adequacy depends on the characteristics of the patients tested, their renal thresholds, the accuracy of measurement and record keeping and the reliability of informants. Sally's urine charts were meticulously kept by her mother and Sally. In order to assess the quality of control for each of the 288 relevant weeks, fourteen tests per week (the specimen before breakfast and the evening meal for each day) were examined and the percentage of tests showing less than 1 per cent of glycosuria was computed (Ludvigsson 1977). This yielded weekly averages of negative urine glucose tests ranging from 8 to 100 per cent with a standard deviation of 22.6 per cent. Thus, an increase in the percentage of negative urine tests per week represents an improvement in blood glucose control and, conversely, a decrease of the index of glycosuria represents a deterioration of diabetic control. To validate this index the correlation between all available random blood glucose measures taken at the hospital over the period of the psychoanalysis and the corresponding weekly index of glycosuria was computed yielding a Pearson product moment correlation of 0.84 (d.f. = 7, $p < 0.005$).

Results

The association between diabetic control and the therapist's ratings of the seven reliable psychoanalytic themes was calculated and six of the seven correlations reached statistical significance (Table 5.2). The highest correlation with urine sugar levels was of the variable concerned with Sally's feeling unloved by her father and her conflict deriving from anger with him. This implies that during periods when Sally's feeling unloved and in conflict about her anger with her father were prominent in the analytic work, glycosuria tended to be low.

Oedipal conflict showed a smaller but still significant positive association

Table 5.2 Correlation coefficients between urine glucose measures and ratings of analytic themes over 167 weeks

Variables	Correlation coefficients	Significance ($p <$)
Conflicts		
1. Feeling unloved by father and angry with him	0.41	0.001
2. Oedipal conflict	0.26	0.001
3. Diabetes as an expression of psychic conflict	0.15	0.04
4. Conflicts associated with the experience of mother's breakdown	0.06	n.s
Symptoms		
5. Phobic anxiety	−0.15	0.04
6. Imitation of boys and related fantasies	0.14	0.05
7. Deliberate self-punishment	0.27	0.04

with good diabetic control. Finally, the identification of the intertwining of diabetes with other areas of psychological conflict was also positively associated with improvements in diabetic control in terms of glycosuria. One of the conflict dimensions, conflicts associated with the experience of mother's breakdown, was not significantly associated with glycosuria.

In contrast with the analytic themes concerned with the presence of psychic conflict in the analysis, the association of Sally's symptoms with diabetic control was predominantly negative. The association between phobic anxiety as manifest in the psychoanalysis and glycosuria was significant and negative. This implies that weeks during which Sally's material evidenced an irrational fear of persons or situations, urine glucose was relatively high. A negative association was also found between glycosuria and Sally's symptom of imitating her male objects. The symptoms of deliberate self-punishment showed a positive correlation with urine glucose that was of greater magnitude than the relationship between glycosuria and the other two reliable symptoms. This implies that during weeks in which the analyst and patient spoke about Sally's tendency to hurt and punish herself, urine glucose was relatively low.

In order to further examine the nature of the relationship between urine glucose and the analytic themes noted above, lag correlation coefficients were computed between glycosuria and the rating of psychoanalytic themes. For example, in looking at the dimension concerned with Sally's feeling unloved and in conflict about her anger with father, we wished to know if the emergence of this material tended to precede improvements in diabetic control or, conversely, whether an improvement in diabetic control ushered in changes in the nature of the analytic material.

The computation of lag correlations requires the removal of trends (gradual shifts or drifts in the data). This is achieved by the subtraction of the preceding observation from the current one throughout the time series. After thus modifying the data, what remains are the week-to-week fluctuations of diabetic control and analytic themes independent of the general improvement in Sally's diabetic control and analytic themes independent of the general improvement in Sally's diabetic status over the course of the analysis and the expectable differences in the predominance of particular themes in particular phases of the analysis. Cross-lag correlations can then be computed to examine if variations in analytic themes were concurrent with (lag of zero), or were predicted by measures of glycosuria taken one, two or more weeks previously (positive lags of one, two or more). Alternatively, if fluctuations of glycosuria were predicted by the presence or absence of particular psychoanalytic themes one or more weeks previously, correlations at negative lags would be expected. Cross-correlations were computed between the two differenced series at lags of between plus and minus four weeks.

Table 5.3 indicates that when cross-correlations were examined, symptoms and conflicts were found to have a different direction of association to glycosuria. Two conflicts had a significant relationship to the index of urine

Table 5.3 Cross-correlation coefficients (and standardized estimates) between analytic themes and index of glycosuria at lags of −4 to +4 weeks

	Analytic themes predicting glycosuria				Glycosuria predicting analytic themes				
Weeks:	−4	−3	−2	−1	0	1	2	3	4
Conflicts									
Feeling unloved by father and angry with him	0.01 (0.13)	0.03 (0.39)	0.12 (1.55)	0.17[a] (2.20)	0.19[a] (2.46)	0.09 (1.17)	0.04 (0.04)	0.08 (1.03)	0.11 (1.40)
Oedipal conflict	0.15 (1.91)	0.27[a] (3048)	0.19[a] (2.45)	0.10 (1.30)	0.13 (1.69)	0.04 (0.52)	−0.02 (0.25)	−0.05 (0.64)	−0.10 (1.28)
Diabetes as an expression of psychic conflict	0.10 (1.28)	0.03 (0.39)	0.04 (0.52)	0.09 (1.17)	0.07 (0.91)	0.10 (1.30)	0.10 (1.29)	0.06 (0.77)	0.07 (0.89)
Conflicts associated with mother's breakdown	0.00 (0.0)	0.05 (0.64)	0.02 (0.20)	−0.06 (0.78)	−0.12 (1.56)	−0.15 (1.94)	0.00 (0.00)	0.08 (1.03)	0.01 (0.13)
Symptoms									
Imitation of boys and related fantasies	0.04 (0.05)	−0.08 (1.03)	0.01 (0.13)	0.09 (1.17)	0.13 (1.69)	−0.03 (0.39)	−0.07 (0.90)	−0.03 (0.39)	−0.06 (0.77)
Phobic anxiety	0.10 (1.28)	0.07 (0.90)	0.03 (0.39)	0.01 (0.13)	−1.05 (0.65)	0.02 (0.25)	0.11 (1.42)	0.23[a] (2.97)	0.25[a] (3.19)
Deliberate self-punishment	0.08 (1.02)	0.09 (1.16)	0.11 (1.42)	0.10 (1.30)	0.10 (1.30)	0.13 (1.68)	0.25[a] (3.23)	0.24[a] (3.09)	0.24[a] (3.06)

Note: a Statistically different from zero.

sugar at negative lags. The verbalization and interpretation of Oedipal conflict in the psychoanalysis was associated with reduced glycosuria (i.e. an improvement in diabetic control) two to four weeks later. The related conflict concerning anger with father showed a similar relationship at a lag of minus one week. By contrast, two of the three symptoms showed a correlation with glycosuria at positive lags. This implies that, following improvements in diabetic control, Sally experienced an exacerbation of her phobic reactions and her tendency to punish and hurt herself deliberately. The time lags at which these associations were most prominent were three to four weeks and two to four weeks, respectively (Table 5.3).

We can more rigorously examine the temporal association between psychoanalytic themes and glycosuria by constructing statistical models to describe their relationship. Transfer functions (the statistical model used originally described by Box & Jenkins 1976) have been recommended for $n = 1$ psychotherapy research (Gottman 1981, Barlow & Herson 1984). This statistical model is conceptually analogous to multiple linear regression. It allows us to identify what part of the variation in a continuously evolving dependent variable (glycosuria) can be explained by fluctuations in analytic themes, independent of the predictable fluctuations of glycosuria across time. We attempted to construct such a model for each of the psychoanalytic themes. In two of the models, psychoanalytic themes reached statistical significance as independent predictors of glycosuria when regular fluctuations in urine glucose were statistically controlled for.

The first model shown in Table 5.4 represents a statistical description of the association between Oedipal conflict and glycosuria. The first two components of the model refer to the variability in glycosuria that may be pre-

Table 5.4 Transfer functions for Oedipal conflict and diabetes (causer variable) and the index of glycosuria (effector variable)

Variable	Lag (weeks)	Estimates	Standard error of the estimates (df = 160)	t ratio	Significance (p <)
Model I[a]					
Oedipal conflict	3	4.14	1.3	3.2	0.005
Glycosuria	1	0.67	0.07	8.9	0.001
Glycosuria	2	0.21	0.07	2.8	0.01
Model[b]					
Diabetes as an expression of conflict	4	0.83	0.32	2.4	0.02
Glycosuria	1	0.16	0.05	−3.2	0.005
Glycosuria	2	0.78	0.05	16.1	0.001

Notes:
a Total percentage of variance accounted for by Model I = 46.
b Total percentage of variance accounted for by Model 2 = 33.

dicted on the basis of past observations of glycosuria one and two weeks previously. The third component represents the rating of Oedipal conflict in the psychoanalytic material that is shown independently to predict glycosuria over the three weeks following its ratings in the analysis. The second model concerned the analytic theme of diabetes as an expression of psychic conflict. Ratings of this conflict also predicted fluctuations of glycosuria independently of the regular fluctuations in the latter variable over the somewhat smaller time lag of one week. The models accounted for 46 and 33 per cent of the variation in glycosuria, respectively.

Discussion

Our study had three aims. First, we intended to demonstrate that psychoanalytic data may be organized and examined in a way that is consistent with the canons of eliminative inductivism. Second, we aimed to test our hypothesis concerning the value of specific psychoanalytic insights in the dissolution of neurotic structures. Third, we hoped to utilize this method of investigation to elaborate the neurotic processes underlying brittle diabetes. These three ambitions were in part fulfilled by the study.

The findings demonstrated that the working through of psychic conflict predicted an improvement in diabetic control, both in the long and the short term. The association of analytic themes and the measure of diabetic control over the entire period of the psychoanalysis is of limited importance, as the association may be accounted for in terms of common long-term trends. The association in the short term, when common underlying trends were removed, is of far greater theoretical interest. Grünbaum (1984) argues that symptomatic improvement in association with insight may be totally accounted for by the intensification of the analyst's demand on the patient for improvement in association with self-understanding. Whilst it may be argued that the analyst unwittingly and consistently made such demands on Sally, it is very difficult to imagine how he could have made a consistent demand on Sally to improve blood glucose regulation in the absence of knowledge of her diabetic control. Yet relevant analytic material was found regularly to precede changes in glycosuria. Furthermore, the temporal relationship of Sally's symptoms and glycosuria, although not initially predicted, is highly consistent with the psychoanalytic theory of neurosis and ill fits Grünbaum's model of the pschoanalytic process. Temporary improvements in Sally's diabetic control were regularly followed by an increase in other neurotic symptomatology. The increase in phobic avoidance and deliberate self-harm consequent upon improvement in diabetic control may be understood as a dynamically meaningful reaction, reflecting the patient's relative incapacity to tolerate states of well-being. We may assume that during certain phases of the analysis, particularly during its early years, good blood glucose control could only be achieved through temporary inhibitions that exacerbated psychological conflict and led to a significant intensification of other psychological symptoms. A non-dynamic account of such a temporal association is difficult to formulate.

Thus, overall, the findings lend some support to the Freudian model of therapeutic change. The support, however, is limited. It could be argued that emotional responses associated with insight, rather than insight *per se*, were primarily responsible for changes in blood glucose control associated with analytic themes. A number of workers (e.g. Hinkle & Wolf 1950, Baker, Barcai, Kaye & Haque 1969, Minuchin, Rosmon & Baker 1978) have demonstrated that metabolic balance may be adversely affected by the physiological concomitants of emotional arousal, particularly anxiety. It is plausible that a relative reduction in anxiety associated with the interpretation of unconscious conflict, rather than the interpretation of unconscious conflict *per se*, accounts for the temporal association of psychic conflict and glycosuria. Further studies are needed to examine this possibility. Even if emotional reaction to interpretation was shown to be the critical variable mediating the short-term effects of psychoanalysis on diabetic control, the long-term trend for such reactions to decrease as a result of psychoanalytic treatment could not be denied.

A more serious limitation of the technique we adopted concerns our inability to operationalize some psychoanalytic themes which we regarded as potentially crucial to the understanding of Sally's improvement. These included the manifestation of Sally's relationship with her parents and brothers as these emerged in her relationship with her analyst. Similarly, the relevance of psychoanalytic interventions that addressed experiences and conflicts from earlier phases of Sally's development to changes in diabetic control could not be investigated because the material available did not lend itself to operational definitions or quantitative ratings. It should be emphasized that the present study is viewed as an initial step towards the increased systematization of the treatment of psychoanalytic data and that other workers using similar methodologies may be able to explore psychoanalytic hypotheses that eluded the current authors.

The findings also lend support to a psychosomatic formulation of the aetiology of brittle diabetes. They run counter to may current formulations of the determinants of diabetic control within behavioural medicine (Fisher, Delameter, Bertelson & Kirkley 1982, Surwit & Genglos 1982, Wing, Epstein, Nowiak & Lamparski 1986). The models of diabetic control put forward by these authors fall short of exploring the personal meaning underlying the symptoms of poor diabetic control and focus simply on the pragmatic question of which methods may be most suitable for modifying behaviour. We do not wish to recommend five-times-weekly psychoanalysis as the treatment of choice for children with brittle diabetes but we would like to argue in favour of the consideration of dynamic factors that may underlie the condition. The present findings of a close temporal link between two specific psychological conflicts and glycosuria diabetes is relevant to the formulation of treatment strategies for such children. The case of Sally serves as an illustration of our assumption that brittle diabetes may be understood as a neurotic symptom of persons with diabetes who turn to their illness in the hope of obtaining relief from anxiety and guilt feelings. The expression of neurotic structures in diabetic mismanagement is, we believe, an important consideration in the effective treatment of brittle diabetes.

Acknowledgements

The authors wish to express their gratitude for the interest and support of Professor Albert J. Solnit, Dr Antony Kurtz, Dr Peter Neubauer, Mrs Maria Berger, Dr Charles Brook, The Anna Freud Foundation, The Special Trustees of Middlesex Hospital, The Rayne Foundation and to Steven Marans and Miss Claudia Lament for providing independent ratings of the clinical material.

References

Baker, L., Barcai, A., Kaye, R., Haque, N. (1969) Beta adrenergic blockade and juvenile diabetes: Acute studies and long-term therapeutic trial. *Journal of Pediatrics*, *75*, 19–29.

Barlow, D. H., Herson, M. (1984) *Single case experimental designs* (2nd edn). New York: Pergamon.

Box, G. E. P., Jenkins, G. M. (1976) *Time series analysis, forecasting and control* (2nd edn). San Francisco: Holden-Day.

Edelson, M. (1986) Causal explanation in science and in psychoanalysis: Implications for writing a case study. *The Psychoanalytic Study of the Child*, *41*, 89–128.

Fisher, E. B., Delamater, A. M., Bertelson, A. D., Kirkley, B. G. (1982) Psychological factors in diabetes and its treatment. *Journal of Consulting and Clinical Psychology*, *50*, 993–1003.

Fonagy, P. (1982) The integration of psychoanalysis and experimental science: A review. *International Review of Psychoanalysis*, *9*, 125–145.

Gottman, J. M. (1973) N-of-one and n-of-two research in psychotherapy. *Psychological Bulletin*, *80*, 93–105.

Gottman, J. M. (1981) *Time-series analysis: A comprehensive introduction for social scientists*. Cambridge: Cambridge University Press.

Grünbaum, A. (1984) *The foundations of psychoanalysis: A philosophical critique*. Berkeley, CA: University of California Press.

Hinkle, L. E., Wolf, S. (1950) Studies in diabetes mellitus: Changes in glucose, ketone, and water metabolism during stress. *Research in Nervous and Mental Disease*, *29*, 338.

Ludvigsson, J. (1977) Socio-psychological factors and metabolic control in juvenile diabetes. *Acta Paediatrica Scandinavica*, *66*, 431–437.

Minuchin, S., Rosmon, B., Baker, L. (1978) *Psychosomatic families. Anorexia nervosa in context*. Cambridge, MA: Harvard University Press.

Moran, G. S. (1984) Psychoanalytic treatment of diabetic children. *The Psychoanalytic Study of the Child, 39*, 407–447.

Schade, D. S., Drumm, D. A., Duckworth, W. C., Eaton, R. P. (1985) The aetiology of incapacitating, brittle diabetes. *Diabetes Care, 8*, 12–20.

Surwit, D. A. W., Genglos, M. N. (1982) The role of behaviour in diabetes care. *Diabetes Care, 5*, 337–342.

Tattersall, R. B. (1985) Brittle diabetes. *British Medical Journal, 291*, 555–556.

Thrall, T., Engelman, L. (1981) Univariate and bivariate spectral analysis. In W. J. N. Dixon (ed.) *B M D P Statistical Software* (pp. 604–638). Berkeley, CA: University of California Press.

Wallerstein, R. S. (1985) *Forty-two lives in treatment: A study of psychoanalysis and psychotherapy*. New York: Guilford Press.

Wallerstein, R. S. (1986) Psychoanalysis as a science: A response to the new challenges. *Psychoanalytic Quarterly, 55*, 41–451.

Wing, R. R., Epstein, L. H. Nowiak, M. P., Lamparski, D. M. (1986) Behavioral self-regulation in the treatment of patients with diabetes mellitus. *Psychological Bulletin, 99*, 78–89.

Chapter 6

Exploring change processes in psychodynamic child psychotherapy: The therapist's perspective

Gunnar Carlberg

Introduction

The concept of 'change' in a broad perspective has been discussed through the history of psychotherapy and psychoanalysis (e.g. Strachey 1934, Kris 1956, Blum 1992, Cooper 1992, Klimovski, Bekman Vainer, de Goldberg, de Kuitca, de Liberman & Siniavsky 1994). The question as to what constitutes good conditions for change in psychotherapy and psychoanalysis is constantly recurring (e.g. Rogers 1957, Strupp 1973, Stewart 1990, Pine 1992, Stern et al. 1998). Descriptions of what can be regarded as change agents show that many perceptions exist side by side. For example, an important dividing line is the one that runs between the emphasis on the relationship as an important ingredient in the change process and the emphasis on the necessity of the verbal interpretation that leads to insight.

The analysis of change processes can be carried out at different levels. Stern and colleagues in The Process of Change Study Group (Stern et al. 1998) introduced a micro-perspective by which the details in the individual moments in the therapeutic process are analysed. Cooper (1992) put a contrasting macro-perspective forward where a central issue is the therapist's attitude and basic values.

The discussion about what constitutes good conditions for change has been less intense in the field of child psychotherapy. Important contributions suggest that technique and attitude must be adapted according to the child's developmental level and disorder (e.g. Fonagy & Moran 1991, Lanyado & Horne 2006).

The overarching aim of this chapter is to illustrate how change processes and conditions promoting change in child psychotherapy can be explored. In several studies, psychotherapists' experiences of crucial, data-rich points in child psychotherapies have been examined. Against this background, results from an ongoing study, the Erica Process and Outcome Study (EPOS), will be presented.

Previous research

Systematic research in the domain of change in adult psychotherapy is an established field of research with well-developed methods (e.g. Rice & Greenberg 1984, Mahrer & Nadler 1986, Elliott & Shapiro 1992, Stiles Barkham, Shapiro & Firth-Cozens 1992, Mergenthaler 1996, Timulk 2007). However, there is a great lack of such studies within psychodynamic child psychotherapy (Fonagy 2003, Kennedy & Midgley 2007).

'Turning points' in child psychotherapy have been analysed in some studies (Carlberg 1997, Terr et al. 2005, 2006a, 2006b, Andersson, Boalt Boëthius, Svirsky & Carlberg 2006). Examples of turning points are when a child shows an ability to play for the first time, or the relationship changes from the child avoiding contact to mutual interplay. In a broader perspective, turning points can be seen as a part of a change process.

Psychotherapists' experiences of change processes were investigated in four consecutive studies (Carlberg 1999, 2007). The focus of the analysis was a session or a part of a process the therapist identified as a 'turning-point'. Data were collected from fourteen child psychotherapies through interviews, process records and questionnaires. In addition, examples of changes in 102 psychotherapies were collected through a questionnaire. The aim of the studies was to investigate the nature and content of change, and factors underlying change processes. It was concluded that different kinds of turning point could be described. A few were turning points in the sense of a sudden, unexpected change that persisted. Some were better categorized as 'the process goes on'. It was often possible to reconstruct a process leading up to the change. How one categorizes an identified change is dependent on factors such as 'the severity of the child's disorder' and on 'the way the psychotherapist organizes his or her experience of psychotherapy processes'.

Therapists' experiences of turning points can be seen as a part of their way of creating meaning. In the beginning of therapy, turning points were connected with 'the therapeutic alliance' and later with 'conflict' and 'working through'. From the analysis of factors seen as underlying change processes, a description of conditions beneficial for change was given. For example: The psychotherapist is psychologically present and offers firm frames and continuity. The psychotherapist 'as a new object' is an important change agent. He or she becomes a model for how to relate and the child internalizes the psychotherapist's reflecting attitude and quest for meaning. Change was often identified when the therapeutic frame was broken. Something unpredictable and/or unusual happened in the usually predictable process. The meeting between two subjects, mutually influencing each other, could be considered the nucleus of change. The emotional meeting can be described in terms of 'the creation of a new intersubjectivity'.

The experiences from the four studies of turning points led to questions about how the described changes can be related to actual outcome and the children's own experiences of the therapies. A new project was started in 2000.

The Erica Process and Outcome Study

The Erica Process and Outcome Study (EPOS) encompasses several sub-projects that mirror a variety of aspects in psychodynamic child psycho-therapy, i.e. children's expectations and experiences of being in psychotherapy (Carlberg, Thorén, Billström & Odhammar 2008). The material from nine-teen therapies forms the basis of the results on psychotherapists' descriptions of change processes that will be presented below. The description of the proj-ect's sample group and method is concentrated on what is deemed relevant to provide a picture of this aspect.

Aim of the study

The aim of the EPOS-study was, through a combination of qualitative and quantitative methods, to increase our knowledge about change processes in child psychotherapy. Outcome and process were studies in *'goal-formulated, time-limited psychotherapy with parallel work with parents'*.

Participants

Extensive data have been collected from nineteen therapies. Child guidance clinics from different parts of Sweden assessed the children in a standardized way and decided that *this* form of therapy was suitable for the specific child and family. The following inclusion criteria were applied: The children should be between five and ten years of age at the start of therapy. The scale of the therapy was one or two sessions per week with a duration of between one and two years. The parents were to attend another therapist regularly once a week or at least every fortnight. Goals and frames for the therapies were to be formulated and documented according to a detailed plan.

One child psychotherapist conducted two of the therapies. All eighteen child psychotherapists (fourteen women and four men) participating had a psychodynamic orientation. The psychotherapists' experience from working as child psychotherapists ranged between one and thirty years (median = 19). Fourteen psychotherapists had specialist training in psychoanalytic child psychotherapy; the four who did not have specialist training received supervi-sion from an experienced child psychotherapist. Table 6.1 presents an overall picture of the participating children and the therapies.

At the start of the therapy, the participating children can be described as relatively highly weighted with regard to the initial assessments made with the Children's Global Assessment Scale (CGAS). After completed therapy, four-teen of the nineteen children were assessed by the child psychotherapists as

Table 6.1 Participating children and the therapies

Cases	19	6 girls
		13 boys
Children's age	Median 8 years	5–10 years
Children's CGAS, start of therapy	Median 55	(range 41–70)
Children's CGAS, end of therapy	Median 72	(range 52–91)
Therapy frequency	11 once a week	
	8 twice a week	
Therapy duration	Median = 1½ year	Range 1–2 years
Number of child therapy sessions	Median 59	37–140 sessions
Number of sessions with parents	Median 42	18–91 sessions

Note: CGAS, Children's Global Assessment Scale.

being on or above the problem limit of 70 points on the CGAS (CGAS scores of 80–71 indicate 'no more than slight impairment in functioning . . .' and scores of 70–61 indicate 'some difficulty in a single area but generally functioning pretty well . . .').

At the start of therapy, the most frequent Axis 1 diagnoses were attention disorder, disruptive behaviour and anxiety disorder. Seven of the nineteen children were assessed as fulfilling more than one diagnosis. After completed therapies, certain diagnoses remained but the co-morbidity had sunk to zero.

In a termination questionnaire the therapists were requested to describe the three most important changes regarding the child and family during the contact. For example, it was noted that several children have developed their contact ability and self-esteem. Thirteen of nineteen had increased their ability to manage and express feelings and seven had developed their peer relationships. More than half of the children had achieved better relations with their parents, according to the therapists.

In summary, the quantitative data, as well as the qualitative judgements made by the child therapists, showed that important changes had taken place in a majority of the children. The assessment was supported by a collective analysis of different informants.

One interesting question can be formulated: How can the process leading up to these considerable changes, described by the child psychotherapists, be captured?

Methodology

Collection of data concerning various aspects of the processes in child and parent contacts were made regularly. Every third month questionnaires were distributed to the therapists and the parents. The questionnaires focused on important themes and changes inside and outside therapies during the time period studied; furthermore, the therapeutic alliance and changes in the goals of therapies were investigated. Data from these questionnaires is now presented. First, answers to the following questions:

- Think back to the three-month period in question. What was *the most important change* in the therapy? If possible specify:

  1   *when* the change occurred (approximate date), and describe as carefully as possible
  2   what it was that was *new*, and
  3   circumstances and *significant* factors that may have been underlying the change.

When the answers were divided into meaning-bearing units, the number of text sections per therapy varied between 14 and 116 (median 52). The text was analysed with the help of the computer program QSR NUD•IST (Non-numerical Unstructured Data Indexing, Searching and Theorising; Qualitative Solutions and Research Pty, Melbourne, Australia). The program was originally developed for work according to 'Grounded Theory'.

The analysis followed these questions:

1   How can *the nature of change* be described and analysed?
2   How can *the content of change* be described and analysed?
3   Which *factors underlying change* can be described and analysed?

Results

The nature of change

Commonly, the therapists reported that a change had taken place every three-month period. The therapists primarily selected positive changes. In only three therapies did comments such as 'the period is without decisive changes' occur.

Descriptions were seldom given of episodes that were spontaneously called turning points or that were characterized as turning points in terms of 'something unexpected happening that leads to a lasting change'. A process perspective was the most common. However, in sixteen of the nineteen therapies a point in time where the change occurred was specified. Several episodes that were specified in time were described in the majority of these therapies. For the most part, a date is given or statements such as: 'after the Easter break, the twenty-third session' or 'the day after the terrorist attack in NY'. There was no systematic difference in the frequency depending on whether the changes were reported at the beginning, in the middle or at the end of the therapy period.

A smaller group described an approximate point of time such as:

'somewhere at the beginning of the term', 'the last sessions during the period before the summer break were characterized by a mutual interplay' or 'the child has been more relaxed, calmer and happier during the whole period'. One group described clearly how the change evolved. For example: 'a change that has been going on a long time and with small steps'. The majority of these descriptions came from a stage of the therapy in which the contact was being built up. In other words, these occurrences were similar to what the earlier studies described as 'the process goes on'. They are changes that are sometimes steps on the way towards a deepened therapeutic alliance and the more turning-point-like changes later in the therapy. The data do not provide an opportunity to clearly see differences between different therapists' experiences of the nature of change. One hypothesis from earlier studies claims that therapists differ with regard to their views of processes that consist of parts or are like a continual, gradual development.

In five of the nineteen therapies, a negative change was sometimes described as the most important change. For example: 'a sudden return to negativism . . . and aggressivity'. The most common negative change concerned 'active resistance towards coming to therapy'. All the statements about negative changes were described as an element in the second half of the therapy process.

To summarize, we see that therapists are able to identify and describe changes with the help of the questionnaire. The process perspective is emphasized in a closer scrutiny of when something changed.

The content of change

Changes related to the child were reported by three-quarters of the therapists. Usually, the child expressed a feeling for the first time or in a new way. Many examples were given of expressions of aggression. For example: 'he hurts me on purpose by hitting me in the face with the boxing glove', 'began to show anger and irritation' or 'a greater openness regarding the aggressive force'. Sometimes the feeling was expressed via play: 'she lets the soft toys have aggressive feelings and they are boisterous and try to bite her'. There were also examples of new openness, laughter and thoughtfulness: 'the child laughs contentedly', 'he has begun to show humour, make jokes sometimes', 'I notice greater openness and happiness in him' or 'he showed thoughtfulness about me when I was going to lie on the floor and have a pillow under my head'.

Many examples can be collected under the heading 'the child'. A common denominator was the descriptions of play in various forms. It can be that the child invited the therapist into the game or that the new theme was expressed, i.e. 'gestalted' in symbolic form. The content of the play could be anything from football to simpler ball games. Some therapists summarized what many expressed: 'the game has begun and new possibilities are being created', 'play is significantly less locked and is filled with pleasure and curiosity'. That the child 'gestalts' in pictures was also a recurring theme. For example: 'he drew events in his life situation that he had earlier tried to defend himself against' and 'draws happy pictures, rainbows, people'.

The child therapists often experienced an important change in the therapy when the child verbalized something. This can be the first time the child was able to convey a narrative about something that happened outside the therapy but also that the child was able to put feelings into words. To talk about being angry instead of acting out in the room recurred as a narrative under the heading 'the child verbalizes'. One saw in the answers that the child gained a new Gestalt for the therapist by talking about earlier events. The child was able to convey the feeling in school or what the child thought about the contact with the absent parent. Play could sometimes facilitate verbalization: 'he talks about when he was adopted whilst we are throwing a ball to each other'.

Certain descriptions of changes concerned the therapist seeing something new in the child, such as, 'increased self-esteem', 'she had gained a perspective regarding that time and wanted to see all her drawings that I had saved', 'what was new was chiefly the decisiveness in the child' or 'he has gone on his own to therapy for the first time, an important symbolic action'.

In approximately three-quarters of the therapies the content of the change was described in terms of the relation between the child and the therapist having changed. There was a recurrence of descriptions of the dialogue between the child and the therapist having deepened. Example: 'the new thing is the warm feeling between us that was created in the dialogue about a drawing', 'a process, created in the contact' or 'the period has been character-ized by a more mutual interplay'. Words used to capture this were: 'eye con-tact' or descriptions of how the child for the first time said 'hallo' to the therapist.

In summary, the results of the analysis are in accord with findings of earlier studies. The emphasis of the content of the change focuses on changes in the child and on the relation that is changed. Examples are given of intense moments of meeting between the child and the psychotherapist.

Factors underlying change

Work in the therapy with the firm frame as a point of departure was described as a basis of change. There were recurring descriptions of work that was deepened after sometimes major testing of the therapist. Time was described as important, and that the child gained experience of seeing someone again after a break: 'the therapy continues despite interruption'. One therapist noted that: 'the relation between us became stronger and therewith also more intense transference and countertransference reactions'. Work took place in relation to the child, and the therapist constantly paid attention to his or her attitude. Sometimes a change in attitude was reported as an important factor. For example: 'I went over to adopting a waiting, wordless attitude', 'I relinquished the ambition to attain a flow during the session', or 'put words to his feelings'. A direct interpretation as a factor underlying change was mentioned only in occasional examples. This is congruent with earlier findings.

The therapy's frame is confirmed as the basis for the work. For example, one therapist talked about: 'a result of maintaining a therapeutic frame that shows itself to be strong enough to hold, despite hate and destructiveness'. Examples were also given of how the therapist's assurance that 'we shall continue' gives security. In one therapy, the therapist's assurance that the therapy would continue longer than the designated period was that which was reported as leading to development.

A break in the frame was often reported as a factor underlying a positive change. The phenomenon that changes are often identified after a break, as highlighted in previous studies, can be confirmed. For example: 'three weeks had passed since the last session' and 'after the Christmas break she felt secure in the fact that I remained and she was able to show more of her painful feelings'. Therapy sessions before and after a break received special attention. Examples were also given of how an altered time, cancelled session or the therapist's late arrival could lead to a change. A non-planned break that occurred against a background of the firm frame becomes a factor underlying change. Something happening unpredictably creates the potential for a moment of meeting (Stern et al. 1998).

One recurring theme is events in connection with separation and the termination of therapies. This could be thought of in relation to the impending separation before the summer break, or that the child and the family saw the therapist's belief in the ability of the child and the family to manage things now without therapy as the termination approached.

In several of the therapies in question it is possible, through the therapist's responses, to follow how the child's current situation in relation to the parents affects the work in the psychotherapy. Events such as the child 'has met his/her biological mother during a vacation, for the first time for a long time', or perhaps 'the meeting with an absent dad did not take place' were events that directly affected the work in the therapy. Better cooperation between divorced parents, or that a parent expressed that he or she accepted that the child goes to treatment, could directly and apparently impact on the therapeutic work according to several therapists. Other events were also reported as factors underlying change. For example: 'she was able to come to therapy by bus on her own', 'calmer since he began taking medication' or 'has received help in applying to another school'. In two cases the meetings that were held between the child, child therapist, the parents and the parents' therapist were described as very positive for the development in the child's therapy.

In summary, the child therapists identify the most important factors in the work in the therapy room. The firm frame is the foundation. Certain changes become clear in relation to the frame. In the material in question it is clarified how relations to parents and external events also evidently affect the inner work in the therapy room.

Discussion

The results from this substudy from the EPOS project corroborate findings from previous studies (Carlberg 1997, 1999). The clinical experiences of a group of skilled child psychotherapists were captured. The process of change in psychodynamic child psychotherapy is best described as a gradual process rather than as a chain of turning points. This is in line with Nahum (1998) and a comment by Mary Boston (1998) about earlier studies of turning points. She says: thinking of change processes will remind therapists of '. . . those steady, plodding cases where nothing new seems to happen yet some gradual change occurs' (Boston 1998 p. 201). The content of change is from the child psychotherapists' view focused on changes in the child or changes in the relation between the child and the therapist. Results point to that work in therapy and its firm frames as the most important prerequisite for change.

Three findings can be commented on:

1   In the therapists' narratives, play is often mentioned as an important ingredient in the mechanisms underlying change. This is in line with the growing interest in play as a powerful part of therapy. The therapist's ability to stimulate affective engagement and play activity as agents of change are highlighted in literature and conferences (e.g. Barish 2004, Desmarais 2006, Terr et al. 2006a). We need to further investigate these issues. Some instruments are already available for systematic descriptions of play in child psychotherapy (Kernberg, Chazan & Normandin 1998). By studying play we could develop the capacity of therapists to be aware of the impact of different ways of participating in play interaction, timing and how receptive attention can be valuable for the child.

2   In this study, many examples are given of how powerful intersubjective encounters, 'moments of meeting' (Stern et al. 1998, Stern 2004) are connected to the identified changes. I hope that we will in the future have more systematic studies of child therapists' experiences of these kinds of phenomena. Interesting questions can be formulated concerning work in the transference relationship and work in the present relationship with the therapist as a new object.

3   In our data, encounters with the child psychotherapist and the parents, sometimes with the child participating in the room, are seen as having influenced the process in a positive way. Events and processes outside of the therapy room are repeatedly mentioned in the answers to the question of factors underlying change. In Sweden it is more and more common that the child psychotherapist has the sole responsibility for both the

child psychotherapy and the parallel contact with the parents. This makes the external world come into the therapy room in a more explicit way. Perhaps this kind of departure from the traditional model for the child psychotherapy could be developed and examined in a more systematic way? In a time when the space for long-term child psychotherapy in the public sector is narrowing, this type of intervention can be used in a more planned way to support processes of change. Cohen (1997) talks about an increasing attention in the practice of child psychotherapy to external factors in the life of the child as a significant advance.

Limitations of the study

The study has some methodological limitations. The group of participating children, families and psychotherapists is small. Nevertheless, results can form a basis for further study, as suggested above. No control group was used. The child psychotherapists' subjective views were the focus of the study and one has to be aware of this when interpreting the data.

The descriptions of the outcome of the therapies has to be valued from the knowledge that it is the therapists' own judgements that form the base for the assessments. Work was done to secure the reliability of these findings through independent ratings (Sundin, Carlberg & Odhammar 2008). In the forthcoming work we will also have the possibility to compare parents', therapists' and sometimes teachers' descriptions of clinical significant changes.

Some comments can be made about the content of the results and the methodology of the study. The reported substudy shows that questionnaires can yield important information about how psychotherapists think about their work. At the same time, we can note that earlier studies emphasized changes in the relationship in a more distinct way. One possible reason for this may be that the questionnaire used in this study focused respondents' attention in a different way to questions raised in a conversation during an interview. The details of the interplay were sometimes lost and events outside the therapy room came into focus in a more apparent way. In earlier studies, data were collected from deep interviews, sometimes even two or three recurring interviews.

Therapists as informants

By analysing other material we can see how all eighteen therapists became deeply committed to the study. They also described participation in the research as something positive that gave scope for reflection about the therapies. As researchers, we can state that it is not always easy to receive completed questionnaires according to schedule. A great deal of work has been invested in seeking missing information. Nevertheless, the final assessment, from the therapists' side, was that participation was positive for the therapists themselves and many times for the therapeutic work. One therapist thought that 'the fear that has existed – amongst psychodynamically oriented psychotherapists that research disturbs the therapeutic process is unwarranted and based on a lack of knowledge' . . . 'through scrutinizing myself, my attitude, by completing the questionnaire I have become more stringent and focused . . . it has helped me'.

Concluding remarks

Currently we analyse outcomes, processes and formulated goals from various perspectives. Hopefully, more certain conclusions can be drawn about which children and families have benefited the most from this form of therapy. One strength in this type of study is that data were collected from various sources to illuminate the same course of events in the therapies. Different data-collection methods complement one another and make it possible to present multiperspective outcome assessment from the point of view of the patients, parents and therapists.

References

Andersson, G., Boalt Boëthius, S., Svirsky, L., Carlberg, G. (2006) Memories of significant episodes in child psychotherapy: An autobiographical approach. *Psychology and Psychotherapy: Theory, Research and Practice, 79*, 229–236.

Barish, K. (2004) What is therapeutic in child psychotherapy? 1. Therapeutic engagement. *Psychoanalytic Psychology, 21*(3), 385–401.

Blum, H.P. (1992) Psychic change: The analytic relationship(s) and agents of change. *International Journal of Psychoanalysis, 73*, 255–265.

Boston, M. (1998) Correspondence. Letter to the editors. *Journal of Child Psychotherapy, 24*, 201–202.

Carlberg, G. (1997) Laughter opens the door: Turning points in child psychotherapy. *Journal of Child Psychotherapy, 23*, 331–349.

Carlberg, G. (1999) *Vändpunkter i barnpsykoterapi. Psykoterapeuters erfarenheter av förändringsprocesser*, [*Turning points in child psychotherapy. Psychotherapists' experiences of change processes*]. Dissertation, Department of Education, University of Stockholm. Edsbruk: Akademitryck.

Carlberg, G. (in press) Focused systematic case studies. An approach linking clinical work and research. In J. Tsiantis & J.Trowell (eds) *Child and adolescent psychodynamic psychotherapy research*. London: Karnac, EFPP Clinical Book Series.

Carlberg, G., Thorén, A., Billström, S., Odhammar, F. (2008) Children's expectations and experiences of psychodynamic child psychotherapy. Submitted.

Cohen, J. (1997) Child and adolescent psychoanalysis: Research, practice and theory. *International Journal of Psycho-Analysis, 78*, 449–520.

Cooper, A.M. (1992) Psychic change: Development in the theory of psychoanalytic techniques. *International Journal of Psychoanalysis, 73*, 245–250.

Desmarais, S. (2006) A space to float with someone: Recovering play as a field of repair in work with parents of late-adopted children. *Journal of Child Psychotherapy*, *32*(3), 349–364.

Elliott, R., Shapiro, D.A. (1992) Client and therapist as analysts of significant events. In S.G. Toukmanian & D.L. Rennie (eds) *Psychotherapy process research. Paradigmatic and narrative approaches* (pp. 163–186). London: Sage.

Fonagy, P. (2003) The research agenda: the vital need for empirical research in child psychotherapy. *Journal of Child Psychotherapy*, *29*(2), 129–136.

Fonagy, P., Moran, G.S. (1991) Understanding psychic change in child analysis. *International Journal of Psychoanalysis*, *72*, 15–22.

Kennedy, E., Midgley, N. (2007) *Process and outcome research in child, adolescent and parent-infant psychotherapy: A thematic review*. London: North Central London Strategic Health Authority.

Kernberg, P.F., Chazan, S.E., Normandin, L. (1998) The children's play therapy instrument (CPTI): Description, development, and reliability studies. *The Journal of Psychotherapy Practice and Research*, *7*, 196–207.

Klimovsky, G., Bekman Vainer, S., de Goldberg, D. B., de Kuitca, M. K., de Liberman, J.F., Siniavsky, M. (1994) Change in psychoanalysis: Epistemological aspects. *International Journal of Psychoanalysis*, *75*, 51–58.

Kris, E. (1956) On some vicissitudes of insight in psychoanalysis. *International Journal of Psychoanalysis*, *37*, 445–455.

Lanyado, M., Horne, A. (2006) *A question of technique*. London: Routledge.

Mahrer, A. R., Nadler, W.P. (1986) Good moments in psychotherapy: A preliminary review, a list, and some promising research avenues. *Journal of Consulting and Clinical Psychology*, *54*, 10–15.

Mergenthaler, E. (1996) Emotion – abstraction patterns in verbatim protocols: A new way of describing psychotherapeutic processes. *Journal of Consulting and Clinical Psychology*, *64*, 1306–1315.

Nahum, J.P. (1998) Case illustration: Moving along . . . and, is change gradual or sudden? *Infant Mental Health Journal*, *19* (special issue): 315–319.

Pine, F. (1992) From technique to a theory of psychic change. *International Journal of Psychoanalysis*, *73*, 251–254.

Rice, L. N., Greenberg, L. S. (1984) *Patterns of change: Intensive analysis of psychotherapeutic process*. New York: Guilford Press.

Rogers, C.R. (1957) The necessary and sufficient conditions of therapeutic personality change. *Journal of Consulting Psychology*, *21*, 95–103.

Stern, D.N. (2004) *The present moment in psychotherapy and everyday life*. New York: W.W. Norton & Company.

Stern, D.N., Sander, L.W., Nahum, J.P., Harrison, A.M., Lyon-Ruth, K., Morgan, A.C., Bruschweiler-Stern, N., Tronick, E.Z. (1998) Non-interpretive mechanisms in psychoanalytic therapy. The 'something more' than interpretation. *International Journal of Psychoanalysis*, *79*, 903–921.

Stewart, H. (1990) Interpretation and other agents for psychic change. *International Review of Psychoanalysis*, *17*, 61–69.

Stiles, W.B., Barkham, M., Shapiro, D.A., Firth-Cozens, J. (1992) Treatment order and thematic continuity between contrasting psychotherapies: Exploring an implication of the assimilation model. *Psychotherapy Research*, *2*, 112–124.

Strachey, J. (1934) The nature of the therapeutic action of psycho-analysis. *International Journal of Psychoanalysis*, *15*, 127–159.

Strupp, H.H. (1973) On the basic ingredients of psychotherapy. *Journal of Consulting and Clinical Psychology*, *41*, 1–8.

Sundin, E., Carlberg, G., Odhammar, F. (2008) Eighteen children in psychodynamic child psychotherapy. Changes in global functioning. Submitted.

Terr, L.C., McDermott, J.F., Benson, R.M., Blos, P.Jr., Deeney, J.M., Rogers, R.R., Zrull, J.P. (2005) Moments in psychotherapy. *Journal of Academic Child and Adolescent Psychiatry*, *44*(2), 191–197.

Terr, L.C., Deeney, J.M., Drell, M., Dodson, J.W., Gaensbauer, T.J., Massie, H., Minde, K., Teal, S., Winters, N.C. (2006a) Playful 'moments' in psychotherapy. *Journal of Academic Child and Adolescent Psychiatry*, *45*(5), 604–613.

Terr, L.C., Beitchman, J.H., Braslow, K., Fox, G., Metcale, A., Pease, M., Ponton, L., Sack, W., Wasserman, S. (2006b) Children's turn-arounds in psychotherapy. The doctor's gesture. *Psychoanalytic Study of the Child*, *61*, 56–81.

Timulk, L. (2007) Identifying core categories of client-identified impact of helpful events in psychotherapy: A qualitative meta-analysis. *Psychotherapy Research*, *17*(3), 305–314.

Part III

Evaluating the outcomes and the clinical effectiveness of child psychotherapy

Introduction

When Freud (1909) first made use of psychoanalytic principles to try and help a young child, 'Little Hans', almost one hundred years ago, concern was immediately expressed about the impact such treatment would have on him. Would Little Hans be 'corrupted' by his encounter with psychoanalysis? Or could it actually strengthen him in his future life, both in enabling him to deal with his immediate childhood difficulties (a phobia about horses) and in preparing him to deal more effectively with the emotional challenges of his adult life?

For many years, this question about the effectiveness of psychodynamic child psychotherapy was answered on the basis of a growing body of clinical experience and single-case studies that illustrated the impact that psychotherapy could have on children lives. But since the 1950s – especially following the publication of Hans Eysenck's famous paper (1952), in which he argued that there was no evidence that (adult) psychotherapy was effective – there has been growing pressure to examine the effectiveness of child psychotherapy using more scientific and 'objective' measures. This pressure has increased considerably with the growth of the evidence-based medicine movement, which has argued that no treatment should be made available (especially when funded by public finances) unless there is sufficient evidence that such treatment works.

This part of the book is not an attempt to summarize the cumulative information about the effectiveness of psychoanalytic psychotherapy with children, nor does it deal with all the complex methodological issues about how best to judge whether a treatment is effective or not. Such information is available elsewhere, both for the general field of child mental health treatments (Fonagy, Target, Cottrell, Phillips & Kurtz 2002) and more specifically for psychoanalytic child psychotherapy (Kennedy 2004).

Instead, the chapters in this part of the book raise some of the key issues about how the effectiveness of treatment can be most meaningfully assessed, and give examples of a variety of different ways in which the outcome of treatment can be explored. Grainger et al. give an account of one of the earliest systematic studies of the outcome of psychodynamic child psychotherapy for looked-after children. The study was a landmark in the history of child psy-chotherapy treatment evaluation. Although it would not meet the rigorous methodological requirements of modern evaluation research, it has had con-siderable impact on the field – not least in making people aware of the important role child psychotherapists can play in the lives of looked-after young people.

The study by Trowell et al. is an example of one of the latest, and most impressive, attempts to investigate the effectiveness of child psychotherapy – this time, for adolescents suffering from depression. Twenty years after the study described by Grainger et al., this team of international researchers made use of mainstream scientific research design to produce the kind of findings that will be accepted by organizations such as the National Institute of Health and Clinical Excellence (NICE), whose guidelines only refer to evidence gathered from certain types of research.

The other two chapters in this part – by Schachter and Target and by Cathy Urwin – take rather different approaches to evaluating the effectiveness of treatment. Schachter and Target look at the longer-term consequences of being in psychotherapy as a child, from both a quantitative and qualitative perspective. Urwin, meanwhile, describes one way of incorporating the evalu-ation of treatment into routine clinical practice, in a way that may be of direct relevance to practising clinicians.

Taken together, we hope that the chapters in this part of the book will open the door to an awareness of the variety of approaches that are needed to explore the question of 'what works for whom' in child psychotherapy.

References

Eysenck, H. (1952) The effects of psychotherapy: An evaluation. *Journal of Consult-ing Psychology*, *16*, 319–324.

Fonagy, P., Target, M., Cottrell, D., Phillips, J., Kurtz, Z. (2002) *What works for whom? A critical review of treatments for children and adolescents.* New York: Guilford Publications.

Freud, S. (1909) Analysis of a phobia in a five-year-old boy ('Little Hans'). In *Penguin Freud Library, Vol 8*. London: Penguin Books (1977).

Kennedy, E. (2004) *Child and adolescent psychotherapy: A systematic review of psycho-analytic approaches.* London: North Central London Strategic Health Authority. Available as a free download at www.acp.uk.net

Chapter 7

Evaluation of psychoanalytic psychotherapy with fostered, adopted and 'in-care' children [1]

Mary Boston, Dora Lush and Eve Grainger

Introduction

This chapter describes a research project that was undertaken between 1988 and 1994 to evaluate the outcome of psychoanalytic psychotherapy with fostered, adopted and in-care children. It was a ground-breaking study at the time, both because it evaluated psychotherapy with children in care, a group that had previously been thought to be untreatable, and because it was one of the first attempts to develop a research methodology for psychotherapy that would not interfere with clinical practice (Boston 1989). In the twenty years that have followed this project, psychotherapy with 'looked-after children' has become a core part of the child psychotherapist's caseload, and is an area of special interest for many therapists undertaking doctoral research. The chapter draws particularly on two previously published papers: Lush, Boston & Grainger (1991) and Boston & Lush (1994).

Background to the project

This research project arose from an earlier, descriptive study of psychotherapy with severely deprived children (Boston & Szur 1983), which had utilized the workshop method of clinical research as described by Rustin (1984). Up until the 1980s, it was generally thought that psychotherapy could not help children who had experienced extreme emotional and social deprivation. The stereotypical child psychotherapy patient until that time was seen as

---

1 Parts of this chapter were previously published in:

> Boston, M., & Lush, D. (1994). Further considerations of methodology for evaluating psychoanalytic psychotherapy with children: reflections in light of research experience. *Journal of Child Psychotherapy, 20* (5), 205–229.

and

> Lush, D., Boston, M., & Grainger, E. (1991). Evaluation of psychoanalytic psychotherapy with children: therapists' assessments and predictions. *Psychoanalytic Psychotherapy, 5* (3), 191–234.

a 'middle-class' child who could primarily communicate through talking, drawing and orderly symbolic play. By contrast, it can be difficult for many deprived children to enter the therapy room at all. Large periods of their therapy may have to focus on what the child is communicating through chaotic action both in and outside the therapy room. This was thought at the time to make these children 'untreatable'. However, through following the course of these children's therapy, the Tavistock workshop identified that many of them had been able to achieve, in time, a considerable amount of hopeful progress. This was evidenced by reports from current carers and social workers on the external relationships and behaviour of the children, and by the therapists' own observations of the process of change in the treatment material, reinforced and checked by discussion in the workshop.

These observations led to the formulation of tentative hypotheses that psychotherapy might begin to modify the internal images of abandoning and rejecting parents, which most of these children held, and which they projected on to current carers, precipitating further breakdowns of substitute care. It might therefore facilitate permanent placement, decreasing the placement-breakdown rate, as well as improving the general functioning, well-being, and relationships of these children.

It was also at this time in the 1980s that the debate about the evidence for the effectiveness of psychotherapy was beginning. This research project was one of the first attempts by the profession to engage with that debate in order to try to differentiate improvements, as a result of therapeutic efficacy, from maturational and environmental causes of change (Rutter 1981, Stevenson 1986). At the same time, there was a concern that the research process should not interfere with, or distort, clinical practice.

Aims of the project

The study had two main aims:

1   To test the hypothesis that severely deprived children could benefit from psychotherapy, and that their adjustment in family placements might therefore be facilitated; and
2   To devise a suitable methodology for evaluating psychoanalytic psychotherapy with children in general.

It was decided to include children known to be adopted at referral, because of the increasing tendency for severely deprived children to be offered adoptive placements. Some of the adopted children had been adopted in early infancy, and this offered a further advantage in providing a possible 'within-group' comparison.

Developing a suitable methodology

As researchers, we were not at this time primarily concerned with the relative efficacy of different treatments, but to make public therapists' aims in psychotherapy for their particular patients, to develop ways of assessing to what extent these aims had been achieved, and to see how well progress in psychotherapy could be predicted. External changes in the patient's behaviour would be noted, but, more importantly, evidence of qualitative changes in personality organization, and in the structure of the inner world, would be systematically described. This dimension can often be missing from outcome studies, but we believed that description of the processes of change was essential for a valid assessment of the degree of improvement. Confidence in the future progress of patients depends on the quality of internal development judged to have occurred, and not solely on external change. A further aim was to develop a method of evaluation that did not interfere with ordinary clinical practice.

Method

Stage I. The identification of the study group

During a three-year period, all referrals of children in care, and of those known to be adopted, to the Tavistock Clinic's Child and Family Department were monitored to identify all those proceeding to individual psychotherapy. A form (Form 1; Lush, Boston & Grainger 1991, Appendix I) asking for factual data on the child's age, placement, family background, significant historical factors, and ethnic matching in the placement, was issued to the person (known as case consultant), to whom the case was initially allocated for exploration.

From this total group of 203 in care and adopted referrals, a series of fifty-one consecutive cases who had been recommended for psychotherapy during the three-year period and who were between the ages of two and eighteen inclusive, was identified. These were the cases that, following the recommendation, were judged to be ready to start psychotherapy. The remainder of the 203 were identified as not ready to start psychotherapy for a variety of reasons, e.g. changes of placement or social worker, refusal of the offer of psychotherapy, or unavailability of therapist. In the event, only thirty-eight children actually started therapy. The reasons why thirteen of the fifty-one cases did not proceed to therapy varied. There were sometimes practical reasons, such as change of placement to one too far from the clinic; or it was considered that therapy should be delayed until decisions about placement were made. In one case, adoptive parents refused treatment and three adolescents refused to have therapy. In some cases there was no therapist available.

The thirty-eight constitute all those who actually started psychotherapy in the specified three-year period and were therefore unselected by the researchers. However, seven of these dropped out after one or two sessions, and we were left with thirty-one whose therapy could be followed through. Of this final sample, there were nineteen girls and twelve boys. Half the children were under ten. Thirteen were adopted, thirteen were fostered and five were in children's homes. Only four had had early adoption with the minimum of discontinuity of care so that our hoped-for comparison between those with and without a disrupted background was not possible. We had expected that the very disturbed children would have needed fairly intensive psychotherapy for much impact to be made. In the event the majority (nineteen) were given once-weekly work for practical reasons, even though the therapists invariably said they needed more frequent sessions; twelve had two- or three-times-weekly therapy.

We attempted to investigate the issue of whether the group who proceeded to psychotherapy were a self-selected group or whether they differed in motivation, placement or background from the non-psychotherapy group through:

• comparisons between the two groups in respect of age, sex, placement and background; and
• a study of the thirteen of the original fifty-one recommended for psychotherapy who had not actually started it within the two years; these constitute the contrast group.

Comparisons between psychotherapy and non-psychotherapy group

A great variety of work was offered in response to these referrals by the clinical teams involved (e.g. consultation to professionals, work with natural parents, foster parents, adopted parents and families). Psychotherapy for the child was recommended in only about twenty-five per cent of cases, but allocation to different interventions was determined not at random but by the needs of the particular cases, the practical possibilities and the preferences of the clinical team.

From the information requested with the form, indicating the number of moves or changes of placement during the course of the child's life, an 'Index of Discontinuity of Past Care' was calculated for each child in the psychotherapy group, for the first year's intake of other looked-after/adopted children who attended the service, and for the contrast group. This was intended to be a rough guide to the kind of disruption of care each child had experienced. Points were given for numbers of moves of home, giving increased weight to those occurring earlier in life and to the strangeness of the new carers. Additional points were given for adverse factors of a traumatic kind, such as physical and sexual abuse, or murder of parents (for details, see Lush, Boston & Grainger 1991, Appendix I). In addition, an estimate of the

'Stability of the Current Placement' was requested from the clinician carrying out the initial assessment. This was rated by the researchers on a five-point scale, 1 being the most stable (no moves likely) to 5 (further moves already certain) (Lush, Boston & Grainger 1991, Appendix II).

These ratings were made independently from the forms by three different research workers, and then compared. Ninety per cent agreement was reached, and in the remaining ten per cent discrepancies were minor and recourse to the files for further information sufficed to obtain agreed ratings.

We checked if the backgrounds and placements of the psychotherapy cases differed from those of the rest of the referrals by comparing the indices of discontinuity and current placement ratings for psychotherapy and non-psychotherapy groups. The groups were similar in sex and age distribution. Both had a wide range on the index of discontinuity. There was very little difference in the stability of current placement ratings. We concluded that the psychotherapy group did not differ substantially in background or current placement from other adopted and in-care referrals.

The contrast group

We tried to investigate all thirteen cases where psychotherapy was recommended but had not been carried out. As we had initial assessment material on these cases they were potentially a suitable comparison group, although not randomly selected.

Regarding discontinuity of past care and stability of current placement, there was very little difference between the past care of the contrast group and that of the psychotherapy group. There was a small difference in the stability of their current placement, with the contrast group's placement being, on average, a little less stable.

We found only seven cases where information was available for at least two years after psychotherapy was recommended, and we investigated how these children fared during this time. None of these children did well during the period of two years and over without psychotherapy. The reasons for not having therapy varied. Sometimes no therapist was available, or it had been decided that stable placement should be found first. In one case, adoptive parents did not accept therapy until two years later. The only common factors we could find in this group were that therapy had been recommended but had not taken place; and that their problems had not disappeared but were still causing concern. As sixteen of the psychotherapy cases improved, the evidence suggests that it was the psychotherapy rather than the environmental change or developmental progress that led to the improvement. Of the seven children, four did eventually start psychotherapy.

There was no information obtainable on the other six of the thirteen cases, mostly because they refused to return to the Clinic, or were referred elsewhere.

The psychotherapy group

Seven of the thirty-eight children starting psychotherapy stopped in less than three months. These were omitted from the main study because the plan was to compare initial material with descriptions two years later. It was not anticipated that processes of change could be identified in a period as short as three months, especially as the initial material on the cases in general tended to be based on several weeks' work.

The psychotherapists

Twenty-three different therapists participated in the project. Some were highly experienced staff members and some less experienced, in training, with opportunities for supervision or discussion with experienced staff. They were all trained in a similar method of therapy, the essence of which is the provision of a predictable setting (in terms of a regular time, place and a space in the therapist's mind) in which attempts can be made to understand the communications of the patient, verbal or non-verbal, as they occur in the context of the developing relationship between patient and therapist (for a fuller description of the method, see Boston & Daws 1988, Boston & Szur 1983). The interaction was a non-directive one, with non-specific play and drawing materials available to facilitate communication for younger children.

Stage II. Gathering the baseline data for measuring change

The psychotherapy group having been identified, the case consultants were then given a questionnaire (Form 2, Lush, Boston & Grainger 1991, Appendix III), which, in conjunction with any processed records of initial interviews, psychological tests or school reports available, constituted the baseline data for each case. This semi-structured questionnaire was devised to elicit both factual material and more subjective qualitative material, as in a number of follow-up studies of foster children and adopted children (e.g. Triseliotis 1980, Rowe, Caine, Hundleby & Keane 1984, Triseliotis & Russell 1984). Form 2 was filled in as near to the completion of the exploration/assessment process as possible, either by the person assessing the case or by the psychotherapist at the start of psychotherapy. In most cases this was the same person, but in a few the assessment was not done by the person who subsequently took the child on. In accordance with our policy of interfering as little as possible with the ordinary clinical practice in the Department, we tried to work with the existing records, except for the questionnaires to the therapists. We had to accept that formal assessment data, e.g. psychological tests or psychiatric interviews, were not always available. Established and validated interview schedules of that time, such as Rutter–Graham scales

(Rutter, Tizard & Whitmore 1970) were not appropriate to our purpose of highlighting the processes of psychotherapy. We therefore devised our own schedule. This allowed space for the therapists to fill in reports on the child's behaviour by referrers, parents, or current carers, as well as for the therapist's own initial observations on a number of categories of external behaviour and personality qualities. The main purpose of the questionnaire was to allow clinical judgements to be described systematically and in detail. In addition, therapists were asked to state their aims for the therapy, to specify the criteria that would need to be met for improvement to be judged to occur, and also to rate the anticipated progress on a five-point scale. We were interested to know how well therapists could predict the use their patients would make of psychotherapy. This might be important in assessment, especially where resources are limited. As many of these patients were extremely disturbed and deprived to start with, it was also important to be able to compare actual progress with the prognostic indications. The ratings in addition provided a means of making comparisons between the therapists' and independent assessors' judgements of improvement.

Stage III. Gathering the outcome data

At approximately two years after the start of psychotherapy, or at termination if it occurred earlier than this, a further form (Form 3, Lush, Boston & Grainger 1991; Appendix IV) was given to the therapists, who were asked to rate the actual progress made on a six-point scale (this includes an extra point for 'worse', which was inappropriate for rating of anticipated progress). The questions on Form 3 cover similar areas to those of Form 2, so that the research team was in a position to assess any changes, and whether the criteria for improvement had been met, both in terms of external behaviour and also in terms of personality change and structure of the inner world.

If the case continued in psychotherapy, Form 3 was given again at termination, or at the next two-year point.

Administration of forms

The forms were originally given to the therapists to fill in, with researchers offering to be available to discuss or help if required. Therapists varied a good deal in how easy or time-consuming they found it to fill in the forms. We therefore decided that Form 3, and in future Form 2, should be filled in during an interview with one member of the research team.

The main purpose of the interview was for the interviewer to act as a 'live' manual of instructions to ensure that the questions on the form were clearly understood by the interviewees, and to prevent forms not being returned because of failure to understand the requirements. It was felt to be particularly hard to rate the outcome of therapy, as this invariably involved some feeling of the therapist rating him- or herself as a therapist. The position of the researcher as outside the clinical team, unfamiliar with the particular child described, was thought to have helped the therapist towards an objective assessment of the material.

However, despite the initial anxiety and the thoroughness of the forms, which were experienced by all the interviewees as very rigorous, most therapists found filling in the form a useful opportunity to bring together their thoughts about their patients, and some interviewees asked for copies of the form to help with their thinking about other patients. Strikingly, the interviewer did not feel that anxieties about confidentiality affected the interviewees' responses at all. However, all patients were, of course, given pseudonyms and codes throughout in order to protect their confidentiality.

Reliability and validity

The internal consistency of the completed questionnaires was assessed independently by two researchers, who agreed in considering it good in all cases. We had no way of knowing how far two different therapists would agree in completing the forms, except in a few cases where Form 2 happened to have been filled in by two different people. In these cases there was good agreement.

The degree of internal consistency of responses to the forms and variations in profiles of progress led the researchers to have some confidence in the validity of the therapists' assessments. Anonymity given to therapists by codenames and pseudonyms for the patients also facilitated frank and honest recording. It might be thought that therapists would be prone to overestimate the success of their work, but Kissel (1974) found that therapists' ratings of improvement were not as high as those of parents, a finding that has since been confirmed in more recent studies.

In addition to the questionnaire, we had two checks on the validity of the therapists' responses:

- External reports on progress: Therapists' ratings were compared with reports available from parents or current carers, school or social worker. External evidence was also afforded by factors such as maintenance of foster placements, becoming fosterable or adjusting to school.
- Independent clinical ratings: In order to obtain further independent measures of the degree of change shown by these patients, processed records of early interviews were being compared with sessions at the later stage by an experienced therapist outside the Clinic, to whom both the patients and therapists were unknown. These ratings were done 'blind' in the sense that the clinical rater was told nothing about the cases, except the age and sex of the child, the frequency of therapy and the position of the session in question in the course of the therapy. The clinical rater

was given the initial sessions first and asked to fill in relevant parts of Form 2, including a rating of anticipated progress. When this was completed, later material was given for an assessment of any change to be made. Form 3 was filled in, including a rating of progress, and comments were invited.

Results

Despite this being a series of very deprived children, judged both by the information about their internal worlds, and by their experiences and behaviour in the external world, at the Form 3 stage (therapists' rating at the end of treatment), twenty-six were rated 1, 2 or 3 (some degree of improvement). Twenty-three of these were rated 1 or 2 (definite or considerable improvement). Four were rated 4 (doubtful progress) and one 'no change'. None was rated worse.

Thirteen therapies stopped well before the two-year stage, sometimes for external reasons and sometimes because the child terminated the treatment. All except one of these children who terminated therapy before the two-year mark were in once-weekly treatment. Although the numbers are too small for statistical treatment, the figures do indicate a tendency for more frequent and longer therapy to be more effective for this group of children.

There was also a tendency for good progress to be related, as one would expect, to more stable current placements and to good external 'support' for the therapy. 'Support' meant both agreement with, and backing of the therapy by the network, and regular (weekly or fortnightly) sessions for parents and carers with Clinic staff. In the twenty-one cases where there was good support for the therapy, all cases showed improvement.

In twenty-six of the thirty-one cases, according to the independent assessment of the children's material by the external raters, the external criteria for improvement were met. The alleviation of referral problems was confirmed in most cases by parents. The children's relationships were said to have improved in most cases in all aspects, including depth. Therapy was said to have helped the intense jealousy and rivalry with siblings and peers that had been noted in over half the cases. Twenty-five of the children were said to show some inner change, mostly in the direction of increased strength and supportiveness of internal figures. This led to an increase in trust, confidence and security, and a decrease in depression even in those still searching for more sustaining internal objects. On referral, over half the children were said to have disturbances in intellectual functioning. These included learning difficulties, poor capacity to think, confusion and inhibitions in play, imagination and fantasy. Improvement in sessions in these areas was noted by therapists in most cases, usually confirmed by reports from parents, teachers and social workers.

Although there was an improved image of the self in most cases after some therapy, we found that this was an area in which change did not come as easily as in other areas, and therapists often said 'still low in self-esteem'. Many of these children had been the recipients of unconscious hate or rejection, and had internalized images of themselves as deserving hate or rejection, feeling 'I was not loved and therefore am not lovable'. The findings suggest that the level of damage to the self caused by these experiences has a profound impact on the personality of the young person. Depression about the self was seen in half the children and was often linked to the low self-esteem already mentioned.

Discussion of the results

The findings confirmed those of an earlier study (Boston & Szur 1983) that severely deprived children are able, in many cases, to make good use of psychoanalytic psychotherapy. Furthermore, the use of a questionnaire demonstrated more systematically, and in detail, the kinds of change in personality that had occurred.

Most children showed considerable improvement in their relationships with adults, and often also with peers, which is a crucial area of change if successful placement is to be maintained. Concomitant changes in the inner world, necessary for a more confident prediction of future adjustment, were also judged to have occurred in many cases, although it naturally takes time to achieve such fundamental change. Most of the therapists thought a longer period of therapy would be required for the strengthening of internal parental images to be consolidated. In view of the prevalence of learning difficulties in deprived children, it is encouraging to note that improvement in learning and thinking processes was observed in most cases. Most therapists reported an increased tolerance of mental pain, which made the patients more emotionally accessible and less prone to defensive strategies. This is important, considering the painful experiences that many children had undergone, and the 'hard-to-reach' quality often observed initially. Self-esteem seems slow to improve in this group of children, not surprising in those who have experienced severe rejection and abandonment.

There were too few cases to enable a comparison to be made between early-adopted children and those with disrupted backgrounds. There is an impression that the differences between the groups is not as great as we anticipated, and that self-esteem, for example, can be low even among early-adopted children. These observations suggest that being adopted when very young does not necessarily ensure good internal parental figures, as the images persist of the original parents who have not kept the child (see Chapter 13).

One advantage of this attempt to make children's responses to psychotherapy more open to scientific inquiry is that although it makes a substantial demand on therapists' time it does not require any departure from their normal clinical practice and does not involve patients directly. In the researchers' view there is, therefore, a greater likelihood that such a model can be incorporated into ongoing clinical work, and for clinical research to be conducted rather than avoided. Although this project was on adopted and in-care children, this method could be used with any children in psychotherapy, and possibly, in an adapted form, with adults.

An obvious limitation of these results is that they depend mainly on the therapists' own assessments, and therefore can be considered subject to bias. The separation of initial from later assessments, and the use of a large number of different categories to describe the children, go some way towards making the data available for scientific scrutiny, and towards making possible a somewhat more objective, and certainly more discriminative, evaluation of outcome, the differing sources of information offering a form of triangulation.

The spectrum of personality change observed by the therapists in the course of their work with the patients is not obtainable, by definition, for a non-treatment control group. However, the contrast group does provide some comparison data and an indication of how similar children are likely to fare without psychotherapy.

The collection of more systematic data to meet research requirements would entail a greater degree of active participants with the therapists as co-research-workers. Similar routine data collected on all cases seen in a clinic would obviously facilitate research, but even then the kind of qualitative data on individual children required for our baseline on psychotherapy cases cannot be obtained outside the individual psychotherapeutic interview, and is therefore not practical where many children may be seen in a family context only.

Conclusions

In a naturalistic research, such as this, it may not be possible to achieve methodological exactitude without sacrificing the meaningfulness and clinical relevance of the results. However, the ongoing tension between these different perspectives has serious implications for the development of a fully-informed 'evidence base'. This study does not meet the research criteria that The National Institute for Health and Clinical Excellence in the UK (NICE) requires in order to be included in their evidence-based guidelines. Nevertheless, this work has had a huge impact on the child psychotherapy profession, and on the therapeutic help that is now made available to 'looked-after children', because the relative success of the therapeutic work confirmed the hypothesis that this group of extremely traumatized children can make significant progress, both in the quality of their attachments and of their general developmental functioning, with the help of psychoanalytic psychotherapy. The research has confirmed the phenomenological insights of Boston and Szur, and helped to describe and delineate in greater detail the internal worlds of 'looked-after children'. It has inspired a number of child psychotherapists to undertake further studies of 'looked-after children', and to lead the field in describing the difficulties and help required for these children (e.g. Hunter 2001; Hindle 2000; Canham 2003).

References

Boston, M. (1989) In search of a methodology for evaluating psychoanalytic psychotherapy with children. *Journal of Child Psychotherapy, 15*, 15–46.

Boston, M., Dawes, D. (eds) (1988) *The child psychotherapist and problems of young people*. London: Karnac.

Boston, M., Lush, D. (1994) Further considerations of methodology for evaluating psychoanalytic psychotherapy: reflections in the light of research experience. *Journal of Child Psychotherapy, 20*, 205–229.

Boston, M., Szur, R. (eds) (1983) *Psychotherapy with severely deprived children*. London: Routledge.

Canham, H. (2003) The relevance of the oedipus myth to fostered and adopted children. *Journal of Child Psychotherapy, 29*, 5–19.

Hindle, D. (2000) The Merman: recovering from early abuse and loss. *Journal of Child Psychotherapy*, 26, 369–391.

Hunter, M. (2001) *Psychotherapy with young people in care*. Hove, UK: Brunner-Routledge.

Kissel, S. (1974) Mothers and therapists evaluate long-term and short-term child therapy. *Journal of Clinical Psychology, 30*, 396–299.

Lush, D., Boston, M., Grainger, E. (1991) Evaluation of psychoanalytic psychotherapy: therapists' assessments and predictions. *Psychoanalytic Psychotherapy, 5*, 191–234.

Rowe, J., Caine, M., Hundleby, M., Keane, A. (1984) *Long-term foster care*. London: Batsford.

Rustin, M. (1984) *Clinical research: The strengths of a practitioner's workshop as a new model*. London: Tavistock, document EN 1926.

Rutter, M. (1981) Stress, coping and development: some issues and some questions. *Journal of Child Psychology and Psychiatry, 22*, 323–356.

Rutter, M., Tizard, J., Whitmore, K. (1970) *Education, health and behaviour*. London: Longman.

Stevenson, J. (1986) Evaluation studies of psychological treatment of children and practical constraints on their design. *Association of Child Psychology and Psychiatry Newsletter, 8*, 2–11.

Triseliotis, J. (ed) (1980) *New developments in foster care and adoption*. London: Routledge.

Chapter 8

Childhood depression: An outcome research project

Judith Trowell, Maria Rhode and Ilan Joffe[1]

Introduction

This chapter presents the findings of a prospective, randomized comparative outcome study of the effect of time-limited individual child psychotherapy and systemic family therapy on severely depressed young people funded by a BIOMED ERC grant. The current trend for combining the use of quantitative and qualitative approaches (Midgley 2006) addresses the need both to provide evidence of effectiveness in terms that are accepted in the wider professional community of non-psychoanalytic workers and to examine the process of treatment in a manner that is meaningful to psychotherapists and may shed light on what factors contribute to improvement.

The project[2]

A randomized controlled trial was conducted in London (Tavistock Clinic), Athens (Aghia Sophia Children's Hospital) and Helsinki (Children's Hospital), with seventy-two patients aged between nine and fifteen years allocated to either Individual Therapy (FIPP) or Family Therapy (SIFT), based on standard randomization methods. Patients in each centre were randomly allocated to one of the two treatments.

Childhood depression has only recently begun to be recognized and it was

1 Part of this chapter was previously published in Trowell J et al. Childhood depression: A place for psychotherapy. An outcome study comparing individual psychodynamic psychotherapy and family therapy. *European Child and Adolescent Psychiatry* **16**(3) 2007:157–167.
2 This project was conceived by the late Professor Issy Kolvin, and built on previous European studies. Funding was secured from Brussels, a Biomed ERC grant, conditional upon three EU centres participating in the research project, these were London, Helsinki and Athens, making it possible for there to be cross-cultural comparisons. The Tavistock Clinic in London agreed to host the lead team, which would support the research and clinical work and supply expert statistical advice. Senior child psychotherapists who provided a service in London, Helsinki and Athens had been trained in London, the family therapists had been trained in their own countries by visiting senior family therapists.

hoped that this project would not only give evidence about the effectiveness of these two treatments but also lead to an understanding of the intrapsychic (individual) and interpsychic (family) components in depression in young people. Cognitive behavioural therapy (CBT) had been shown to be helpful (Kovacs 1981, Parloff 1986, March et al. 2004) for young people with depression but there was no evidence of the effectiveness of child psychotherapy or family therapy for this presentation. This study was designed to provide evidence of the effectiveness of child psychotherapy and family therapy for severely depressed young people, and this would use quantitative methodology; qualitative methodology would be used to examine thematic issues in the young people and their families.

Cases that fulfilled the inclusion criteria were randomly allocated to either treatment: child psychotherapy or family therapy. It was not possible to have additional streams for CBT and drug treatment due to concerns about the safe use of selective serotonin reuptake inhibitors (SSRIs) in young people with depression (Harrington & Dubicka 2002) and the lack of experienced CBT therapists in some of the centres. The use of placebo groups was ruled out on ethical grounds (Shaffer, Gould & Brasic 1983). The study gained ethical approval in each of the three centres.

Young people who had been randomly assigned to child psychotherapy were seen individually for thirty sessions and their parents were seen in parallel to the individual work by parent workers. These were predominantly social workers (in London, they had an adult psychotherapy qualification). Regular contact was maintained between parent and child workers. Those young people who were randomly allocated to Family Therapy were seen by the therapist with their family for fourteen sessions. Manuals were written for the individual psychoanalytic work (Trowell & Rhode 1999), parallel parent work (Trowell & Miles 1999) and family therapy (Byng-Hall, Campbell & Papadopoulos, unpublished data).

Children were included in the study if they lived with at least one biological parent and scored over/under a predetermined threshold in the instruments, e.g. Childhood Depression Inventory (CDI) score of 13 or over. Any antidepressants or other psychotropic medication must have ceased at least four weeks prior to commencement of therapy, to ensure the exclusion of confounding variables. Exclusion criteria included: depressive disorders meriting urgent hospitalization, bipolar and schizoaffective disorder, severe conduct disorder (considered likely to respond only moderately to psychotherapy) and parents with psychotic disorder or severe personality disorder. Children who were too ill to receive once-weekly treatment were excluded from the study.

Out of 110 referrals, twelve were excluded and twenty-six declined to take part. Seventy-two patients entered the study, following screening (Fig. 8.1): twenty-four cases entered into therapy in each country, divided equally between therapy types in London and Helsinki, with eleven in

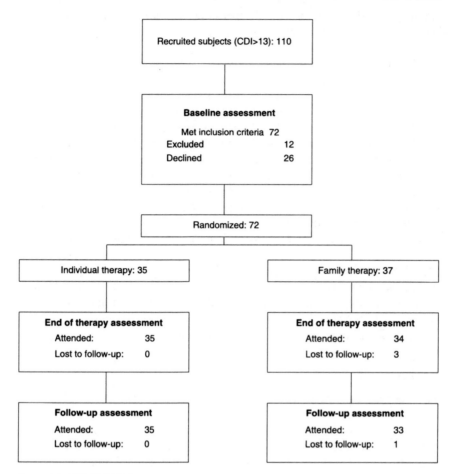

Figure 8.1 CONSORT diagram.

Individual Therapy and thirteen in Family Therapy in Athens. The excluded cases were either not clinically depressed or so ill they needed more than once-weekly treatment. Those who declined to take part were mainly in Athens, where the stated reason for referral was learning problems in school and the diagnosis of depression was felt to be stigmatizing.

A battery of instruments was used prior to inclusion in the project, in the course of therapy and at the 'End of therapy' (primary endpoint), and again six months later, 'Follow-up' (secondary end point). Patients 'Lost to follow-up' were those who did not return for 'End of therapy' or 'Follow-up' assessment. They had attended a variable number of therapy sessions.

An extensive battery of instruments (including the Childhood Depression Inventory and the Moods and Feelings Questionnaire) was administered at each time point, collecting information about the child, the parents, their families, as well as relevant school measures. The findings of the following instruments are reported here:

- The Demography Interview (Kolvin, Barrett, Bhate & Berney 1991): a semi-structured interview.
- The Kiddie-SADS (Chambers et al. 1985): this semi-structured clinical interview provides a measure of major depressive disorder (MDD) and dysthymia (based on DSM-IV criteria), and of psychiatric co-morbidity. These included anxiety disorders (generalized, phobias, separation anxiety and panic disorder), behavioural disorders (oppositional defiant disorder (ODD), conduct disorder), obsessive-compulsive disorder (OCD), attention deficit hyperactivity disorder (ADHD) and anorexia nervosa.
- The Children's Global Assessment Scale (C-GAS, Shaffer et al. 1993): this clinician-rated scale provides a measure of overall impairment of child functioning [range of scores: 0 (lowest) to 100 (highest)].

Mixed-model repeated measures ANOVA was used to examine the extent of depression at each of the three time points. Chi-square and Exact tests were used for the comparison of the presence/absence of depression using cut-offs and the Kiddie-SADS. Due to the small sample size in each country, most of the analysis was done for the three countries combined.

Results

The mean age of participants was twelve years, almost two-thirds (62%) were male, the majority were white and they represented all social class groups (Table 8.1). Almost two-thirds (62%) came from two-parent families (although not necessarily both biological parents). Just under half (44%) had a history of maternal psychiatric illness whereas 15% had a history of depression in their extended family (siblings, grandparents, aunts and uncles). Three-quarters (76%) of the referred young people had been depressed for more than six months.

Overall, the sample characteristics were similar in each therapy type, except for a significantly higher percentage of males in the Individual Therapy group (x^2 = 4.036; df = 1; P < 0.05) and a significant higher prevalence of paternal psychiatric history in the Individual Therapy group (x^2 = 5.449; df = 1; P < 0.05). A possible explanation for these findings is that demographic factors were not taken into consideration at randomization. These differences might have disappeared had the sample size been larger.

Prevalence of depressive disorders

The prevalence of cases of MDD and/or dysthymia, only MDD, only dysthymia, and both MDD and dysthymia ('double depression') have been

Table 8.1 Characteristics of the sample[a]

		Individual therapy (n = 35) (%)	Family therapy (n = 37) (%)	Combined (n = 72) (%)	Chi-square/ t-test
Age	Mean (years)	11.57	11.97	11.71	NS
	Standard deviation	1.17	1.52	1.38	
	Range (years)	9–14	10–15	9–15	
	Mode (years)	11,12	10,12	12	
Gender	Male	26 (74)	19 (51)	45 (62)	$x^2 = 4.036$; df = 1; P < 0.05
	Female	9 (26)	18 (49)	27 (38)	
Ethnicity	White	29 (82)	34 (92)	63 (87)	NS
	Asian	2 (6)	2 (5)	4 (6)	
	Other	3 (9)	1 (3)	4 (6)	
	Missing	1 (3)	0 (0)	1 (1)	
Socioeconomic status[b]	Class 1	1 (3)	1 (3)	2 (3)	NS
	Class 2	7 (20)	11 (30)	18 (25)	
	Class 3	12 (34)	13 (35)	25 (35)	
	Class 4	5 (14)	6 (16)	11 (15)	
	Class 5	4 (12)	1 (3)	5 (7)	
	Missing	6 (17)	5 (13)	11 (15)	
Parental marital status	Single/ widowed/divorced	11 (31)	14 (38)	25 (35)	NS
	Married/living with partner	24 (69)	21 (57)	45 (63)	
	Missing	0 (0)	2 (5)	2 (2)	
Maternal psychiatric history	Yes	16 (46)	16 (43)	32 (44)	NS
	No	19 (54)	21 (57)	40 (56)	
Paternal psychiatric history	Yes	7 (20)	1 (3)	8 (11)	$x^2 = 5.449$; df = 1; P < 0.05
	No	28 (80)	36 (97)	64 (89)	
Depression in extended family (excluding parents)	None	29 (83)	32 (86)	61 (85)	NS
	One family member	5 (14)	3 (8)	8 (11)	
	Two family members	1 (3)	2 (6)	3 (4)	
Duration of depressive illness	0–6 months	9 (26)	8 (22)	17 (24)	NS
	> 6 months	26 (74)	29 (78)	55 (76)	

Notes:
a Demography Interview (Kolvin *et al.* 1991).
b UK Register Registrar General's Classification (social class 1 = highest, social class 5 = lowest).

examined in order to pick up any differences in treatment effects in these clinically distinct groups of patients.

Prevalence of depression (major depressive disorder and/or dysthymia) before and after therapy based on the Kiddie-SADS

At baseline assessment all the participants were diagnosed as depressed, with either MDD and/or dysthymia, based on the Kiddie-SADS. By the end of therapy, of those receiving Individual Therapy, 74.3% were no longer diagnosed as depressed and none was diagnosed as depressed at follow-up (see Table 8.2). Of those receiving Family Therapy, 75.7% of cases of depression had improved by the end of therapy, and at follow-up only 18.9% were still diagnosed as depressed.

The prevalence of depression in the two groups was similar at the end of therapy. At follow-up there were significantly more cases with depression in the Family Therapy group ($x^2 = 7.335$; df = 1; P < 0.01). However, when the 'Lost to follow-up' cases were excluded, the prevalence of depression in the Family Therapy group at 'End of therapy' was 13.4%, and at 'Follow-up' 8.1%. The comparison at 'Follow-up' between the therapy types was not statistically significant when the 'Lost to follow-up' cases were excluded.

Table 8.2 Presence of depression [major depressive disorder (MDD) and/or dysthymia], MDD, dysthymia and double depression (MDD and dysthymia) at three time points by therapy type, based on the Kiddie-SADS (percentages in brackets)

	Individual Therapy (N = 35) (%)		Family Therapy (N = 37) (%)		Total (N = 72) (%)	
	Present	Absent	Present	Absent	Present	Absent
Depression						
Baseline	35 (100.0)	0 (0.0)	37 (100.0)	0 (0.0)	72 (100.0)	0 (0.0)
End of therapy	9 (25.7)	26 (74.3)	9[a] (24.3)	28 (75.7)	18 (25.0)	54 (75.0)
Follow-up	0 (0.0)	35 (100.0)	7[a] (18.9)	30 (81.1)	7 (9.7)	65 (90.3)
MDD						
Baseline	32 (91.4)	3 (8.6)	34 (91.9)	3 (8.1)	66 (91.7)	6 (8.3)
End of therapy	6 (17.1)	29 (82.9)	8[a] (21.6)	29 (78.4)	14 (19.4)	58 (80.6)
Follow-up	0 (0.0)	35 (100.0)	7[a] (18.9)	30 (81.1)	7 (9.7)	65 (90.3)
Dysthymia						
Baseline	20 (57.1)	15 (42.9)	20 (54.1)	17 (45.9)	40 (55.6)	0 (44.4)
End of therapy	6 (17.1)	29 (82.9)	7[a] (18.9)	30 (81.1)	13 (18.1)	54 (81.9)
Follow-up	0 (0.0)	35 (100.0)	4[a] (10.8)	33 (89.2)	4 (5.6)	65 (94.4)
Double depression						
Baseline	17 (48.6)	18 (51.4)	17 (45.9)	20 (54.1)	34 (47.2)	38 (52.8)
End of therapy	3 (8.6)	32 (91.4)	6[a] (16.2)	31 (83.8)	9 (12.5)	63 (87.5)
Follow-up	0 (0.0)	35 (100.0)	4[a] (10.8)	33 (89.2)	4 (5.6)	68 (94.4)

Notes:
a Including imputed data for four 'lost to follow-up' cases.

*Prevalence of major depressive disorder before and after therapy
based on the Kiddie-SADS*

At the start of therapy, more than 90% of the participants were diagnosed as
having major depressive disorder (MDD; Table 8.2.). By the end of therapy,
only six (17.1%) still had this diagnosis in the Individual Therapy group, and
by 'Follow-up' none received this diagnosis. In the Family Therapy group, the
proportion with a diagnosis of MDD had dropped from thirty-four (91.9%)
at baseline to eight (21.6%) at 'End of therapy' and seven (18.9%) at the
'Follow-up' contact.

The prevalence of MDD in the Individual Therapy group compared to
the Family Therapy group at 'End of therapy' was not statistically significant.
However, at 'Follow-up' there was a statistical significance ($x^2 = 7.335$; df = 1;
P < 0.01). This difference resulted from the inclusion of the four 'Lost to
follow-up' cases in the Family Therapy group (there were no 'Lost to follow-
up' cases in the Individual Therapy group). When the 'Lost to follow-up'
cases were excluded, the prevalence of MDD in the Individual Therapy
group compared to the Family Therapy group at 'Follow-up' was not statistically significant.

*Prevalence of dysthymia before and after therapy based on the
Kiddie-SADS*

At the start of therapy, more than 50% of the participants were diagnosed
as having dysthymia (Table 8.2). By the end of therapy, only six (17.1%) still
gained a diagnosis of dysthymia in the Individual Therapy group and by
'Follow-up' none received this diagnosis. In the Family Therapy group, the
proportion with a diagnosis of dysthymia had dropped from twenty (54.1%)
at baseline to seven (18.9%) at the 'End of therapy' and to four (10.8%) at
the 'Follow-up' contact.

The prevalence of dysthymia in the Individual Therapy group compared
to the Family Therapy group at 'End of therapy' was not statistically significant. The prevalence of dysthymia in the Individual Therapy group compared to the Family Therapy group at 'Follow-up' was slightly statistically
significant ($x^2 = 4.006$; df = 1; P < 0.005). However, this difference resulted
from the inclusion of the four 'Lost follow-up' cases in the Family Therapy
group (there were no 'Lost to follow-up' cases in the Individual Therapy
group). When the 'Lost to follow-up' cases were excluded, the prevalence of
dysthymia in the Individual Therapy group compared to the Family Therapy
group at 'Follow-up' was not statistically significant.

Prevalence of 'double depression' (major depressive disorder and dysthymia) before and after therapy based on the Kiddie-SADS

At the start of therapy, 48.6% in the Individual Therapy group and 45.9% in the Family Therapy group were diagnosed as having double depression (Table 8.2). By the end of therapy, only three (8.6%) still gained a diagnosis of double depression in the Individual Therapy group and by 'Follow-up' none received this diagnosis. In the Family Therapy group, the proportion with a diagnosis of double depression had dropped from seventeen (45.9%) at baseline to six (16.2%) at the end of therapy and to four (10.8%) at the 'Follow-up' contact.

The prevalence of double depression in the Individual Therapy group compared to the Family Therapy group at 'End of therapy' was not statistically significant. The prevalence of double depression in the Individual Therapy group compared to the Family Therapy group at 'Follow-up' was slightly statistically significant ($x^2 = 4.006$; df = 1; P < 0.05). However, this difference resulted from the inclusion of the four 'Lost to follow-up' cases in the Family Therapy group (there were no 'Lost to follow-up' cases in the Individual Therapy group). When the 'Lost to follow-up' cases were excluded, the prevalence of double depression in the Individual Therapy group compared to the Family Therapy group at 'Follow-up' was not statistically significant.

Measure of impairment/level of functioning

Children's Global Assessment Scale (C-GAS)

There was a significant difference in the mean C-GAS scores for both therapy groups at the different time points, with the scores increasing for both types of therapy (P < 0.001, power > 99%). There was no significant difference between the Individual Therapy and Family Therapy groups by 'Follow-up'. There was also no significant difference between the two therapy groups over time, specifically at 'End of therapy'.

In the Individual Therapy group, the mean rise in C-GAS score from baseline to 'End of therapy' was 16.13, with a further rise of 3.84 from 'End of therapy' to 'Follow-up' (total rise: 19.97). In the Family Therapy group, the mean rise in C-GAS score from baseline to 'End of therapy' was 17.05, with a further rise of 2.03 from 'End of therapy' to 'Follow-up' (total rise: 19.08).

Co-morbidity

The presence of co-morbid conditions was assessed using the Kiddie-SADS (based on DSM-IV criteria).

The change in prevalence of cases with co-morbidity over the three time points in the Individual Therapy group, as depicted in Table 8.3, was

Table 8.3 Cases with one or more co-morbid conditions at three time points, by therapy type, based on the Kiddie-SADS

	Individual therapy (N = 35) (%)		Family therapy (N = 37) (%)		Total (N = 72) (%)	
	Co-morbidity	No co-morbidity	Co-morbidity	No co-morbidity	Co-morbidity	No co-morbidity
Baseline	29 (82.9)	6 (17.1)	29 (78.4)	8 (21.6)	58 (80.6)	14 (19.4)
End of therapy	16 (45.7)	19 (54.3)	19ª (51.4)	18 (48.6)	35 (48.6)	37 (51.4)
Follow-up	11 (31.4)	24 (68.6)	19ª (51.4)	18 (48.6)	30 (41.7)	42 (58.3)

Notes: a *Including imputed data for 4 'lost to follow-up' cases*

statistically significant (x^2 = 19.821; df = 2; P < 0.001). The change in prevalence of cases with co-morbidity over the three time points in the Family Therapy group was not statistically significant, because of the absence of any decrease from 'End of therapy' to 'Follow-up'. The prevalence of cases with co-morbidity in the Individual Therapy group compared to the Family Therapy group at each of the three time points, however, was not statistically significant.

Discussion

In the Individual Therapy group, 74.3% of cases were no longer clinically depressed following therapy, and 100% of cases were no longer clinically depressed six months later. Individual therapy appears to have been effective in cases of MDD, dysthymia and 'double depression'. This effectiveness appears to have been persistent, with no relapses six months after therapy. In addition, all remaining cases of depression (MDD, dysthymia and 'double depression') had resolved at the follow-up point. This suggests an ongoing response to therapy following completion, the 'sleeper effect' (Kolvin, Macmillan, Nicol & Wrate 1988).

In the Family Therapy group, 75.7% of cases were no longer clinically depressed following therapy, and 81% of cases were no longer clinically depressed six months later. Family therapy also appears to have been effective in cases of MDD, dysthymia and 'double depression'. Again, this appears to have been persistent, with no relapses six months after therapy. In addition, further improvement in some of the remaining cases of depression (MDD, dysthymia and 'double depression') was found at the follow-up point, particularly in cases of dysthymia and 'double depression'.

Response rates for depression in the Individual Therapy and Family Therapy groups were not significantly different by 'End of therapy'. Whereas response rates appear to have been approximately 20% greater in the

Individual Therapy group, compared to the Family Therapy group, at 'Follow-up', this is very largely influenced by the inclusion of the four 'Lost to follow-up' cases in the Family Therapy group, who were considered as unsuccessfully treated cases following therapy. Without these four cases, the differences in response rates between the two groups are not statistically significant.

In addition to improvement as measured by cases no longer meeting diagnostic criteria for MDD or dysthymia, similar improvement was found in both treatment groups in terms of level of impairment and level of functioning.

Whereas final outcome appears to have been similar in the two groups in many respects, the results from the Childhood Depression Inventory and Moods and Feelings Questionnaire (MFQ) (Angold, Costello, Messer, Pickles, Winder & Silver 1995) suggest a different pattern of response or improvement. With regard to the MFQ, the Family Therapy group had a lower score at 'End of therapy', despite having had a higher score than the Individual Therapy group at baseline. Although the power of this test was low (< 80%), it does reflect the slightly different 'path' for each of the therapy groups. The Family Therapy group appears to have made greater improvement, in some respects, by End of Therapy, compared to the Individual Therapy group. However, at 'Follow-up', many of the Family Therapy trajectories appear to have plateaued, whereas the Individual Therapy group trajectories suggest the possibility of further, and possibly more rapid, improvement to follow. What evidence is there for this?

The population groups in the three countries appear to have responded similarly to the treatment. Although not presented here, virtually no significant differences were found when similar analysis was done comparing the three treatment centres (London, Athens, Helsinki), in terms of response rates and patterns.

Almost a third of cases in the study had three or more co-morbid conditions. Following therapy, there was a decrease in co-morbid conditions; particularly anxiety disorders and conduct disorders, which are often associated with depressive disorders. This occurred in both therapy groups.

The results of this study suggest both Individual Therapy (response rate 74% by 'End of therapy') and Family Therapy (response rate 75% by 'End of therapy') may be more effective in the treatment of depression than other forms of treatment. Previous studies have found a response rate in the region of 60% to CBT (Brent et al. 1997) and 52–56% to fluoxetine (Emslie et al. 1997, 2000) and 71% to CBT and fluoxetine combined (March et al. 2004). A more recent study (Goodyear et al. 2007) has shown that with 208 adolescents, aged 11–17 years, half of whom received SSRI plus routine care and half SSRI plus routine care plus CBT, there were no differences at 12-week follow-up, and 57% were much improved and 28% unimproved at 28 weeks.

The chronicity and severity of the depression in our study led us to believe that spontaneous remission was unlikely to have occurred in the vast majority of cases, particularly in light of the extent of coexisting dysthymia. Furthermore, the TADS study demonstrated a response rate of only 35% to placebo. The Brent/Birmaher study (Brent et al. 1997, Birmaher et al. 2000) found that CBT did not confer any long-term advantage over family therapy or supportive therapy with regard to rates of remission, recovery, recurrence or level of functioning. In that study, the median onset of recurrence was four months after recovery, whereas in this study, there had been no recurrences, and ongoing improvement, six months after psychotherapy.

It is perhaps worth noting at a human level that in the London sample many of the children were out of school at the start of the project, mainly at home, some even staying in bed. By the end of the project, they were all back at school and were reported to be learning. Many of the parents, however, were left troubled either in themselves or in their relationships. Some needed further help in their own right.

A longer follow-up was planned at each centre; despite lack of funds Athens and Helsinki have been active in this phase. In London, most of the young people declined to be visited or did not respond to written or telephone contact.

A small follow-up in London was undertaken, the twenty-four subjects were contacted and five agreed to be interviewed, this was over four years after the start of the project. These subjects and their parents spoke positively about the help received. Their main criteria were the education outcome for the young person and this was positive (twenty cases).

In addition, the seven London excluded cases were reassessed. Those not sufficiently depressed to be included had improved with usual CAMHS conciliation over two to five sessions. Those too troubled (three) had needed inpatient admission and were still receiving services at two-year follow-up.

The process of psychotherapy[3]

Unsurprisingly, aggression and the management of it were of central importance across cases. When they began treatment, most of the children presented a picture of living in a world of fragile significant people and destroyed relationships. By the end, they were much more able to own anger and to distinguish it from a proper assertiveness, although the path by which they reached this varied from case to case. No consistent correlation could be established between the themes appearing in the sessions and the children's scores on the MFQ, although, interestingly, the beginnings of play

---

3 This section is based in part on the section on themes and interventions in Trowell, Rhode, Miles & Sherwood (2003):157–168, which contains two brief case histories and a more detailed discussion of themes and interventions. Clinical papers by some of the therapists appear in Trowell, J. (ed.) *Depression in Young People: Psychotherapy Works* (in press).

involving role reversal coincided with a noticeable drop in one girl's 'True' score on the MFQ.

What was surprising was the prominence of themes concerning existential anxiety, living in 'no man's land', not being believed and so on. The theme of identity was particularly to the fore: children spoke about not having their own room or clothes, or said explicitly that their lives were their parents' to dispose of until they left school. Some emphasized their resemblance to a parent or grandparent of the same sex, as though these transgenerational factors were immutable and inescapable. A quotation from one girl (Gretton, in Trowell (ed.) in press) serves to convey the atmosphere:

> I feel like a tramp – someone who doesn't have a proper home, who lives in the street, looks for shelter, doesn't have any proper clothes, doesn't know what to wear, nothing fits. I don't belong anywhere.

This girl's remarkable articulacy was exceptional among the young people in this project; the feelings she described, however, were not.

In view of this central importance of the sense of identity, it is interesting that the overwhelming majority of therapists' interventions consisted of mirroring of various kinds: in which the child's statements, experiences, feelings or behaviour was reflected back to them. On the most basic level, as Winnicott (1967) has argued in his paper *Mirror Role of Mother and Family in Child Development*, such mirroring conveys the message that the child's individuality is recognized and validated. Description, elucidation and linking were important too; transference interpretations were infrequent, except around holidays and, particularly, termination. This emphasis on mirroring was something that all the therapists arrived at intuitively, but it makes sense in terms of the children's problems concerning identity. As one therapist put it, 'I feel that if I talk about myself, there's no room for her'.

Several whole-project meetings of all professionals involved made it possible to run focus groups of workers within the project's individual psychotherapy arm. This way of collecting recurrent themes provided some way of counteracting the expectable differences between supervisors with regard to issues that seemed most significant across cases. The main themes were:

- identity and sexual identity
- having nothing of one's own/being a have-not
- living in a black hole
- living and growing at someone else's expense
- inability to perform
- fear of damaging the parents' marriage
- fear that aggression was unmanageable/intolerable
- fear of being terrorized/murdered by a Mafia-type gang (generally at school).

Interestingly, workers on the family therapy arm of the study also formulated a list of significant themes (Campbell, Bianco, Dowling, Goldberg, McNab & Pentecost 2003). Although they arrived at these by working on 'significant moments', and although the differing theoretical framework meant that the themes were couched in very different language, discussion in more depth during joint presentations revealed a marked degree of convergence between the issues that were thought to be significant. The very fact that this convergence (between, for example, 'living in a black hole' and the family therapists' 'attractive force of sadness') was not immediately obvious without discussion of examples seems to provide good evidence that different approaches were tapping into at least some similar constellations.

Conclusion

These first qualitative approaches to the material confirm the importance of the management/treatment of aggression in depressive states. They also suggest that the instruments used in the study selected for a particular type of depression, one in which existential issues were central. This would fit with the age of the young people, at which the main developmental task is the construction of a sense of identity and sexual identity. It would also fit with the predominance of mirroring interpretations, which may have allowed the young people to feel seen and recognized relatively quickly.

In the future, a more thorough analysis of themes might allow these to be correlated with scores on the MFQ. It may also be fruitful to apply the techniques of analysis described by Emde (1994), which seem particularly well suited to capturing some of the complexities of change brought about by psychoanalytic interpretation (see also Philps 2002). The preliminary findings are beginning to influence practice, both on the level of technique and in terms of offering time-limited psychotherapy for serious problems.

Further research

Further analysis will look at whether differential predictors of response can be identified in the two therapy groups, and whether there are any significant differences across the three different cultural settings. Data from additional instruments about the child, his or her parents and family, and his or her environment will provide further insight into the current findings. It will also be important to establish if any specific components of the respective forms of therapy were likely to have contributed to the patients' response, analysis of the video and audio-tapes and the individual process notes could be helpful in answering this.

A book on the clinical aspects of the work is forthcoming (Trowell in press).

Acknowledgements

We would like to thank the young people and their families, as well as the therapists who took part, for their contribution to the study.

References

Angold, A., Costello. E. J., Messer S. C., Pickles. A., Winder F., Silva D., (1995) The development of a short questionnaire for use in epidemiological studies of depression in children and adolescents. *International Journal of Methods in Psychiatric Research, 5,* 237–249.

Birmaher, B., Brent, D., Kolko, D., Baugher, M., Bridge, J., Holder, D., Iyengar, S., Ulloa, R.E. (2000) Clinical outcome after short-term psychotherapy for adolescents with major depressive disorder. *Archives of General Psychiatry, 57*(1), 29–36.

Brent, D.A., Holder, D., Kolko, D., Birhamer B., Baugher R., Iyenger S., Johnson B. A. (1997) A clinical psychotherapy trial for adolescent depression comparing cognitive, family, and supportive therapy. *Archives of General Psychiatry, 54,* 877–885.

Campbell, D., Bianco, V., Dowling, E., Goldberg, H., McNab, S., Pentecost, D. (2003) Family therapy for childhood depression: Researching significant moments. *Journal of Family Therapy, 25,* 417–435.

Chambers, W., Puig-Antich, J., Hirsch, M., Paez, P., Ambrosinium, P., Tabrizi, M., Davies, M. (1985) The assessment of affective disorders in children and adolescents by semi-structured interview: Test-retest reliability of the schedule for affective disorders and schizophrenia for school-age children, present episode version. *Archives of General Psychiatry, 42,* 696–702.

Emde, R. (1994) Developing psychoanalytic interpretations of experience. *Infant Mental Health Journal, 15,* 42–49.

Emslie, G. J., Rush, A. J., Weinberg, W. A., Kowatch, R.A., Hughes, C.W., Carmody, T., Rintelman, J. (1997) A double–blind randomised placebo-controlled trial of fluoxetine in children and adolescents with depression. *Archives of General Psychiatry, 54,* 1031–1037.

Emslie, G. J., Heiligenstein, J. H., Hoog, S., Wagner, K.D., Nilsson, M.E., Jacobsen, J.G., Hoog, S.L., Ernest, D.E., Brown, E. (2000) *Fluoxetine for acute treatment of depression in children and adolescents: A placebo controlled trial.* Paper presented at the 39th annual meeting of the American College of Neuropsychopharmacology, 10–14 December 2000, San Juan, Puerto Rico.

Goodyear, I., Dubicka, B., Wilkinson, P., Kelvin, R., Roberts, C., Byford, S., et al. (2007) Selective serotonin reuptake inhibitors (SSRIs) and routine specialist care with and without cognitive behaviour therapy in adolescents with major depression: A randomised controlled trial. *British Medical Journal,* 7 June, 17556431.

Harrington, R., Dubicka, B. (2002) Adolescent depression: An evidence-based approach to intervention. *Current Opinion in Psychiatry, 15,* 369–375.

Kolvin, I., MacMillan, A., Nicol, A.R., Wrate, R.M. (1988) Psychotherapy is effective. *Journal of the Royal Society of Medicine, 81,* 261–266.

Kolvin, I., Barrett, L., Bhate, S.R., Berney, T.P. (1991) The Newcastle child depression project: Diagnosis and classification of depression. *British Journal of Psychiatry, 159*(11), 9–21.

Kovacs, M. (1981) Rating scales to assess depression in school aged children. *Acta Paedopsychiatrica*, *46*(5–6), 305–315.

March, J., Silva, S., Petrycki, J.C., Curry, J., Wells, K., Fairbank, J., et al. (2004) Fluoxetine, cognitive-behavioural therapy and their combination for adolescents with depression. Treatment for adolescents with depression study (TADS) randomised controlled trial. *Journal of the American Medical Association*, *292*(7), 807–820.

Midgley, N. (2006) The inseparable bond between cure and research: Clinical case study as a method of psychoanalytic inquiry. *Journal of Child Psychotherapy*, *32*(2), 122–147.

Parloff, M.B. (1986) Placebo controls in psychotherapy research: A sine qua non or a placebo for research problems. *Journal of Consulting and Clinical Psychology*, *54*, 79–87.

Philps, J. (2002) *Case studies and their scrutiny: Developing a process chart of psychoanalytic therapy sessions.* Paper presented at the Symposium on Qualitative Methods in Psychoanalytic Research, Tavistock Clinic, London.

Shaffer, D., Gould, M.S., Brasic, J. (1983) A children's global assessment scale (C GAS). *Archives of General Psychiatry*, *40*, 1228–1231.

Trowell, J. (ed.) (in press) *Depression in young people: Psychotherapy works.* Tavistock Clinic Book Series. London: Karnac Books.

Trowell, J. A., Miles, G. W. (1999) Parent work Manual. EFPP Book Series, *Psychotherapy research.* Trowell, J. (eds). London: Karnac Books.

Trowell J. A., Rhode M. (1999) Individual psychoanalytic psychotherapy manual. EFPP Book Series, *Psychotherapy research.* Tsiantis, J., Trowell, J. (eds). London: Karnac Books.

Trowell, J., Rhode, M., Miles, G., Sherwood, I. (2003) Childhood depression: Work in progress. Individual child therapy and parent work. *Journal of Child Psychotherapy*, *29*(2), 147–169.

Trowell, J., Joffe, I., Campbell, J., Clemente, C., Almquist, F., Soininen, M., Koskenranta-Aalto, U., Weimtraub, S., Kolaitias, G., Tomaras, V., Anastasopoulos, D., Grayson, K., Barnes, J., Tsiantis, J. (2007) Childhood depression: A place for psychotherapy. An outcome study comparing individual psychodynamic psychotherapy and family therapy. *European Child and Adolescent Psychiatry*, *16*(3), 157–167.

Winnicott, D. W. (1967). Mirror role of mother and family in child development. In: *Playing and reality.* London: Tavistock/Routledge.

Chapter 9

The adult outcome of child psychoanalysis: The Anna Freud Centre Long-term Follow-up Study

Abby Schachter and Mary Target

An introduction to outcome research at the Anna Freud Centre

Traditionally, research on the outcome of psychological treatments for children and adolescents has lagged behind research on adult therapies. This gap has been particularly pronounced in the case of psychoanalytic child psychotherapy and child psychoanalysis (Kazdin 2003). Over the past two decades, the Anna Freud Centre (AFC) has pioneered a series of innovative and ground-breaking studies on the outcome of psychoanalytic treatment for young people. These studies have contributed a body of important findings and novel methodologies to the field at the same time that they have underscored the challenges and difficulties facing outcome research.

The need for meaningful outcome studies has in part been spurred on by the increasing call for accountability or evidenced-based treatments in the field of mental health (Gabbard 2000). In addition, epidemiological evidence regarding the persistence of childhood disorders into adolescence and adulthood (Kim-Cohen, Caspi, Moffett, Harrington, Milne & Poulton 2003) has further highlighted the need for effective treatments. Given that children are in the midst of ongoing developmental processes, it is important to conduct outcome research using a life-span perspective in order to see whether therapeutic help in childhood may also prevent later risk and disturbance. To this end, the AFC embarked on the Long-term Follow-up Study of adults who received psychoanalytic treatment in childhood. This study, which is the focus of the chapter, is presented within the broader framework of the AFC's tradition of outcome research, which has included studies of particular clinical groups, such as children with poorly-controlled diabetes (Moran & Fonagy 1987, Fonagy, Moran & Higgitt 1989, Fonagy & Moran 1991) and young adults diagnosed with personality disorders (Gerber 2004). It was a major retrospective study of the outcome of child psychoanalysis, however, which formed the immediate context for the follow-up study, so this research will be described in greater detail.

The retrospective study of child psychoanalysis

The AFC Retrospective Study represents a first attempt to investigate the outcome of child psychoanalysis, moving beyond the individual case study toward a systematic and methodologically well-designed large-scale and comprehensive body of research. Under the leadership of Dr Mary Target, the outcome of 763 children and adolescents treated over a forty-year period at the AFC was studied, comparing those who received psychoanalysis four or five times a week with those who received psychodynamic psychotherapy between one and three times per week. The study compared the efficacy of these two types of treatment for children suffering from emotional (Target & Fonagy 1994a) and disruptive (Fonagy & Target 1994) disorders among three age groups (under six, six to twelve, and adolescents; Target & Fonagy 1994b).

A major contribution of the Retrospective Study was the creation of the Hampstead Child Adaptation Measure (HCAM; Target, Fonagy, Schneider, Ensink & Janes 2000), which assesses children's overall levels of adjustment. In keeping with psychoanalytic theory, the HCAM was designed to assess a child's pro-social functioning and broad emotional development as well as impairment, defined mostly by level of adaptation and ability to function in appropriate ways rather than in terms of psychiatric symptoms or diagnoses. A comparison of children's HCAM scores at the beginning and end of treatment enabled the tracking of changes in functioning and impairment during the course of treatment.

Overall, the findings of the retrospective study underscore the importance of a differential approach to treatment based on the patient's primary diagnosis and age, suggesting that psychoanalysis is not necessarily the treatment of choice for all individuals. By examining predictors of outcome, among a wide range of child, family and treatment variables, the study also sheds light on moderating factors influencing treatment outcome within this particular sample. Although the findings of the Retrospective Study significantly enhance our knowledge regarding the immediate outcome of child psychoanalysis, they are unable to tell us whether treatment gains are maintained over time, from childhood into adulthood. To this end, the Long-Term Follow-Up Study was developed with the aim of contributing a life-span perspective to outcome research.

The adult outcome of child psychoanalysis

Background and rationale

In its initial conception, the Long-term Follow-up Study, led by Dr Abby Schachter, aimed to follow-up a proportion of the subjects assessed in the Retrospective Study in order to examine their adult functioning. Overall, the study aimed to assess the adult outcome of a group of disordered children and the extent to which treatment in childhood may have mitigated the negative life trajectories of children diagnosed with early psychological disturbances (Champion, Goodall & Rutter 1995). More specifically, the study hoped to explore potential trajectories from childhood to adulthood.

Several scenarios were envisaged. It is possible that patients who benefited from early treatment may continue to develop in a healthy and functional manner. Alternatively, treatment gains may be transient. Patients who did not seem to benefit from treatment in childhood may continue to suffer psychological disturbance, in keeping with epidemiological findings on the natural history of childhood disorders. However, it is also possible that assessment in adulthood finds that 'unsuccessful' patients turned into well-functioning adults, perhaps as a result of treatment, pointing to the so-called 'sleeper effect', or as a result of other subsequent life events.

Beyond the investigation of outcome, the follow-up study aimed to explore some of the mechanisms that underlie individual pathways of development. Specifically, the authors hypothesized that the capacity to mentalize productively on the psychological state of self and others (reflective functioning; Fonagy, Target, Steele & Steele 1998) and a secure attachment status (Main & Goldwyn 1994) would serve as important protective mechanisms for the development of psychiatric disorder across the life span (Cyranowski et al. 2002). In addition, the study aimed to examine some of the potential moderators that interact with these mechanisms, ultimately leading to differential therapy outcomes. To this end, the study examined the relationship between a range of childhood variables (including family background, individual characteristics and treatment variables) and adult outcome in order to increase our understanding of individual responses to treatment.

Sample, methodology and measures

Sample

Research assistants reviewed the 763 case files of former child patients, treated at the AFC between 1952 and 1991, whose data were analysed in the retrospective chart review. They selected for tracing subjects between the ages of twenty-five and fifty who did not have a history of mental retardation, autism or psychotic illnesses, as these syndromes are known to have poor long-term outcomes and are not expected to benefit significantly from child psychoanalysis. Roughly 400 subjects met the inclusion criteria. Of these, nearly 50% could not be traced. Of the sixty individuals who agreed to participate in the study, only thirty-four completed all of the outcome interviews. This sizable attrition rate raises important questions regarding the degree to which the participants were representative of the total sample and demonstrates a major challenge to outcome research.

For most of the childhood variables, the follow-up sample appeared representative of the retrospective sample. However, because of the small sample size, statistical comparisons were of limited value and, for the most part, were not powerful enough to detect differences. Comparisons of the two samples cautiously suggest that the follow-up subjects may be a slightly more advantageous group. For example, the lower end of child HCAM scores was underrepresented in the follow-up sample as compared to the overall sample. So, too, the follow-up sample had a relatively higher prevalence of anxiety disorders than the full sample. This is a potentially meaningful difference given that anxiety disorders tend to respond better to treatment than disruptive disorders (Fonagy & Target 1994, 1996) and also serve as a protective factor against the long-term persistence of disruptive disorders when co-occurring with them (Vander Stoep, Weiss, McKnight, Beresford & Cohen 2002). Finally, in nearly half of the follow-up subjects, the decision to end treatment was based on a mutual agreement between therapist and family. Indeed, research has shown that treatments terminated by mutual agreement are associated with greater benefit to patients (Bachrach 1993).

Methodology

Initially, the study planned to compare subjects who had received intensive psychoanalytic treatment in childhood (four or five sessions per week) with those who had received psychoanalytic psychotherapy (one to three sessions per week), in keeping with the findings of the Retrospective Study. In addition, treated subjects were to be compared with two control groups: (1) a group of untreated siblings who were perceived as providing the closest match to family background and psychosocial circumstances; and (2) a group of subjects who had been referred for treatment due to childhood disorders but who had remained untreated (from the AFC case files and from records of local mental health services), matched with treated subjects on demographic and broad clinical variables. Unfortunately, many of these comparisons had to be abandoned. Of the thirty-four treated subjects who participated in the study, most (twenty-six) had received intensive treatment. Only eleven siblings within a six-year age range of the treated subjects participated in the study. In addition, access to subjects from local clinics was problematic, primarily for ethical reasons. As a result, the findings below primarily reflect an analysis of the adult outcome of thirty-four treated subjects who participated in the study, along with individual case comparisons of pairs of treated subjects and their siblings.

Measures

Subjects participated in a comprehensive interview process comprised of three or four sessions, each lasting between two and three hours. Interviews were conducted by extensively trained interviewers and were audio-taped for later coding and analysis. The lack of long-term follow-up studies on child psychoanalysis necessitated the creation of a battery of adult outcome measures. It was important that instruments be of proven reliability and validity and, at the same time, consistent with psychoanalytic concepts that view an individual's functioning across a broad range of developmental tasks. Outcome measures covered multiple key areas of adult adjustment: psychopathology and use of mental health services since treatment; physical health and use of medical services in adulthood; personality functioning across a range of domains; attachment status; reflective functioning; coping skills; planning for transitions; stressors and adversity across the life span; estimated IQ; and memories of psychoanalytic treatment (for a more detailed description of the measures, see Schachter 2004). In addition to analysing the results of subjects for each of the adult outcome measures, the information from five of the outcome measures was synthesized into an overall functioning index, the Adult Functioning Index (AFI). Like the HCAM, the AFI integrates both symptomatology and adaptation into a more comprehensive and integrated global score.

Findings regarding the adult outcome of treated subjects

The findings of the follow-up study indicate that, overall, subjects treated in childhood were not characterized by severe adult psychopathology or poor adult functioning, despite the risk for impairment in adulthood. The majority of treated subjects reported the presence of at least one significant support figure, relatively low levels of adversity throughout their adult lives, and relatively few severe life events in the five years preceding the interviews. They also reported relatively good health and minimal use of medical services. Subjects evidenced a low rate of personality disorders, although they did report a somewhat higher than average rate of lifetime adult psychopathology than that reported for non-clinical populations (Kringlen, Torgersen & Cramer 2001). However, subjects seemed to seek appropriate professional help in response to these difficulties and, in most cases, interventions tended to be brief. They demonstrated adequate personality functioning across several domains, an ability to successfully plan and negotiate important transitions in several areas, and good coping skills in some domains. Finally, the sample's distribution of attachment classifications fell somewhere between that of clinical and low-risk samples.

Individual analyses of treated subjects and their siblings lend support to the view that successful treatment in childhood enhances resilience in later life. Whereas, in childhood, treated subjects were more likely to have experienced greater adversity than their siblings, in adulthood the untreated siblings were more likely to experience negative life events. Regarding personality functioning, all of the subjects, except those whose childhood treatment outcome was poor, were functioning well in the work domain. In the area of intimate relationships, subjects who were treated successfully in childhood appeared to be doing somewhat better than their siblings. Not surprisingly, none of the subjects who were unsuccessfully treated in childhood had an adequate love relationship.

In relation to attachment status, children whose treatment outcome was relatively good were as likely to be as securely attached as their siblings. Those whose childhood treatment was unsuccessful tended to be insecurely attached as adults, predominantly 'preoccupied', whereas the untreated siblings were predominantly 'dismissing'. Reflective functioning capacity was somewhat better among those subjects whose childhood treatment was successful than other subjects. Those whose treatment in childhood was unsuccessful remained unable to mentalize accurately about their own and others' mental states. Thus, overall, treatment in childhood seems to have been a protective factor. However, successfully treated subjects appeared to be somewhat disadvantaged with regard to friendships relative to their siblings. So, too, treated subjects were more likely than their siblings to have depressive or anxious personalities, although not in an overtly disturbed manner.

Statistical analyses looking at the relationship between the Adult Functioning Index (AFI) scores and adult demographic and outcome variables yielded several interesting results. Subjects with higher AFI scores tended to be involved in long-term cohabiting relationships, highlighting the protective role of marital or long-term cohabiting relationships (Rutter 1990). In addition, AFI scores were negatively correlated with the number of severe life events. Although this finding does not tell us whether adversity leads to poor functioning or vice versa, it does underscore the strong link between the two. Interestingly, higher AFI scores were significantly related to a secure attachment status and higher capacity for reflective functioning.

Given the study's assumption that attachment is a potentially significant mediator of adult outcome, special attention to the relationship between security of attachment and adult functioning was explored in greater detail. Overwhelmingly, the secure attachment group demonstrated significantly better scores than the insecure groups on four of the five AFI subscales. The insecure/preoccupied group emerged as the more troubled of the two insecure groups (in contrast to the insecure/dismissing group). In particular, the findings underscored the relationship between adult functioning and secure attachment with regard to psychopathology, life events and intimate relations.

Furthermore, the overall coping skills of securely attached individuals were significantly better than those of their insecure counterparts. This is in keeping with the growing body of research demonstrating a strong relationship between security of attachment and overall adaptation throughout development (e.g. Roche, Runtz & Hunter 1999). Indeed, the findings support the view of security of attachment as a resilience factor, one that mitigates the degree and extent of adversity and enhances the individual's ability to cope more effectively when faced with adversity (Svanberg 1998).

A further set of analyses among the treated subjects examined the relationship between childhood variables and adult outcome. Specifically, correlation and regression analyses were used to explore the relationship between childhood variables taken from two points in time – assessment (pretreatment) and termination (conclusion of treatment) – and adult outcome. A central finding of the study was that the best predictor of adult outcome was a child's overall level of functioning (HCAM score) *before* receiving treatment. Children with less than adequate functioning levels prior to psychoanalytic intervention tended to remain poorly functioning adults, despite therapeutic intervention in childhood. Moreover, individuals whose global functioning at the end of treatment had improved did not necessarily maintain these gains into adulthood. However, about one-third of the sample, despite an expected poor adult outcome due to low assessment HCAM scores overcame their poor prognosis, receiving superior AFI scores. A further analysis, which examined termination variables alone, found that the number of termination diagnoses emerged as the best predictor of long-term adaptation in adulthood. This is in keeping with studies highlighting co-morbidity as a significant risk factor associated with poor long-term outcome of childhood disorders (Fonagy, Target, Cottrell, Phillips & Kurtz 2002).

A qualitative analysis of the different pathways from childhood to adulthood demonstrated several interesting trends. For example, the four subjects whose global functioning in childhood was assessed as severely impaired (HCAM scores ranging from 41 to 50) received the lowest overall functioning scores in adulthood, despite intensive treatment in childhood. This sobering finding suggests that there may be a qualitatively different level of psychopathology for which psychoanalysis is ineffectual. The fact that pretreatment levels of psychosocial functioning better predicted adult outcome than post-treatment levels may come as a bit of a surprise and disappointment. It raises questions regarding the relative effect of treatment in childhood on adult outcome as compared to premorbid traits or abilities. Indeed, 'premorbid competence' (Vander Stoep et al. 2002), including an individual's functioning across occupational, educational and social domains before the onset of mental illness, is strongly associated with prognosis (Giaconia, Reinherz, Silverman, Pakiz, Frost & Cohen 1994). Because of the small sample size, it is important that these findings be replicated within a larger sample. However, as they stand, the findings raise important questions regarding the extent to which personality and resilience are innate or environmentally influenced, changeable or enduring and, to what extent psychoanalytic interventions can impact on pre-existing traits.

An examination of the pathways from poor childhood functioning to positive adult outcome yielded a more optimistic finding. Despite an expected poor adult outcome based on low assessment HCAM scores, a group of eleven individuals (nearly a third of the sample) managed to transcend their poor prognosis and receive high AFI scores. Common to these individuals was a secure adult attachment status. This finding suggests that security of attachment may play a pivotal role in the development from poor childhood prognosis to positive adult outcome. A qualitative analysis of two individuals who were referred for treatment in childhood because of an inability to invest productively in crucial aspects of functioning and severe levels of emotional distress found that their early inhibitions no longer hindered their psychosocial development. Both had developed effective ways for dealing with stress. Despite very troubled early relationships with their primary caregivers, both were involved in supportive intimate relationships in adulthood and were assigned a secure adult attachment status.

Can the positive adult outcome of these at-risk children be attributed to their psychoanalytic treatment in childhood? On the theoretical level, Fonagy and colleagues (1995) have argued that early psychoanalytic treatment enhances the individual's mentalizing and reflective capacities, resulting in more coherent internal representations of early attachment relationships. As such, psychoanalysis in childhood, by fostering secure attachment and reflective capacities, may serve as an important mediator between childhood pathology and adult functioning. However, without a control group and without measures of attachment and reflective functioning in childhood (before and after treatment), the subjects' treatment in childhood cannot be credited solely with the fostering of a secure adult attachment status.

In order to explore this concept more fully, outcome research needs to look more closely at the process of psychoanalysis, focusing specifically on concepts and constructs related to attachment and reflective functioning as manifested before, during and after treatment. Process measures that assess the development of reflective capacity and the use of attachment ratings may potentially shed important light on whether psychoanalytic treatment indeed enhances and improves this capacity and whether it is maintained over time. Indeed, the salience of the attachment concept supports the use of attachment as a process measure of psychoanalytic treatment.

Conclusions and future directions

The AFC Long-term Follow-up Study offers a unique look at the lives of thirty-four adults who received psychoanalytic treatment in childhood. The study provides a life-span perspective on the adult outcome of childhood disorders, going far beyond the usual short-term time frame typical of most follow-up studies (Eyberg, Edwards, Foote & Boggs 1998). In addition, the study contributes a much-needed interview protocol for long-term assessment of psychoanalytic treatment. The findings support the view that intervention in childhood may help a majority of high-risk individuals overcome a poor prognosis, leading to well-functioning adult lives. Specifically, children with average or above average intelligence, from middle to upper-class socio-economic brackets, and suffering primarily from emotional disorders seem to have benefited most from psychoanalysis in childhood. In particular, the findings emphasize the strong association between positive adult outcome and a secure attachment status.

However, the study's unique and small sample, and lack of a control group, clearly limit the ability to generalize these findings or to be fully confident that positive adult functioning is due to the therapeutic intervention this sample received. The use of underpowered parametric statistics on a small sample size may have rendered unreliable some of the findings, particularly negative ones. In addition, the low participation response rate raises issues regarding the effect of attrition and the introduction of biases inevitably introduced by those subjects who agreed to participate in the study. It is therefore difficult to determine whether demonstrated change is a result of therapeutic intervention or the passage of time and subsequent development. Moreover, without a non-treatment control group, it is difficult to know whether changes in symptomatology reflect the natural life-course of a particular disorder, the introduction of a new disturbance, a change due to naturally occurring developmental growth or the positive result of treatment. Although the treated subjects were often (blindly) rated more positively than their siblings, suggesting that psychoanalytic treatment in childhood may have enhanced their resilience and served as a protective factor, these findings can only be tentative due to the small sample size.

The Long-term Follow-up Study, together with the body of outcome research conducted at the Anna Freud Centre, has contributed methodological innovations and interesting findings regarding the outcome of psychoanalytic treatment among young people. The studies have also highlighted many of the difficulties and challenges involved in outcome research. Given the differential responses to treatment evidenced by outcome research, the AFC research staff has embarked on additional studies that go beyond the question of 'does treatment work' to examine the specific ingredients and processes that contribute to change (Kazdin 2006). The AFC Child Psychotherapy Outcome Study (CPPOS), under the leadership of Dr Nick Midgley, aims to focus on the process of psychodynamic psychotherapy through an intensive analysis of five children, aged eight to twelve, diagnosed with depression and/or generalized anxiety, who received individual psychotherapy at the AFC as part of a pilot study for a proposed prospective outcome study comparing child psychotherapy and cognitive behavioural therapy (Fonagy, Target & Ensink 2005). The CPPOS study will apply state of the art methodologies from the field of adult psychotherapy in order to identify key mechanisms involved in therapeutic change (Boston Change Process Study Group 2005, Kachele et al. 2006). Data have been collected through the use of video-recording and therapist process notes, together with a battery of standardized measures used before, during and after termination of treatment. This pioneering work has the potential to contribute a more sophisticated understanding of change processes in treatment and clinically relevant findings to the evidence-based practice of child treatments.

Likewise, the Young Adults Study (Gerber 2004), referred to at the start of this chapter, aimed to go beyond outcome measures to explore the process of psychoanalysis and to discern some of the components of treatment that make it effective. For this purpose, the study introduced two new methods for evaluating the therapeutic process and structural change: (1) the Young Adult Weekly Rating Scale (YAWRS), created for the study, designed as a therapist-report measure of psychoanalytic process covering a wide range of themes likely to emerge in a week of analytic sessions; and (2) the Adult Attachment Interview and its attachment classification scheme (Main & Goldwyn 1994).

As with the Follow-up Study, the findings of the Young Adult Study are limited by the small sample size and the many missing assessments at follow-up and follow-along time points. However, a factor analysis of data from the YAWRS questionnaires yielded interesting trends. For example, in psycho-analysis, as compared to psychodynamic psychotherapy, therapists reported using more general interpretation, more transference interpretation and more negative patient transference. The study also explored the ability of YAWRS data from the first year of treatment to predict symptomatic outcome.

The findings confirmed the hypotheses that dynamic therapeutic technique (i.e. interpretation, transference interpretation and relationship interpretation) is associated with better outcome. Regarding attachment, the study found a high proportion of secure classifications at initial assessment and, in successful treatment, a move towards a preoccupied-entangled attachment pattern, which began to resolve by termination. Based on these findings, the authors suggested that in effective, intensive psychotherapy, particularly psychoanalysis, patients appear more preoccupied-entangled with respect to their childhood relationships as part of the therapeutic process involving regression and transference neurosis. Only at termination and beyond are these states of mind appropriately resolved, leading to increased security and symptomatic improvement.

A further outgrowth of the Follow-up Study is the in-depth, clinically based qualitative analysis of detailed autobiographical narratives taken from the follow-up interviews. This approach applies Interpretative Phenomenological Analysis (IPA), a qualitative method for systematically extracting personal meanings from interview narratives (Smith, Jarman & Osborn 1999). One study employed the IPA to qualitatively explore subjects' recollections and understandings of the treatment they received in childhood and the ways in which they feel the treatment impacted on their current lives (Midgley & Target 2005, Midgley, Target & Smith 2006). Researchers at the AFC are now attempting to extend the IPA method to look not only at subjects' conscious beliefs about their life experiences but also to identify subjects' self-representations and the way in which they have integrated their experiences of childhood disorders and child psychoanalysis into their experience of themselves and their life stories. In particular, this qualitative study aims to explore differential treatment outcomes, focusing in-depth on various pathways and trajectories. The first such analysis of an individual whose childhood treatment terminated successfully but who demonstrated poor functioning and psychopathology in adulthood has yielded some interesting clinical insights (Target & Fonagy 2002). Three additional analyses exploring alternative trajectories (i.e. a subject with a healthy adult outcome despite poor treatment outcome in childhood, a subject with a positive treatment outcome and positive adult functioning, and a subject with poor child and adult outcomes) are currently in progress. These analyses aim to bring out some of the unconscious processes underlying outcome in keeping with psychoanalytic theory. Together with large-scale empirical outcome studies using a life-span perspective (ideally comparing different types of treatment with non-treatment control groups), and along with improved assessments of the treatment process, these qualitative analyses should provide a much richer and clinically meaningful understanding of the process and outcome of child psychoanalysis.

References

Bachrach, H. M. (1993) The Columbia Records Project and the evolution of psychoanalytic outcome research. *Journal of the American Psychoanalytic Association, 41*, 279–297.

Boston Change Process Study Group (2005) The 'something more' than interpretation revisited. *Journal of the American Psychoanalytic Association, 53*, 693–729.

Champion, L.A., Goodall, G., Rutter, M. (1995) Behaviour problems in childhood and stressors in early adult life: I. A 20-year follow-up of London school children. *Psychological Medicine, 25*, 231–246.

Cyranowski, J.M., Bookwala, J., Feske, U., Houck, P., Pilkonis, P., Kostelnik, B., Frank, E. (2002) Adult attachment profiles, interpersonal difficulties, and response to interpersonal psychotherapy in women with recurrent major depression. *Journal of Social and Clinical Psychology, 21*, 191–217.

Eyberg, S., Edwards, D., Foote, R., Boggs, S. (1998) Maintaining the treatment effects of parental training: The role of booster sessions and other maintenance strategies. *Clinical Psychology: Science and Practice, 5*, 544–554.

Fonagy, P., Moran, G.S. (1991) Studies on the efficacy of child psychoanalysis. *Journal of Consulting and Clinical Psychology, 58*, 684–694.

Fonagy, P., Moran, G., Higgitt, A. (1989) Psychological factors in the self-management of insulin-dependent diabetes mellitus in children and adolescents. In J. Wardle & S. Pearce (eds) *The practice of behavioural medicine.* Oxford: Oxford University Press.

Fonagy, P., Steele, M., Steele, H., Leigh, T., Kennedy, R., Mattoon, G., Target, M. (1995) Attachment, the reflective self, and borderline states: The predictive specificity of the Adult Attachment Interview. In S. Goldberg, R. Muir & J. Kerr (eds) *Attachment theory: Social, developmental, and clinical perspectives.* Hillsdale, NJ: The Analytic Press.

Fonagy, P., Target, M. (1994) Efficacy of psychoanalysis for children with disruptive disorders. *Journal of the American Academy of Child and Adolescent Psychiatry*, *33*, 45–55.

Fonagy, P., Target, M. (1996) Predictors of outcome in child psychoanalysis: A retrospective study of 763 cases at the Anna Freud Centre. *Journal of the American Psychoanalytic Association*, *44*, 27–78.

Fonagy, P., Target, M., Cottrell, D., Phillips, J., Kurtz, Z. (2002) *What works for whom? A critical review of treatments for children and adolescents.* New York: Guilford Press.

Fonagy, P., Target, M., Ensink, K. (2005) *The efficacy of psychodynamic and cognitive-behavioural therapies for children with complex mental health disorders.* London: Anna Freud Centre.

Fonagy, P., Target, M., Steele, H., Steele, M. (1998) Reflective functioning manual for application to Adult Attachment Interview (version 5). Unpublished manuscript, London.

Gabbard, G.O. (2000) Psychodynamic psychotherapy of borderline personality disorder: A contemporary approach. *Bulletin of the Menninger Clinic*, *65*, 41–57.

Gerber, A. (2004) *Structural and symptomatic change in psychoanalysis and psychodynamic psychotherapy: A quantitative study of process, outcome, and attachment.* PhD Dissertation, University of London.

Giaconia, R.M., Reinherz, H.Z., Silverman, A.B., Pakiz, B., Frost, A.K., Cohen, E. (1994) Age of onset of psychiatric disorders in a community sample of older adolescents. *Journal of the American Academy of Child and Adolescent Psychiatry*, *33*, 706–717.

Kachele, H., Albani, C., Buchheim, A., Holzer, M., Hohage, G., Mergenthaler, E., et al. (2006) The German Specimen Case, Amalia X: Empirical studies. *International Journal of Psychoanalysis*, *87*, 809–826.

Kazdin, A.E. (2003) Psychotherapy for children and adolescents. *Annual Review of Psychology*, *54*, 253–276.

Kazdin, A.E. (2006) Arbitrary metrics: Implications for identifying evidence-based treatment. *American Psychologist*, *61*, 42–49.

Kim-Cohen, J., Caspi, A., Moffett, T.E., Harrington, H., Milne, B.J., Poulton, R. (2003) Prior juvenile diagnoses in adults with mental disorder: Developmental follow-back of a prospective-longitudinal cohort. *Archives of General Psychiatry*, *60*, 709–717.

Kringlen, E., Torgersen, S., Cramer, V. (2001) A Norwegian psychiatric epidemiological study. *The American Journal of Psychiatry*, *158*, 1091–1098.

Main, M., Goldwyn, R. (1994) Adult attachment rating and classification system (version 6). Berkeley, CA: University of California.

Midgley, N., Target, M. (2005) Recollections of being in child psychoanalysis: A qualitative report of a long-term follow-up study. *Psychoanalytic Study of the Child*, *60*, 157–177.

Midgley, N., Target, M., Smith, J. (2006) The outcome of child psychoanalysis from the patient's point of view: A qualitative analysis of a long-term follow-up study. *Psychology and Psychotherapy: Theory, Research and Practice*, *79*, 257–269.

Moran, G.S., Fonagy, P. (1987) Psychoanalysis and diabetic control: A single-case study. *British Journal of Medical Psychology*, *60*, 357–372.

Roche, D.N., Runtz, M.G., Hunter, M.A. (1999) Adult attachment: A mediator between child sexual abuse and later psychological adjustment. *Journal of Interpersonal Violence*, *14*, 184–207.

Rutter, M. (1990) Psychosocial resilience and protective mechanisms. In J. Rolf, A.S. Masten, D. Cicchetti, K.H. Nuechterlein & S. Weintraub (eds) *Risk and protective factors in the development of psychopathology*. Cambridge: Cambridge University Press.

Schachter, A. (2004) *The adult outcome of child psychoanalysis: A long-term follow-up study*. PhD dissertation, University of London.

Smith, J., Jarman, M., Osborn, M. (1999) Doing interpretative phenomenological analysis. In M. Murray & K. Chamberlain (eds) *Qualitative health psychology*. London: Sage.

Svanberg, P.O.G. (1998) Attachment, resilience and prevention. *Journal of Mental Health*, *7*, 543–578.

Target, M., Fonagy, P. (1994a) Efficacy of psychoanalysis for children with emotional disorders. *Journal of the American Academy of Child and Adolescent Psychiatry*, *33*, 361–371.

Target, M., Fonagy, P. (1994b) The efficacy of psychoanalysis for children: Developmental considerations. *Journal of the American Academy of Child and Adolescent Psychiatry*, *33*, 1134–1144.

Target, M., Fonagy, P. (2002) *Attachment theory and long-term psychoanalytic outcome: Quantitative and qualitative approaches and observations*. Paper presented at the Sigmund Freud Insitut, on Pluralism of Sciences, Frankfurt, September 2002.

Target, M., Fonagy, P., Schneider, T., Ensink, K., Janes, K. (2000) *Raters' manual for the Hampstead Child Adaptation Measure (HCAM)*. London: University College London and the Anna Freud Centre.

Vander Stoep, A., Weiss, N.S., McKnight, B., Beresford, S.A.A., Cohen, P. (2002) Which measure of adolescent psychiatric disorder – diagnosis, number of symptoms, or adaptive functioning – best predicts adverse young adult outcomes? *Journal of Epidemiology and Community Health*, *56*, 56–66.

Chapter 10

A qualitative framework for evaluating clinical effectiveness in child psychotherapy: The Hopes and Expectations for Treatment Approach (HETA)

Cathy Urwin

Introduction

Child psychotherapists are under increasing pressure to demonstrate and enrich the evidence base of the discipline. This pressure applies both in the private and public sectors. In the UK, for example, the National Health Service (NHS) requires practitioners to move forward on three fronts: to demonstrate the evidence (1) for clinical effectiveness, (2) for the processes that psychotherapy assumes and illuminates, and (3) for the use made of research findings in improving practice.

This requirement contains many conflicting views about appropriate research models, what counts as evidence and what is in patients' best interests. For example, on the one hand the National Institute of Health and Clinical Excellence (NICE), the national body responsible for issuing guidelines on treating particular pathologies in the UK, adopts a hierarchy that places randomized controlled trials (involving evaluating treatments of single pathologies against no-treatment controls) at the top, with patients' own experiences at the bottom. On the other hand, the new government-led National Service Frameworks explicitly require managers and practitioners to seek out and attend to patients' views, encouraging feedback and involvement. The development of such frameworks aims to address well-recognized regional and local variations. A further and somewhat different priority reflects the impact of critical analyses of medical autocracy, the hegemony of expert knowledge and a one-size-fits-all model of care.

Within this somewhat contradictory context, there are few guidelines about how to undertake research that enhances the knowledge-base of the discipline, benefits patients and takes their experience into account. This chapter describes a framework for evaluating and auditing clinical effectiveness that aims to rise to some of these challenges. It involves parents' and children's views and experiences of treatment and is compatible with the use of standardized methods. Here, the aim is to show how it can enable clinicians to monitor technique, incorporating research evidence into this process.

The Hopes and Expectations for Treatment Approach

The Hopes and Expectations for Treatment Approach (HETA) is intended for use in routine practice in child and family clinics, where other professionals within the service usually refer children for psychotherapy (Kam & Midgley 2006). HETA can also be used in private work. It is based on using the assessment and feedback process normally preceding child psychotherapy to derive a set of 'hopes and expectations for treatment', to be reviewed at the end of each year or agreed period of treatment.

Within a public-sector child mental health service, a typical assessment might involve an initial meeting between psychotherapist and parents or family followed by three individual sessions with the child, in which the psychotherapist hopes to gain some sense of the child's attachments, internal world, developmental level and dominant defences, and an idea of what contributes to the presenting problems. The psychotherapist is also interested in how the child responds to a 'taster' of psychotherapy and may ask the child whether he or she would like to come for further work and what he or she hopes will change.

This process enables the psychotherapist to put together a formulation that illuminates the presentation and indicates whether psychotherapy is the treatment of choice. In my view, the justification for this relatively intensive treatment includes some expectation about areas of development that may be opened, internal or structural changes that will be brought about and likely areas of resistance. These factors affect recommendations about intensity and likely length of treatment.

A feedback meeting with the parents and worker who referred the child follows the individual sessions. One aim of this is to make a bridge with the parents so that they recognize that their concerns have been taken on board and feel that the psychotherapist understands their child. Another is for the psychotherapist to explain the formulation in an accessible way and suggest why, if it is considered to be the case, psychotherapy might be useful. Within this evaluation framework, if the parents agree to start psychotherapy, a further appointment is scheduled in order to complete a Hopes and Expectations for Treatment Form (HETA). This is in two parts:

- **Part 1** records the parents' three main concerns before psychotherapy, any new information about the child and whether there were any changes during the assessment period. It also records three factors about the child that made an impression on the psychotherapist, what has been agreed in terms of work with parents or carers and the frequency and length of the psychotherapy, for example, 'once a week for one year in the first instance'.
- **Part 2** requires the parents and the psychotherapist to record their hopes

and expectations about what might be different by the end of treatment. This is not a 'wish list'. Rather, the aim is to capture expectations based on what has been thought about and understood during the assessment process. It is in three sections:

- *Section 1* concerns parents' hopes and expectations for change in the child. Based on the discussion in the feedback meeting, the parents specify three things that they would hope to be different at the end of the agreed treatment period (e.g. one year), giving examples of what change would look like in each case. For example, the parents of a child whose problems include aggressive behaviour that monopolizes family life might hope that the child would 'get on better with his sister', an example being that he would 'let her have her choice of TV programme sometimes without making a fuss'.
- *Section 2* concerns what the psychotherapist hopes to find in the psychotherapy sessions. It requires the psychotherapist to put him- or herself on the line about the psychotherapy process, again specifying three areas, with examples. The aim is to increase the transparency of the psychotherapy process, and also to indicate areas where support from parents and parent worker may be needed. This section also enables the psychotherapist to check on the thinking behind the original formulation.
- *Section 3* records three areas where the psychotherapist hopes to see change at home or at school by the end of the year, giving examples.

Once the HETA form has been completed, it is not returned to again until a feedback meeting between parents and psychotherapist at the end of a set period (e.g. one year), when the child's progress is discussed. Using a three-point scale where 0 = no progress, 1 = some progress and 2 = considerable progress, parents and psychotherapist together reach an overall total score *based on the review discussion*. This indicates the degree of relative change for a particular child. If it is agreed that the child's psychotherapy will continue for a further length of time, the psychotherapist's formulation of *where the child is at this review* will guide the setting of new standards of expectation. As will be described, the formulation may need modifying or fine-tuning in the light of discoveries made through the psychotherapy process. The Strength and Difficulties Questionnaire (SDQ; Goodman 1997) and/or the Child Behaviour Checklist (Achenbach 1991) may be completed by the parents and/or the school before the start of the psychotherapy assessment and administered again every six months or at the end of the year to provide concurrent additional sources of evaluation.

HETA has now been used in several clinics in the UK. We have found that parents appreciate being involved and parent workers have emphasized the value of transparency and of bringing together parent and child work. Child psychotherapists have found that it increases rigour and helps to keep the work on track. A record of the starting point is very useful during phases when the work is difficult. Not returning to the completed form between review meetings helps to counteract the tendency for pre-established hopes to get in the way of the psychotherapist's attempts to rid themselves of 'memory and desire' (Bion 1970) so that the child's own way is respected (Correia & Nathanson 2005, Urwin 2007). Importantly, the expectations are not set up as 'goals'; this is not goal-oriented or focused psychotherapy. HETA aims to set down markers to help establish the terrain and course of movement through psychotherapy and sees the evaluation of clinical effectiveness in terms of the increased capacity to learn from experience in the child, family and psychotherapist.

Focusing on a single case, in which identifying features have been changed, the next section illustrates how using this framework enhanced my understanding of the clinical process. Although the presentation was less severe than in many CAMHS child psychotherapy cases, and the outcome was very satisfactory eventually, initially this case did not go as I expected. I focus on using *Section 2, The psychotherapist's hopes and expectations for the psychotherapy process*, in monitoring my own practice.

Stefan: Using HETA in clinical practice

A GP referred Stefan to our Child and Family Consultation Service at age seven years suffering from nightmares and separation difficulties associated with his father's death two years earlier. Stefan's father was a political refugee living in the UK suffering from symptoms suggesting post-traumatic stress disorder and a progressive physical illness that necessitated a leg amputation. He died at home two years later.

Stefan is an only child. He was born via a forceps delivery after fetal distress. Early milestones were normal. He and his mother were living in their country of origin when the father's illness was diagnosed. Stefan was two years old when his mother managed to travel to the UK to join her husband, leaving Stefan with maternal grandparents. Stefan was flown to the UK, alone, to join his parents when he was four years old. He was met by his mother, who he had not seen for eighteen months, and his father, with an amputated leg.

Family work preceding child psychotherapy enabled Stefan and his mother to begin to tell their story and to obtain practical help. Stefan settled reasonably well at school. However, despite some cognitive behavioural and behavioural interventions, nightmares persisted. At the end of the year the family worker requested a psychotherapy assessment to establish whether individual psychotherapy might be helpful. Stefan's mother was keen for the assessment.

Assessment

The assessment involved three appointments arranged over three consecutive weeks. At the first appointment, as is my usual practice, I met mother and child together for the first part of the session. I then saw Stefan on his own. Stefan had been told in advance that the appointments were to 'think about what might be helpful'. His mother and Stefan's school each filled out an SDQ prior to the first appointment.

To the first appointment, they both arrived eager and determined to tell me they had lots of worries about each other. Stefan said his mother always worried about him and was afraid he would die. 'No, no!' his mother insisted '*He* worries about *me!*' She explained he could not sleep alone, would wake her up to check if she was all right and would not let her go into a shop on her own. She was also afraid that he was an easy target for bullying. He never had other children home.

Stefan's play, involving toy baby tigers fighting with a bear for a bigger share of a pot of honey, reflected some competitiveness between mother and son. On his own, Stefan revealed his anxieties more openly. He *did* worry about his mother. He went visibly pale telling me about recurrent nightmares. He did not know the English word but: 'He wears a long black cloak. His face is covered. He has a long silver sword, curved at the top. He is coming for me. It is very frightening. You have to follow him.'

I said that I thought this was what we call 'the grim reaper'. Stefan thought that the nightmare started after his father died. He remembered his father but he was hard to describe. He told Stefan that he was going to be very brave and that he would not die. I said that he *did* die though. I wondered why Stefan thought this happened. Stefan looked troubled. He did not know. His father had been in a war. He had hurt his leg. His leg was very short. 'His leg was cut off, up here; his leg stopped here', showing me on himself. Stefan agreed that he was very angry that his father had died. He found it hard to leave at the end of the session.

Over the course of the three assessment sessions, Stefan's nightmares stopped. He reported another dream in which he and a group of people were preparing a birthday party for his mother. He wanted her to have a good time. In the last session his play involved a toy crocodile, a bear, a father tiger and two baby tigers. The crocodile was bigger than the father tiger and threatened to overwhelm them all. Stefan insisted that, although the crocodile was bigger, the tiger was stronger, with big muscles. The problem was how the tiger would keep up its strength. Surreptitiously a baby tiger took food from the bear's nipples, and then fed the father tiger, as if this would be 'all right now'.

I interpreted the baby feeling responsible for feeding the father, and Stefan's concern about what was going to happen after this last session. I asked if he had any thoughts. He said that he wanted his sleeping to be better, and added that his mother did not go out shopping anymore. He acknowledged that her anxiety about him made this more difficult. It was important that she did go out to get food to feed the family. He thought that coming for more sessions would help.

SDQs taken over this time showed that the school was less concerned than the parent; Stefan's mother placed the difficulties in the abnormal range. She was very anxious about their effects on family life.

Formulation

The first session showed how mother and son had become entwined due to their difficult circumstances. On his own, Stefan emerged as an intelligent boy who had lost his father at an age when Oedipal urges to compete with and displace the father, with consequent castration anxiety, are normally at their height. Stefan's situation was further complicated by his separation from his parents at two years, and from his grandparents two years later. The presenting problems centred on separation anxiety and fear of death. He held a rather distant and idealized view of his father and voiced little anger spontaneously. It was encouraging that some change took place during the assessment.

I concluded that, through the regularity of the sessions and the therapeutic relationship, psychotherapy could enable Stefan to explore the impact of his feelings as they arose in the relative safety of the therapeutic sessions. This would enable Stefan to re-establish the dependability of internal objects, sort out the limits of his omnipotence and his developmental dilemmas and begin to mourn the loss of father and family life. The process could also free him to make more use of environmental opportunities.

Feedback meeting

At the feedback meeting, to explain the formulation, I said Stefan was a bright, lively boy who wanted help for himself and to make things better at home. I explained that Stefan's father's death had occurred when Stefan was at an age when boys can be very rivalrous with their fathers. Therefore he could be confused about the cause of the tragedy. Stefan's mother understood and added that Stefan loved his father, who could be very strict. He was changed by his illness. She also thought that Stefan clung to her in case he lost her too. He could be very bossy, as if he was her big brother taking charge. She had worried about Stefan since his birth. We noted two sides of Stefan. He could be very grown up; in other ways he was still like a baby or small child.

We arranged that I would see Stefan once-weekly, initially for one year. His mother would be seen every two to three weeks by the family worker to continue to work on things at home. HETA was explained, and during a further meeting both mother and the therapist recorded their hopes and expectations for Stefan (Box 10.1).

Box 10.1 Stefan's initial HETA before beginning psychotherapy

Stefan's mother's hoped that, by the end of the year:

1   Stefan will be less anxious at night.

    a   How would you tell?
    He would be sleeping alone and not wake me up.

2   Stefan will be more confident with people.

    b   How would you tell?
    He would not be so shy or clinging when passing other children.

3   Stefan will deal better with strange situations.

    c   How would you tell?
    Stefan will not panic and will stay calm when something unusual happens, and react in a more graded way. For example, he would not get so anxious if I have a headache.

The psychotherapist hoped that, in the sessions:

1   Stefan would express and communicate more of his baby feelings and his fears in the sessions.

    a   How would you tell?
    His play and drawings will allow us to think and talk about his feelings so that he can become more aware of them. I would expect Stefan to have a strong reaction to separations in his therapy, for example, to holiday breaks and sometimes at the end of sessions.

2   Stefan will show us some of his confusions about whether he is expected to be a grown up man already or a boy needing support and encouragement.

    b   How would you tell?
    This will be shown in play and also in his attitude towards Cathy. For example, he may take command of the session or imagine he is Cathy's partner, as he imagines he is his mother's older brother. He may react strongly when he realizes Cathy sees other children and may need his mother's support to come at these difficult times.

3   Stefan will think more about his father over the year and get a more rounded picture of who he was.

> c   How would you tell?
> I would expect Stefan to play out and talk about different sorts of memories or pictures of his father, for example, as a hero, a super-dad but also as a frightening person. As he gets a more rounded picture of him more feelings of sadness about his death and about being left without a father may come to the fore.
>
> The psychotherapist hoped that, at home and at school:
>
> 1   Stefan would be less anxious at night times.
>
> a   How would you tell?
> The nightmares would be less frequent and Stefan would try to sleep in his own bed.
>
> 2   Stefan would be more confident in difficult social situations at school.
>
> b   How would you tell?
> Stefan would stick up for himself if picked on by other children, and let his mother know about this.
>
> 3   As Stefan is more in touch with his own feelings he will worry about his mother less when it is not appropriate.
>
> c   How would you tell?
> If his mother is unwell or worried, Stefan will be concerned without being so overanxious.

Stefan's assessment took place in the Summer Term. We started psychotherapy the following week to ensure six sessions before the summer holiday break; this timing was not ideal.

First term of psychotherapy

Stefan began psychotherapy eagerly. From the outset, rivalry and Oedipal themes were uppermost, possibly enhanced by the knowledge of the coming holiday break. Stefan made a large man with one leg shorter than the other, covering several sheets of paper. But as the holiday approached he became very anxious, afraid of the nightmares restarting. In his play animals were set up for slaughter and picked off one by one. I interpreted Stefan's experience of the cruelty of breaking so soon. Stefan agreed that he did not like this but denied his anxiety about what sort of person I had become.

Second term of psychotherapy

Given his accessibility and his liveliness, I was unprepared for how changed Stefan was at the start of the Autumn Term. He reacted to small changes in the room as if given a body blow and presented like a wizened old man. This was followed over successive weeks by a series of odd presentations. For example, he would come in nodding like a tortoise, or as something I recognized as a snake. In previous sessions there had been several references to fathers; this was now a 'no-go' area. Stefan was emphatically not interested in my life or involvement with anyone when he was not in the room. Stefan was particularly resistant to any talk about 'feelings' or anything that would indicate vulnerability. If I referred to babies, Stefan would be scathing and dismissive. 'Babies don't have feelings; they're too young to have feelings'. Therefore his mother leaving him at two years would not have upset him. It was difficult to tell if he was dismissing vulnerability, protecting his mother or idealizing a state before, he imagined, worry and pain set in.

This denial of feelings went along with an omnipotent control I found hard to manage. He would insist on running the sessions, denying any thoughts about me in the intervening week. He developed a craze for making his own playing cards, consisting of 'Dark' cards that were to be pitched against 'Light'. Each card had various powers for destruction, regeneration or magic. Although I was invariably placed on the Light side, and given lots of chances, the rules were constantly changing, leaving me confused, demoralized and trapped. Excited rather than triumphant, Stefan wanted to be the best card player in the world, to deal with a cynical confusion over what could be achieved through luck, effort or cheating.

Changes at six and twelve months

Despite Stefan's apparent reluctance to take anything in, change nevertheless occurred. At the review meeting at the end of the second term, approximately six months after psychotherapy started, Stefan's mother reported that he had started to sleep in his own bed, although he still wanted the light on. He was still very clinging when passing other children but there were no reports of difficulties at school. She also thought that Stefan had become a little braver, having been able to wait for her outside a shop for ten minutes.

At the end of the year, this progress had been sustained, as indicated by the HETA scores in Table 10.1. However, during the year I had been less satisfied concerning what I had hoped would happen in the psychotherapy sessions. Scores for Section 2 were slower to progress than on the Sections relating to change observable at home and school. At the six months review, Stefan had certainly been reacting strongly to separations, relevant to Item 1, but he appeared very resistant to communicating about his vulnerability. On Item 2, he was indeed 'bossing' me in the sessions, but he was ostensibly uninterested

Table 10.1 HETA scores given per item by parent and psychotherapist at reviews

Section	Item	12-month review	24-month review	6-month follow-up
Section 1	1	2	2	2
	2	1	1	2
	3	1	2	2
	Total score	4	5	6
Section 2	1	1	2	2
	2	1	2	2
	3	1	2	2
	Total score	3	6	6
Section 3	1	2	2	2
	2	1	2	2
	3	2	2	2
	Total score	5	6	6
	Overall score	12	17	18

in any other relationships I might have. This would have required more tolerance of triangularity, that is, the fact that when people significant to him give attention to or have relationships with other people, he will, at times, necessarily feel excluded. As for Item 3, talking and thinking about his natural father had apparently disappeared.

By the end of the year, on Section 2, there was now some indication that things were shifting. Strong reactions to separations remained, but Stefan's approach to the coming holiday was based on the conviction that he would survive it and not be overwhelmed. He was also just beginning to reveal vulnerability. Furthermore, I came to understand that Stefan's attempts to take charge of the sessions (Item 2) were to defend against feelings of vulnerability. Interestingly, a father now emerged in the play occasionally, but in the context of frightening things happening. Where one would hope for a protective father in internal reality, Stefan met something terrifying, like Bion's (1962) concept of the absent object displaced by a present persecutor.

Stefan's mother was pleased with Stefan's progress and wished to continue for a further year, and to keep items in Section 1 the same. Having understood more fully the relationship between avoiding vulnerability and the wish for control, I fine-tuned Items 1 and 2 in Section 2. These now read:

1   Stefan will continue to have strong reactions to separations. Stefan will come to feel safe enough to explore and communicate more about his fears, his baby feelings and his feelings of vulnerability in the sessions.
2   As Stefan becomes safe enough in the sessions to explore his vulnerability, he will feel less need to be in control and will be more able to ask for help, recognizing generational differentiation and showing more curiosity about other children I see and my family.

Monitoring the effectiveness of the clinical process

How can we explain the initial relative difference between what was happening in the sessions and what I had expected? Was something wrong with the original formulation and/or the technique? Was something going on externally that I was not aware of?

It is a common experience that, once a child's psychotherapy starts, vulnerable areas, relative to integration presented in the assessment, become more apparent. HETA allows one to track the ups and downs of this process. Furthermore, in bringing parent and child work together, it is possible to explore the impact of starting psychotherapy on family relationships.

One way of addressing the latter is to compare the content of case notes of the parent work before and after the psychotherapy began. In this case, the initial family sessions were primarily concerned with practical issues and managing Stefan's difficulties. Once psychotherapy started, topics shifted markedly. The mother talked about her own distress, loneliness and depression, suggesting that she was 'letting go'. This may partly explain Stefan's difficulties in revealing vulnerability. It is hard for a child to feel safe to do this if his mother is overwhelmed. Here, containment provided by parent work became crucial to allowing possibilities for change in the child.

But Stefan's development went beyond what supporting the mother could make possible. What else contributed to releasing the initial sense of therapeutic impasse? To explore this I have used a technique used in a research context by Carlberg (1997). This involves identifying a significant session in which the psychotherapist recognizes a distinct change. One can then trace backwards to precursors in previous sessions, allowing the psychotherapist to reflect on and, if necessary, modify technique.

For Stefan a 'lynch pin' session occurred in the third term, roughly nine months after the psychotherapy started. This was the first time Stefan began to own feelings of vulnerability, revealing anxieties about abandonment and loss. Interestingly, he also conveyed feelings about the burden of growing up without his father, and his aggression towards other children:

> Stefan has been drawing a series of 'fighter' robots, explaining they were 'fighting for their freedom'. I said that I was thinking about what it might be like to be under attack and to be totally defenceless. I wondered if that might be a bit like what it feels like when a father dies. Stefan said 'Yes. It was painful, upsetting. Don't talk about it – it was along time ago'. Stefan went on to mention his own and another country in the game. I said that these countries had been at war. Stefan agreed.
>
> The game then changed to include a girl warrior. I was to choose between this and another. 'Which do you like best? You like the girl. Of course you do. You're a girl'. Stefan heard sea gulls outside. He said they were crying. I asked why they were crying. He said they were crying

because one of their flock had been shot. 'You can cry for birds but not for babies'. Stefan wrote on paper:

> 'The birds cry for one of their friends who has been shot-wa-wa
> wa-wa wa-wa wa-wa
> 　　wa-wa wa-wa
> 　　　　wa-wa
> 　　　　　wa-aaaaaaaaaaaaa.'

I said that you cannot cry for babies because that crying might go on for ever.

Stefan did not want to leave at the end of this session. He wanted to take his drawing with him. 'It's *mine*', he insisted, 'I made it!' I said that he didn't trust me to keep his drawings safe for him because he was very angry with the other children. 'Yes,' he said, 'I want to murder them!'

Stefan's pain, expressed rather beautifully in the imagery of the crying gulls isolated from their flock, seemed to symbolize both the baby's terror of abandonment and also his mother's loss of her husband, their future children and the loss of country and countries riven by wars. Tracing back from this material, as Carlberg suggested, I noted in the first instance a shift in my technique away from interpretations aimed at challenging Stefan's denial towards greater emphasis on working through in the countertransference. Initially, this was in part a consequence of recognizing my colleague's concern for Stefan's mother, and the extra burden that Stefan was carrying. Second, as I realized my challenges were counterproductive, I began to attend more closely to the kinds of feelings that Stefan's play and insistent control were bringing about. I began to understand it was important to maintain hope in future effectiveness, and to see the wish to be the 'champion card-player of the world' as a communication about the need to maintain some optimism in the face of life's cruel lotteries.

Thus, I replaced interpretations of the sort 'you feel or intend x or y,' with comments of the sort, 'I wonder how it would feel in such-and-such a situation', responding, as in the above example, to my emotional reaction to the situation that Stefan was depicting. This effectively put the child in charge of exploring, explaining and owning his experience. As Stefan rightly insisted, the drawing was *his* creation; he made it.

The sense of Stefan making an investment in the process was also preceded by a moving and touching expression of positive transference. He made a set of love-hearts instead of cards and put one for me in his box for safe-keeping. There was also a changed reaction to holidays. After the first break Stefan reacted as if violently pushed aside. Approaching the second holiday he took more responsibility for keeping in mind what was his, checking on his return that his things were still there. This anticipation of mindfulness indicates a stronger internal object, of which he was attempting to integrate good and bad aspects.

It is not so much that the initial formulation was wrong but that I underestimated the importance of containing baby aspects of Stefan. It is possible that the first holiday replayed his mother's absence in his infancy during a crucial developmental period.

Second year of treatment

It was in the second year of treatment that, as HETA had originally specified, Stefan became curious about my life and relationships. He also talked about loneliness and how he missed school at the end of term. Although identifying strongly with England, he showed some interest in watching a documentary about his country of origin. This paralleled his mother talking in her sessions about missing her parents back home. Stefan seldom talked about his father but the picture was more integrated. He formed a particularly helpful relationship with his science master.

Stefan had the advantage of a planned ending to the psychotherapy. Patients often produce a version of their original symptoms in the final weeks, as if to test out whether they have found a new solution. Three weeks before the last session Stefan produced a kind of mirror image of the 'lynch pin' session that confirmed my sense that he had grasped what the psychotherapy had been about and that he had a choice over owning or denying his feelings.

Stefan knew there were only three more sessions. He thought he would make the best of it. He liked coming to talk to me, though, about 'Play Station and things'. He had played nearly all of the 'Kingdom Hearts' game (which he had mentioned once before). The thing he liked best about Kingdom Hearts is the beginning, where they are all on the island. It is all about friendship. The struggle of the game is against the Heartless. The hero is severed from his friends and has to fight against the Heartless taking over the planet. And he knows that, in the end, he is going to have to say goodbye to his friends.

Stefan said that he would be sad when his therapy finished. I said he knew it was important to know about these feelings. Stefan talked about a day when there had been terrorist bombs in London. Some people had died, but he thought that you have to 'get on with things'. I said that Stefan knew about death. But it was also important to put things behind him to move forward.

At the end of term review, I gave maximum scores for expectations for change within psychotherapy as well as in the outside world. The mother, although pleased with developments, felt that Stefan was still a bit anxious around other children. However, at a follow-up review six months later, Stefan had now started inviting children round and was going into their houses after school. She gave the maximum score, as Table 10.1 indicates. SDQ scores were in the normal range.

Conclusion

This paper has described an evaluation framework used for the routine monitoring of child psychotherapy's clinical effectiveness. In line with contemporary patient-benefit agendas, parents, patients, psychotherapists, parent workers, and sometimes schools and social services, are involved in the process of establishing realistic expectations. All provide viewpoints on relative progress that contribute to the triangulation necessary to validate qualitative evidence.

Bringing the child and parent work together under one framework can be particularly valuable where loss and trauma have affected both child and family, as in this case, and/or where improving commitment in hard-to-reach families is a priority. Another value is that the framework allows the clinician to modify formulation and technique. Here I have described how the framework allowed me to track interrelationships between understanding psychopathology, developmental level and appropriate intervention, improving my own practice. With minor adjustments, this approach is highly suited to process research, and eventually to contributing to theory generation and more effective treatment of further cases.

References

Achenbach, T. M. (1991) *Manual for the Youth Self Report and 1991 Profile.* Burlington, VT: University of Vermont Department of Psychiatry.

Bion, W. (1962) *Learning from experience.* London: Heinemann.

Bion, W. (1970) *Attention and interpretation.* London: Heinemann.

Carlberg, G. (1997) Laughter opens the door: turning points in child psychotherapy. *Journal of Child Psychotherapy, 23*, 331–349.

Correia, S., Nathanson, A. (2005) Making a contract: formalising our expectations of therapy. *Bulletin of the Association of Child Psychotherapy, 155*, 16–18.

Goodman, R. (1997) The Strengths and Difficulties Questionnaire: A research note. *Journal of Child Psychology, Psychiatry, and Allied Disciplines, 38*(5), 581–586.

Kam, S., Midgley, N. (2006) Exploring 'clinical judgement': How do child and adolescent mental health professionals decide whether a young person needs individual psychotherapy? *Clinical Child Psychology and Psychiatry, 11*(1), 27–44.

Urwin, C. (2007) Revisiting 'What works for whom': A qualitative method for evaluating clinical effectiveness in child psychotherapy. *Journal of Child Psychotherapy, 33*(2), 134–160.

Part IV

Creating connections through interdisciplinary research

Introduction

One of the aims of this book is to give a sense of the distinctive research tradition that exists within child psychotherapy. However, like all areas of research, some of the most interesting work takes place at the borders, where child psychotherapy engages with ideas and approaches from other disciplines. Many child psychotherapists come to the profession of child psychotherapy having already gained extensive training in a variety of academic and professional backgrounds, such as clinical psychology, sociology, medicine, social work and so on. When considering issues pertinent to research into psychoanalytic psychotherapy with children, they inevitably bring to these considerations their understandings and skills gained prior to their clinical training. Researchers from outside the field of child psychotherapy have also chosen to collaborate with child psychotherapists, producing innovative models and methods of child psychotherapy research.

Emerging from such collaboration and cross-fertilization comes a range of very different studies, each of which brings something unique to our way of understanding children from a psychodynamic perspective. This part of the book is particularly concerned with this delicate and sensitive interaction, which involves finding analogies, translations, common concerns and differences between the insights gained in the 'laboratory' of a direct clinical interaction and fields such as developmental psychology, neuroscience, sociology, the other social sciences and medicine.

This field is not without its tensions, as has been discussed in the introduction and the first section of this book. These tensions can perhaps be summarized as hinging on the question of what is considered to be valid scientific evidence, and on the degree to which it is possible to translate the findings from one field (such as studies of the brain) to another (such as a study of the mind). Some authors would consider that for child psychotherapy to gain its legitimate status within the sciences it is crucial that the cross-fertilization is a very direct one, such as, for example, finding a direct link between clinical phenomena and brain functioning. Others, however, would feel that such a direct link is not only unnecessary, but also misleading: one line of argument might be framed along the lines that the functioning of the mind cannot be reduced to the functioning of the brain; another line might be that the attempt at integration is premature.

All authors in this part have attempted to find points of contact between the understanding of clinical phenomena observed in the consulting room and other fields of science concerned with similar preoccupations.

The chapter by Alvarez and Lee takes the form of a debate between a clinician and a researcher, describing the tensions involved in a collaboration aimed at capturing very complex modes of relating between a child affected by autism and his therapist. While describing some of the findings of this particular study, this chapter also gives us a very vivid sense of some of the values and difficulties in such a collaborative venture between people from different cultures.

Anderson uses grounded theory – a methodology developed within sociology – to analyse clinical data. She studies risk-taking dangerous behaviour in childhood, considering both individual and family factors. Grounded theory enables her to develop theory grounded in the clinical data that might explain the origin, structure and meaning of the risk-taking behaviour. This makes it possible to structure thinking around the interventions that might be most effective. The categories discovered by the research are easily accessible to other professionals working with children and take psychoanalytic theory beyond the consulting room.

Hodges and colleagues' starting point is an attempt to develop a tool by which they would be able to capture the psychic states they had observed in their patients in a more systematic way, while also creating bridges with the field of attachment research. The use of narrative story stems as the tool enables them to assess, standardise, compare and follow the measured changes in the internal worlds of young children, in a way that speaks across disciplinary boundaries.

Mayes and Thomas are concerned with trying to understand the neural mechanisms that they believe may be at least in part underpinning certain psychic processes and their possible links with psychic functioning as observed in clinical practice.

In different ways, each of these chapters illustrates the value of dialogue with other disciplines. They also illustrate the potential for richly rewarding collaborations for the child psychotherapy discipline.

Chapter 11

Interpersonal relatedness in a child with autism: Clinical complexity versus scientific simplicity?

Anne Alvarez and Anthony Lee

Introduction

Philip Roth has suggested that politics and literature are not only in an inverse relation to each other, they are positively antagonistic. He wrote:

> To politics, literature is decadent, soft, irrelevant, boring, wrong-headed, dull, something that makes no sense and really oughtn't to be. Why? – because the particularizing impulse *is* literature. How can you be an artist and renounce the nuance? But how can you be a politician and allow the nuance? As an artist the nuance is your task. Your task is *not* to simplify. The task remains to impart the nuance, to elucidate the complication, to imply the contradiction.
>
> (Roth 1998 p. 223)

Clinicians and researchers enjoy similar antagonisms. These can be equally serious where the conflict coexists in the same person! The clinician attends to the nuances of the emotional forces that gather to either connect or disconnect the child in his or her relationship with the therapist. How can quantitative research capture this process, given that every therapeutic encounter is unique?

We would suggest that interdisciplinary studies provide useful bridges or 'third positions' (Britton 1989) in regard to this. The field of autism is especially riddled with controversy, and degeneration or non-generation of mindfulness presents us with some very puzzling and complex problems.

In 1992, the two of us (Anne Alvarez, a Child and Adolescent Psychotherapist, and Anthony Lee, an Academic Psychologist), both experienced in the fields of autism and developmental disorders, drew up a research proposal to examine the changes in a child with autism over four years of intensive psychoanalytic psychotherapy. The project comprised two studies: the first was designed to track the changes over time to demonstrate that the condition of autism was not static, but 'mutable', the second to look more closely at the underlying processes and investigate whether aspects of the intervention might be associated with the observed changes.

The formal results of this research can be found in Alvarez and Lee (2004). In this chapter, we reflect on the evolution of the first study and convey something of our struggles – as clinician and researcher – in reaching a final design. We draw on an aspect of the results to highlight how findings concerning how the child took in his world visually helped both the clinician and researcher to think more carefully about the activity of looking. We will highlight how the tension between a fiery clinician and dogged researcher produced something thought-provoking and creative for each.

Autism

The condition of autism is characterized by atypical functioning in three domains: social interaction and communication are impaired and there is a restricted repertoire of activities and interests. The difficulty in working with children with autism is that they do not ordinarily turn to others. Current guidance emphasizes providing speech and language therapy, educational support and firm structure. This is often a helpful first step in managing behaviour that may be unusual or challenging. In the therapy context, however, we believe that, whether the propensity to avoid others is due to deficit and/or defence, the initial therapeutic undertaking is to draw the child with autism into a relationship. Once the child feels safe and becomes emotionally engaged, the therapist is in a position to think more closely about the child's capacities as well as the internal forces that prevent him or her from ordinarily connecting with people. Alvarez and Reid (1999) describe how, as these children develop, they form a dense structure around a core fragility that becomes knitted into the fabric of their personalities.

Despite a weight of clinical evidence, there is controversy about whether children with autism can benefit from psychoanalytic psychotherapy. The challenge for Child and Adolescent Psychotherapists is to conduct research that not only 'imparts the nuance, to elucidate the complication', but is viewed by the broader scientific community as replicable and valid.

Background to study

Controversies have led to some extreme views, and sometimes correspondingly extreme implications for aetiology, education and treatment. This has not been helpful for the children and their families. Professor Israel Kolvin of the Tavistock Clinic and Royal Free Hospital urged the Tavistock Autism Workshop to devise formal research in the late 1980s to capture both larger changes in relatedness and factors mediating these changes. We were advised to use video-recording, a relatively new medium in clinical research at that time.

The aim of our study was to identify and measure early forms of relatedness in a young child with severe autism and to examine changes in these

forms over a period of three years. We hypothesized that the social functioning of children with autism would include, as well as functional elements of a
deviant nature, some that are spared. Bion (1967) emphasizes the importance
of the non-psychotic part of the psychotic person's personality; here we were
interested in the non-autistic part of the child with autism (Alvarez & Reid
1999). These spared elements may show delay to varying degrees and, indeed,
may be negatively affected by deviant functioning. Under certain circumstances, however, the spared functioning may develop further and allow the
child to relate to others in a manner that is more comfortable and rewarding
for him. In this way autism may be more mutable than is often thought.

The 'good enough' design

How did a design emerge through our various considerations, cogitations and
conflicts? We had been given people's thoughts and advice, but we had to
wrap something hard around our clinical intuitions and ideas.

Single-case or group?

The first issue that we considered was the feasibility of a single-case design.
Scientific enquiry is generally conducted by testing a representative sample
taken randomly from the population. Testing a number of cases in this way
ensures that the different qualities of the individuals making up the sample
('error variance' in statistical terms) do not confound the identification of the
process under consideration. Thus, working with a single case is a high-risk
business: can you really trust that your findings are representative of this
population? But clinically, and particularly in psychoanalytic psychotherapy,
consideration of the single case is time-honoured. Indeed, 'error variance'
may be thought of as the bread and butter of child psychotherapists, who
strive to be receptive to all aspects of what children bring to therapy.

We opted to go ahead with a single-case rather than a group design. This
was partly because we had limited resources. But primarily we wished to
consider the child's development from the perspective of personality growth
and reorganization, as well as symptom presentation. We were unaware of
other research that employed video-recordings of a child with autism in
intensive psychoanalytic psychotherapy. There were thus no precedents. By
focusing on a single case we hoped to remain sensitive to the interplay
between many different factors.

From a research perspective, however, it was essential to capture the child's
presentation through standardized psychometric instruments. At that time,
medical and allied professionals generally viewed autism as relatively immutable. The argument was often levied that if change was detected the child
had been wrongly diagnosed to begin with. To achieve a true baseline, we
decided to apply a battery of standardized measures prior to the child

starting intensive psychotherapy, thus demonstrating irrefutably that the child met criteria for autistic disorder.

Following ethical approval, the next step was to recruit a family who would consent to their child participating. We approached the first family referred with an under-five-year-old child for whom autism was part of the picture. Recruiting in this way blocked the possible charge of selecting to maximize the likelihood of change. We did reason, however, that by working with a younger child we would increase the likelihood of detecting development. Finally, as part of the selection criteria, the child had to undergo an assessment for psychoanalytic psychotherapy and be deemed suitable for this form of work.

The child

The first child to meet these criteria was Samuel, an only child who lived with his mother. A paediatrician gave Samuel a diagnosis of autism when he was three-and-a-half years old. Some four months later, he was referred to the Autism Service of the Tavistock Clinic and underwent an assessment for psychoanalytic psychotherapy. He was just four years of age.

The three-session psychotherapy assessment conducted by Alvarez confirmed autism. She also found that Samuel had a fleeting capacity to respond to her attempts to draw him into something lively and away from repetitive activities. At other moments he showed interest in her interest in him. Primarily for these reasons, psychoanalytic psychotherapy was recommended.

Samuel's mother was supportive of the work and she gave her consent for his inclusion in the study. Lee interviewed her at this time using the Autism Diagnostic Interview (ADI-R; Lord, Rutter & Le-Couteur 1994). From observations Lee made during a free-play session, the Childhood Autism Rating Scale (CARS; Schopler, Reichler & Renner 1986) was also completed. This measure requires judgements on a number of autism-related items. These instruments formally captured the presentation of severe autism.

Subsequently, Samuel attended three-times-weekly individual psychoanalytic psychotherapy with Alvarez over a period of almost four years. Samuel's mother received regular supportive work from Dilys Daws; there was also close liaison with Samuel's school.

Predictions

From a clinical viewpoint, our hypothesis allowed us to predict that certain early forms of relating would develop over time. Scientifically, we could not attribute predicted change to intervention at this stage: hence the breaking of the project into two studies. In this first study, we hoped only to demonstrate that we could reliably measure these social components and detect an increase in their presentation.

We decided to examine this prediction from both clinical and quantitative perspectives. The clinical data were drawn from process notes made after each therapy session. These registered observations were summarized under the headings of general functioning, visual regard, social relatedness, communication and play, but the content of the summaries included as many emotional and countertransferential particulars as were possible. The quantitative data were taken from video-tape recordings of the therapy sessions and focused specifically on visual regard, emotional expression, level of emotional engagement with and level of interest in the therapist. We predicted that these forms of relating would all show an improvement over time. Of course, these quantitative dimensions contribute to just a few of the social components contributing to the orchestra of human engagement and relationships. Furthermore, unlike the clinical descriptions, they do not include any of the personality features and emotional motivation considered crucial in the psychotherapy process.

Method of recording

Recorded shortly after each session, the therapist's process notes are traditionally taken as prime data in psychoanalytic psychotherapy. Apart from capturing closely the therapist's observations, these notes trace the movement in the course of the session through transference and countertransference responses. For clinicians, suggesting using video-tape is contentious to say the least. Apart from the sanctity of the therapy room, using video-recordings is in some ways like having a third person in the room. Will this not have a profound impact on the child, the therapist, the very psychotherapeutic process under investigation? Why not use a careful analysis of process notes?

The difficulty, from a scientific point of view, concerns validation. This indicates the concordance between two independent measures on the same subject matter, where one measure is standardized or reliable. Good concordance gives confidence that the non-standardized measure captures what was intended. A therapist's process notes derive from her specific experience with the child. Although it is not possible to validate her total experience, it can be argued that aspects of what she observes, including what the child does and to some extent of what he feels, can be validated by a third person who observes the interaction. This was one aspect of an argument to video-record the clinical sessions. Another aspect was that video-recordings would allow us to establish the reliability of the instrument we would need to design to validate aspects of the clinician's experience.

So why not video-tape a sample of sessions over time? The video-taping of sessions, not just the presence of a camera, needed to be a constant in the therapeutic milieu. If we had video-taped every third session, say, the knowledge of this by the therapist or sense of it by the child may have influenced the findings, if not the interpretation of them. Thus each and every therapy session was recorded.

This was a good argument, but a hard decision. Alvarez was very much alive to this third presence in the room that had to be worked with. Over time, however, its presence felt less interfering.

The selection of material

This enterprise produced a vast volume of material, recording well over 400 hours of clinical session-time matched with a comparable volume of process notes. Agreeing a design that reduced this material phenomenally created a huge tension between clinician and researcher! The clinician did not want to lose explicit material that demonstrated change. Why not extract and examine particularly rich episodes? The researcher's concern was to avoid claims of selectivity and bias. There was also the problem of how to reduce the volume of information so that the task of inspecting the material became manageable while making sure that meaning was retained.

We decided to take a random sample from the body of video-taped material. The sessions to be rated were selected by first taking the middle session from the first term as baseline (i.e. at two months). It was assumed that the period before this would be a time in which Samuel would become familiar with the new environment and the routine of his clinical sessions. Measures were then taken at this time and once yearly for the following three years. We considered that if development were proceeding as expected, this trend would be detectable from these selected sessions.

On inspection of the material, however, we soon realized that we had to reduce even further! A minute of video-taped material could take up to half an hour for frame-by-frame inspection, there being twenty-four frames in one second of video-recording. We eventually decided to examine the first five minutes and the mid-ten minutes of the selected clinical sessions. The first five minutes captured the entrance into the room and familiarization with the toys; the mid-ten minutes represented a likely time when Samuel would be relatively unaffected by distractions. Each extracted fifteen-minute section was divided into forty-five twenty-second clips. We took it that twenty seconds would be a sufficient sample of time to gauge the social components to be studied. The sections were randomly ordered on video-tape before being rated, to avoid order effects. If the material is presented chronologically, the rater's judgements may be influenced by the ordinary expectation of development.

Alongside the video data, we drew on clinical observations taken from termly summaries written at the time. These were themselves based on the process notes written after each session. Summarizing the summaries clearly meant that many details were sacrificed. However, the termly overviews of Samuel's progress were conceptualized in broad developmental categories that served to capture the meaning behind the psychology of eye contact.

What's in a look?

We predicted that over the course of the period studied we would see an increase in Samuel's capacity to engage and socially relate with the therapist. The frequency and duration of Samuel's looks to the therapist were aspects examined to evaluate this prediction. Typically, children with autism tend to avoid eye contact and may use their eyes to inspect aspects of their worlds in unusual or intense ways. The therapist felt that how Samuel attended to his world revealed different states of mind. She was adamant that to consider simply the frequency and duration of looks would disregard something about the child's strange, seemingly active use of his eyes, and his difficulties in using more ordinary, leisurely methods of visual introjection.

Thus, apart from scoring each and every look to the clinician and measuring its duration in number of video-tape frames, a judgement was made as to whether the look was 'odd' or 'direct'. The researcher worried that, without a clear, unambiguous definition of what comprised 'odd' looks, rater reliability would be poor, making the judgement worthless. 'Odd' looks were defined behaviourally as those where Samuel looked at the clinician with either wide-opened, staring eyes or narrowed eyes. These were considered to represent a possibly deviant component of visual functioning. However, within this there were subtle variations. Sometimes Samuel's eyes rolled wildly, as though in horror or terror; at others they widened hugely, as though in a desperate effort to take something in; sometimes there were instantaneous micro-seconds of peripheral vision – a quick glance at the therapist in the middle of a period of apparent indifference. As interesting as these observations may be, the study was not designed to fully capture this degree of nuance differentially.

All other looks were coded as 'direct' and were understood as a form of visual functioning that was relatively spared. Through close observation in the therapy sessions, the clinician noticed that when Samuel looked at her face he seemed unable, not simply unwilling, to sustain eye contact. Stern (1974) has noted that scanning is generally how eye contact is sustained as babies develop a capacity to maintain longer periods of eye contact in the first months of life. In the beginning, if Samuel met her eyes it was for no more than a peripheral, fleeting instant. When he eventually began to meet her eyes, his gaze seemed very intense, as if too strong for him to bear. At these times he seemed to have to tear his eyes away, as babies do in the early days of life before they have learned to scan (Stern 1974). As with the nuances of odd looks, we had no way of measuring whether Samuel's more 'ordinary' gaze at the therapist involved scanning as the study was not set up to investigate this.

We drew up our definitions and instructions to raters and two raters independently coded the video-taped data. We found good agreement between them. This reliability gave us the confidence that the rating scale was robust.

Results on looks

Clinical findings

At the beginning of the therapy, the clinician observed that apart from those times when Samuel was engaged in his 'hypnotic' preoccupations, he seemed unable to sustain attention to objects or people. He could track moving objects but he seemed unable to attend to immobile, inanimate objects for more than a few seconds. The clinician formed a sense that this was not simply unwillingness on the child's part; it seemed to occur even when he desperately wanted to examine an object. He looked only fleetingly or peripherally at the clinician and such looks were often bizarre (e.g. strange widening and rolling of his eyes).

At the end of the first year, the clinician noted that Samuel was giving her more looks and smiles. Although these were often off-centre, that is, just to one side of her, sometimes they were focused and co-occurring. At times, he appeared to be showing real interest in her eyes and face. He also began to show slightly more sustained interest in inanimate objects. These signs of visual exploration were often accompanied by odd explorative behaviour, scratching and poking of objects as though their very existence and otherness irritated and puzzled him. Nevertheless, he did occasionally begin to explore with some apparent if brief curiosity. He seemed to have particular difficulties with objects that were identical; two identical bricks, for example, seemed both to fascinate and irritate him. He gradually began to examine and explore one object at a time and to introduce some notion of sequencing.

At the end of the second year, Samuel's eye contact was more constant. Sometimes he would study the clinician's face in a leisurely and ordinary manner, at other times with an intense and non-flinching stare. He also appeared to focus on her face from greater distances, just like babies of three or four months who are beginning to manage convergent vision.

At the end of the third year, Samuel was using his eyes more and could meet the clinician's gaze from ever-greater distances. His acute short-sightedness had improved. We learned that his glasses prescription approached the normal! His mother and his teachers confirmed the improvements in Samuel's attention to objects and to other people, where his gaze became more lingering, less bizarre and more coordinated. His smiles were more ordinary and engaging; some turn taking was evident in the third year.

Quantitative findings

The number of looks by Samuel to the other person over three years is shown in Figure 11.1. The frequency is similar in baseline and year 1 (fifty-six and sixty events), but more than doubles in years 2 and 3 (139 and 147 events).

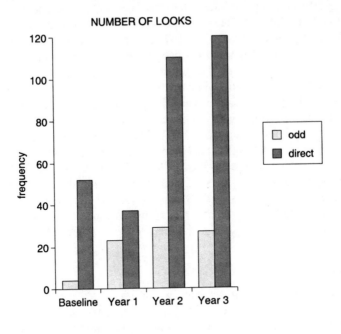

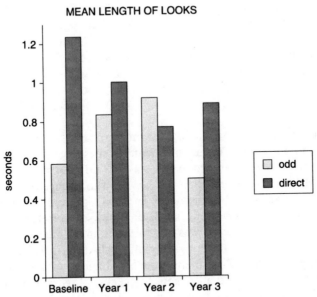

Figure 11.1 Frequency and duration of looks at other.

The proportion of 'odd' to 'direct' looks is 7 per cent at baseline; this increases dramatically in the first year to 38 per cent, then falls to 21 per cent in the second and 18 per cent in the third. The actual number of 'odd' looks runs from four at baseline, then twenty-three, twenty-nine and twenty-seven in the following three years. Thus the number of 'odd' looks over the last three years is relatively consistent, while the number of 'direct' looks increase.

Figure 11.1 also shows the mean length of looks Samuel made to the therapist over the three years. The length is given in seconds. The mean duration of 'odd' look rises from 0.58 s (SD 0.38 s) at baseline to 0.83 s (SD 0.63 s) in year 1, to 0.92 s (SD 0.67 s) in year 2, then falls to 0.50 s (SD 0.33 s) in the final year. The mean duration of 'direct' looks to other falls from 1.24 s (SD 0.83 s) at baseline to 1.00 s (SD 0.58 s) in year 1 and 0.77 s (SD 0.29 s) in year 2, then rises to 0.89 s (SD 0.33 s) in year 3. The approximate proportions of 'odd' to 'direct' looks to other in terms of time increases from 1 : 2 at baseline to 1 : 1 in years 1 and 2, then returns to 1 : 2 in the final year.

Discussion

Through our 'good enough' design, we found evidence that supported our prediction of an increase in early forms of relatedness over a four-year period in a child with severe autism. In this chapter, we have focused on findings on one aspect: looks made by Samuel to the clinician. Clinically, Samuel's looks changed over the course of the study. From mostly bizarre looks that were fleeting and peripheral, Samuel showed a steady improvement in their frequency and quality, so that by the end of the second year his eye contact was more constant and he appeared to be able to focus on the clinician's face from greater distances across the room. By the end of the study, Samuel's looks to the clinician were observed as being longer, more coordinated and less bizarre.

The quantitative findings highlighted an increase in the number of looks over the period of study. Further, the quality of these looks altered to include a far greater proportion of ordinary vis-à-vis 'odd' looks. Interestingly, the duration of looks to the clinician did not seem to change over time. Thus, although there was broad concordance in the clinical and quantitative findings, the clinician's observation that Samuel's looks seemed more lingering towards the end of the therapy was not borne out in the quantitative findings.

Was this discrepancy a result of sampling, or had the clinician not noticed that the apparent durability of the gaze hid frequent escapes? Or was she confusing directness, normality and frequency of gaze with durability? These and other questions force a more careful consideration of clinical judgement *and* experimental design. They sharpen both clinical and research awareness and are the seeds of future studies. Here, we reflect on how the findings might be understood.

Infant research attests to an increase with age in duration of the looks to other people. For example, Stern (1974) found that the average length of look to caregivers by their three- to four-month-old infants was 2.8 seconds and that this length increased as the child developed. Samuel's average length of 'direct' looks over the period of the study ranged from 0.8 to 1.2 seconds. The clinician felt that a combination of factors explains this observation. To start with, Samuel was at times taken over by states of intense irritation with the world. For example, he seemed to have difficulty comprehending that 'two-ness' could be available to him *in time*, that there was enough time to look at two bricks not *precisely* at the same instant. In fact, from the way he first began to look at the clinician's face, she had the impression that he did not scan, which is how most people manage to sustain eye contact. At this time he never met her eyes for more than an instant. As he began to look more closely his gaze was at times too strong, and he would have to tear his eyes away. This is what infants do in the early days of life before they have learned to scan (Stern 1985). Samuel seemed to lack a temporal container that could help him to find out how not to make do with one but to have two *in sequence*, one at a time.

Other states that could explain his short looks were his at times suspicious hypervigilance and at other times his extreme and intolerable excitement. The point here is that the clinical speculation is drawn from countertransference responses that enrich and give meaning to the quantitative research findings. In this way, more refined questions can be posed and other studies designed to increase understanding, and prevent travelling down a 'reductionist' blind alley.

Ordinarily, the persistence of such states of mind in any child would inter-fere with exploratory visual activity (Wolff 1974) and of course bear upon his subsequent representations. Psychoanalytically, the introjection of the interestingness and value of other people for Samuel is likely to have been impaired if the more leisurely taking in of the visible world that scanning implies was absent. Quick snatches and grabs of the visible world must lead to taking in a very different sort of internal object. In this respect, we believe that the developing representations of other people, a 'proto-theory of mind', in a child with autism could be further disrupted.

Another aspect of Samuel's looking was his strange widening and rolling of eyes. These reduced over time relative to the number of direct looks to the clinician, but did not entirely disappear. Bion suggested that certain of his schizophrenic patients used their eyes not for purpose of introjection, but for projection. Certainly, Samuel did seem to be doing something active with his eyes, partly perhaps for purposes of protection against overstimula-tion, but partly also to do something to his visible world: to change it, distort it, control it? The microanalysis of the tapes made the actual content of these 'odd' looks much clearer, but their purpose remains somewhat mysterious. It has led us both to want to carry out further research to see whether studying these microanalytic moments, and the internal states within the child that precede them, could add to the descriptive understanding of autism.

Conclusion

We set out to give a taste of the struggles and tensions that existed between a clinician and researcher, who each held different concerns about what was important to consider in the design of a single-case study. The sanitized description above does not do justice to the creative scuffles that were dotted with expletives and times of gritted teeth! We both believed that the confusing, and at other times terrifying, experience of a child with autism can be gleaned and thought about in the process of psychoanalytic psychotherapy. We each came closer to understanding the other's concerns; but more importantly, through this child we each learned something more about autism.

Yet the gaps between the two worked both ways: for example, the clinician's need to explain to her colleague what she felt deviance meant in this particular child, succeeded in enabling the measurement of 'oddness' to go ahead. It also made her attain greater precision in her own thinking with subsequent patients, and the microanalytic findings made her think much more about the nuances of introjective mechanisms than ever before. The researcher, who had always been interested in nuances, continued to do research but went on to train as a Child and Adolescent Psychotherapist. Need we say more about the usefulness of collaboration?

References

Alvarez, A., Lee, A. (2004) Early forms of relatedness in autism: A longitudinal clinical and quantitative single case study. *Clinical Child Psychology and Psychiatry*, 9, 499–518.

Alvarez, A., Reid, S. (1999) *Autism and personality: Findings from the Tavistock Autism Workshop*. London: Routledge.

Bion, W. R. (1967) *Second thoughts*. London: Heinemann.

Britton, R. (1989) The missing link: Parental sexuality in the Oedipus complex. In J. Steiner (ed.) *The Oedipus complex today* (pp. 83–101). London: Karnac Books.

Lord, C., Rutter, M., Le-Couteur, A. (1994) Autism Diagnostic Interview-Revised: A revised version of a diagnostic interview for caregivers of individuals with possible pervasive developmental disorders. *Journal of Autism and Developmental Disorders*, 24, 659–685.

Roth, P. (1998) *I married a communist*. London: Jonathon Cape.

Schopler, E., Reichler, R.J., Renner, B.R. (1986) *The Childhood Autism Rating Scale (CARS) for diagnostic screening and classification of autism*. New York: Irvington Publishers.

Stern, D.N. (1974) Mother and infant at play: The dyadic interaction involving facial, vocal and gaze behaviors. In M. Lewis & L.A. Rosenblum (eds) *The effect of the infant on its caregiver*. London: Wiley.

Stern, D.N. (1985) *The interpersonal world of the infant: A view from psychoanalysis and developmental psychology*. New York: Basic Books.

Wolff, P.H. (1974) The development of attention in young infants. In L.J. Stone, H.T. Smith, & L.B. Murphy (eds) *The competent infant: Research and commentary*. London: Tavistock.

Chapter 12

The mythic significance of risk-taking, dangerous behaviour[1]

Janet Anderson

Introduction

The purpose of this chapter is to describe and illustrate clinical concepts that were developed in the course of qualitative clinical research into risk-taking, dangerous behaviour in childhood, using grounded theory in a psycho-analytic context. The concepts derived from the clinical material were found to be intimately connected to the myth of Oedipus, and this made it possible to understand the origin, structure and meaning of the risk-taking, dangerous behaviour.

The myth of Oedipus

Laius and Jocasta, King and Queen of Thebes, were warned of the peril that Oedipus, their son, would bring to them. The oracle told them that he would kill his father and marry his mother. Believing the prophecy, yet trying to evade this fate, they distanced themselves from their son and left him where he would surely die; the imputation of danger and wrongdoing to the child led the parents to expel Oedipus from his home and abandon him on a mountainside 'in the twisty thickets' (Sophocles, trans. Grene [1942] *Oedipus Rex*, line 1026) with his feet pinned together. But death was not to be Oedipus's fate. The herdsman who was to 'make away with it' (line 1171) disobeyed his orders because he 'pitied it', and gave the baby to 'this man (who) was from another country'. As an adult, learning of the predictions, Oedipus, like his parents, tried to evade his fate, leaving the only home he had known, which, unbeknown to him was that of his adoptive parents.

At the place 'where three roads meet', he fought and killed a stranger, his natural father, Laius. Later, he confronted the challenge of the sphinx, 'the dark singer' (line 391), who was terrorizing the town. This monstrous

1 The full version of this paper was originally published in the *Journal of Child Psychotherapy* 2003 **29** (1): 75–91. http://www.tandf.co.uk/journals

creature, a combination of genders and species, 'for once in visible form' (line 510), was defeated by Oedipus. Knowing the answer to her riddle, he survived, while she threw herself to her death in the sea. Oedipus was rewarded for ridding the town of the sphinx with the crown and marriage to the queen, the stranger's widow, his mother, Jocasta.

The myth of Oedipus was recognized by Freud (1905, 1926) to have universal significance in emotional development, because emotional well-being depends on the ability to modify the powerful feelings associated with this drama. This is only possible if there are parental figures who can contain and detoxify the psychic contents, rendering them manageable for the child. A child may not have the capacity to tolerate the frustration of the three-person situation, 'where three roads meet', and if the parent is unable to contain her feelings and, rather like Jocasta, only provides her child with either expulsion and likely death or an incestuously intimate partnership, then the experiences that might enable the child to develop emotional maturity are absent. When the Oedipal fantasies, rather than being contained, are constantly reinforced then the scene is set for violent and dangerous consequences.

Research findings

Clinical research was undertaken in a local community Child and Adolescent Mental Health Service. Referred children, aged between three and sixteen years, were offered a place in the research project if their behaviour included risk-taking dangerous acts such as: (1) escaping: running away from parent or home; (2) risk of impact: by falling or collision with a vehicle; (3) firesetting: making a fire in an unsafe situation. While the risk-taking behaviour itself threatened harm to the child, all of the children were also found to make self-harming acts, ranging from self-biting to suicide attempts. None were included in the project if there was only deliberate self-harm. Most children exhibiting risk-taking, dangerous behaviour seen in this project were also described as showing aggressive behaviour. Twelve children and their families participated in this research project. Each child and family was offered an extended assessment by a child psychotherapist. Three children and their parents were offered treatment, two of which were ten-session interventions offered on a weekly basis and one was seen weekly for almost two years. Fortuitously, the cases offered treatment represented each of the categories yet to be discovered in the grounded theory analysis.

Clinical data were analysed using grounded theory (Glaser & Strauss 1967). This method for analysing qualitative data leads to the recognition of categories whose relationships with each other leads to the formation of hypotheses. These hypotheses are tested against the qualitative data by a process called 'constant comparison', which leads to the development of substantive theory that is 'grounded' in the qualitative data (for a full description of this process, see Anderson 2006).

In this research project, the organizing principle, which meaningfully discriminated between cases, was the evident emotion of the parent or primary carer for their child: idealizing, or critical blaming, or both attitudes occurring at different times. An exploration of this revealed different emotional configurations in the parent–child relationship. Three different configurations were identified, emerging from the clinical material, each of which was unsafe for the child. These were called 'no-haven', in which the parent was critical and blaming towards the child; 'illusory-haven', in which there was an apparently positive affect between parent and child and 'perilous-haven' in which an apparently warm and a critical blaming attitude alternate.[2] Both illusory- and perilous-havens are unstable and, without therapeutic help, may deteriorate into the no-haven configuration.

The mythic significance of the three havens

The illusory-haven and no-haven configurations, which were identified through the analysis of the clinical material, can be linked to the two different dispositions of the three main characters in the myth of Oedipus: Oedipus, his father and his mother. First, the parental couple disposes of Oedipus, arranging his death: no-haven. Second, Oedipus kills his father and is united with his mother: illusory-haven. In both situations the third person is eliminated. For the child, this meant either expulsion (no-haven), or partnership with a parent (illusory-haven). In perilous-haven, both the illusory-haven and the no-haven configurations may occur and it is the child's terrifying task to find a way from expulsion to the illusory-haven. Blindness to generational difference pervades the myth and was recognized as a feature for all the children in this research project.

Expelled: no-haven

The research findings show that expulsion from home was a common threat and frequently a reality for a family member, often occurring in the context of violent family relationships. In the no-haven group, the refusal to parent and the critical blame of the child resulted in the parents and child distancing themselves from each other. When away from home the child is vulnerable to harm from a potential abuser or other danger. Mortal danger is often faced when a child risks impact, e.g. with a vehicle or by falling.

---

2 It will surprise the reader no less than it did the author to learn that the three havens (illusory-haven, no-haven and perilous-haven) were named before discovering that Sophocles used the word 'haven', and indeed 'no-haven', in his text.

Incestuous intimacy: illusory-haven

Oedipus and his mother did not know each other (consciously) for who they are. This not-knowing is essential, not only because of the importance of not becoming consciously aware of the incestuous nature of the relationship but also because, if Oedipus recognized his mother, he would know that he was consorting with the mother who planned his death when he was a child. This wishing not to know, the -K relationship (Bion 1962), is an essential feature of the illusory-haven configuration, without which it cannot persist, as is shown in the myth. Not-seeing, not-knowing and not-thinking are features of the families with children showing risk-taking, dangerous behaviour.

The heroic task: perilous-haven

In this context both illusory-haven and no-haven, incestuous intimacy and expulsion, occur. The child is imperiled in two ways, both by the threat of expulsion and by the heroic task required of him, once expelled, to find a way of being reunited with his parent or primary carer.

Clinical evidence showed that expulsion of the child occurred when an intrusive projective identification was made between the mother and another, specifically to exclude the child, to attack or intimidate him. The death-defying feat, in fantasy, is to face and overcome the potentially deadly monster, representing the angry parent; overcoming the sphinx, for Oedipus, or, as will be illustrated later, 'Monstro' the killer whale from the film Pinocchio (Collodi, 1883) for three-year-old Billy. These encounters stir up terrifying fear in the child, who feels himself to be in great danger. The determination of the child to avoid the utter helplessness of expulsion, the exposure of the infantile self to almost certain death, leads to the excessive use of the manic defence with the essential denial of fear. The excitement of the confrontation with the frightening, monstrous object is imbued with the sexual significance associated with the fantasy of being united with the mother. In order to survive, fear must be denied and a move made towards danger. But how can a child approach a frightening parent?

The clinical presentation of the three havens

No-haven

In this configuration it is the child who is in danger. The following vignette illustrates the parent's refusal to parent and the child turning to self-harm or risk-taking, dangerous behaviour in the clinical session. Also illustrated is the use of confusion to try to provide a shield behind which to hide, the contortion of reality by the parent, which is repudiated by the child, and the significance of delinquent acts in the context of the family relationships.

ALAN (10 YEARS), PAUL (8 YEARS) AND STEVE (3 YEARS)

Mrs Cooper had a history of physical, sexual and emotional abuse by both parental figures and went on to make a succession of relationships with violent men. She had had six children and still felt bitter about the loss of her three eldest children, who had been adopted. When Steve was referred for his hyperactive behaviour he lived with his single-parent mother and his two older brothers, Paul and Alan. Both Paul and Steve exhibited risk-taking, dangerous behaviour. The first appointment was attended by the whole family.

Mrs Cooper spoke of all three boys in a critical and blaming way. The descriptions she gave of their behaviour were exaggerated and contorted reality. The boys argued with her, repudiating what she said. Mrs Cooper and the boys used confusion and muddling to try to make certain gains. Paul tried to confuse me, introducing himself with the wrong name, and saying, at the end, that he thought I would not remember what they had all said. Perhaps he thought that I would also be confused. The boys used confusion to divert their mother from knowing what had happened, hoping that she would give up trying to find out who to blame so that they would evade punishment. In the first excerpt, Mrs Cooper tried to discipline Steve by denying reality and hitting him verbally with a barrage of blame.

Mrs Cooper tried to intervene when Steve poured out some water into a play cup. She did not want him to drink it and yelled at him 'That's not water'. 'You'll get wet. . . . We've got to go home and you'll get cold!' Steve's head sank down on the draining board and he wept.

Mrs Cooper told me that Steve might bite himself very hard if she shouted at him. Paul also reacted to his mother's anger by self-harming behaviour at times. Mrs Cooper, jabbing her finger at Paul, said:

> '. . . He tried to hang himself with his belt from the banisters'. I said 'You must have been very worried'. She said, 'Yes', rather weakly and went on to complain that he did this because he could not get his own way. I wondered how she coped with this and she said, 'I shut myself away'. I asked what would happen if she did not shut herself away. She said, 'I'd strangle him'.

The session continued with both mother and sons presenting each other with an impervious object, mother's critical blame being countered by repudiation and criticism by the two elder boys.

I spoke to Alan, listening to his complaints about the awful facilities for play in the town, then both Paul and Alan remembered that their mother had told them of something good she had enjoyed as a child. Mrs Cooper complained angrily that Alan was 'a spoiled brat' because he did not like what he could have. Alan muttered to Paul and Paul publicized what he said. 'Alan said he wanted to use Mum's tits as a punch bag'. Mrs Cooper was appalled.

She appealed to me to see what she meant about their dreadful behaviour and as I was thinking about this Paul began to swing backwards dangerously on his chair. Mrs Cooper told him to stop, first shouting that he would break the chair. He took no notice. She then told him that he would fall and hurt himself. Paul retaliated by saying 'Good' because if he did she would be sorry for him and might say 'Poor Paul'. I said that he wanted his mother to say 'Poor Paul rather than Naughty Paul'. He agreed.

DISCUSSION

Dangerous behaviour that might lead to self-harm, evidenced in this session by Paul rocking backwards on his chair, is an unsuccessful attempt to stir up protective concern and find a sympathetic response in his mother. Steve's collapse into defeated depression when he is criticized for ordinary playfulness is probably the prelude to self-harm, biting himself, which he is known to do when chastised. When the therapist offered a receptive, uncritical space in her mind it was possible to get in touch with something more hopeful, but Mrs Cooper was too angry with the boys to use their interest creatively and soon she and the boys were in a verbal battle. They shocked her by talking of 'attacking her tits', possibly wanting to attack their mother for her lack of emotional nourishment. It is perhaps not surprising to hear that the boys broke windows and milk bottles on their estate and stole from others. The windows possibly represented their mother's eyes, in whose view they were blamed and through which reality was misconstrued, the milk bottles representing 'mum's tits'.

Illusory-haven

Risk-taking, dangerous behaviour occurs in the illusory-haven configuration in order to provide the parents and child with targets for their hostility and this is extremely dangerous to all involved. The illusory-haven is unstable and if it ceases to be maintained the child may experience unbearable loneliness and despair, and may contemplate or attempt suicide.

ANNA (8 YEARS)

Anna lived with both parents in a family that was pervaded with thoughts of sexual abuse. In spite of this, Anna spent a lot of time out of the home dressed as if she was a sexy teenager, which aroused much professional concern, although none in her parents, who thought she 'looked nice'. Anna's parents resisted professional advice, refusing to set boundaries and failing to see the importance of providing these for their 'princess', while organizing the community against her alleged abuser, Colin Smith, hoping to make him move away. Almost light-heartedly they wondered, 'who would move first, us or him?' It was to be hoped they would not both end up on the same estate again! Did Mr and Mrs Price have an intuitive awareness of their inescapable connection with an alleged abuser?

All of Anna's allegations were properly investigated but there was no evidence to substantiate them. Mr and Mrs Price did not change their views when the investigations found that there had been no evidence of abuse by the alleged abuser. They became angry with the authorities, who came to represent a neglectful parent, reminding Mr Price of his despised mother, who 'did not look beneath the surface'. Anna continued to have a favoured place at home, an illusory-haven, being their 'princess' while making relationships that were either to be mutually idealizing or allegedly abusive. The family were re-housed to remove them from the alleged abuser, yet Anna made a further allegation of abuse. Within the month Colin was dead. He appeared to have committed suicide. The death of Colin did not stop Anna's allegations of sexual abuse, which were now made against another stranger.

DISCUSSION

Mr Price was adept at forming a gang, which he did by assuming that others shared his views and acting on this, as described by Bion (1961 p. 153). Harris and Meltzer (1986) identified families that function in this way and referred to this pattern as the 'Gang Family'. Mr Price's powerful, intimidating personality made it difficult for anyone to disagree. Mrs Price was unable to take a different view from that of her husband. Much of the material in Anna's sessions illustrated the way in which she hoped to be a part of an exclusive couple, leaving someone else out. Anna was aware of the envy she might stir up by her freedom, her possessions and her idealized relationships. She could evade taking responsibility for herself, attacking anyone who tried to limit her by making believe that their actions were an expression of their envy and so could be ignored. Anna had internalized the family pattern: attacking the paternal function and using propaganda to prove to herself that she was privileged, when she was actually deprived.

One of the most significant factors obstructing Anna's progress through the Oedipal situation was her strategy for dealing with her intimidating father. In her sessions she occasionally revealed the deadly danger encountered if hostility were expressed between family members. She immediately went to the toilet to evacuate her feelings and restore her manic jollity. To avoid becoming the target for her father's anger, a third person was found who could take the brunt of his rage while she was able to remain his 'princess'. Anna may have anticipated a catastrophe if she were to acknowledge her negative feelings towards her parents, as this might irreparably damage her relationship and threaten her life. When Anna's illusory-haven failed her she was overwhelmed by loneliness and despair. She illustrated this by reading me an excerpt from the story about the Little Mermaid. If the mermaid were not chosen by the prince then she would disperse like 'foam on the sea'. It might have been in this state of mind that she had twice contemplated suicide, and physically given way, falling down the stairs, as she did towards the end of our sessions.

Perilous-haven

In this configuration, parents may be aware that their relationship with their child might play a part in the difficulties experienced and be willing to think about their child in order to try to make changes. The parent (typically mother) finds her child unpredictable and may say 'he's a Jekyll and Hyde', either a delight or frighteningly out of control. A perilous-haven is unstable and may settle into a no-haven in time. The child is able to use the attention of a therapist to explore his feelings. The therapist's capacity to think about the child's aggression is a crucial factor in initiating beneficial change. Parents can cooperate with professionals and can make changes with beneficial results.

BILLY (3 YEARS)

Billy was the youngest child living with both parents and his two teenage brothers. The family had moved house shortly before Billy was conceived. Mrs Heath said 'He came with the house. You know, new house, new baby'. Mrs Heath had not wanted to be pregnant and had cried for months. She told me that her husband did not agree with abortion so they had had to make the best of it. Mrs Heath did not want another boy; she might have found a welcome for a daughter. She would not hold Billy when he was born and suffered from a mysterious illness, which prevented her from caring for Billy in his first weeks. She went to work when Billy was three months old, although the money was not needed. Mrs Heath, whose relationship with her own mother was one in which separation had not been fully achieved, put Billy at a distance from herself. He was cared for by his aunt, where Mrs Heath began to realize that he was exposed to peer violence and neglectful care. In spite of this very difficult start for mother and child, Mrs Heath and Billy's relationship had developed some warmth and affection over time, although she could not understand Billy's dangerous active behaviour and was worried by his lack of fear.

When I saw Mr Heath alone he told me that he had been delighted with the pregnancy and that he wanted more children. It was his wife who did not want them. In spite of this, he was prevailed upon to have a vasectomy. This is perhaps an extreme example of what seemed to be a typical outcome of conflict between Billy's parents. Mr Heath acquiesced, possibly because he feared being made to feel lonely and 'left out'; a feeling he had experienced very painfully in childhood. It seemed that both parents bore considerable anger towards each other, which they could not resolve and which was expressed largely unconsciously.

Ten therapy sessions were planned for with mother and son, which led to beneficial change when Billy was able to experience his negative feelings being contained and thought about. This led to him exclaiming to me 'You like children, don't you!' Size was an important issue for three-year-old Billy, who claimed to be bigger than mummy and me. Interpretations of his wish to be invulnerable and his determination never to be afraid enabled him to begin to see reality more clearly. He was fascinated by this and urgently wanted to draw 'little me'. Two clinical vignettes have been selected to illustrate important aspects of Billy's situation. The first is one in which risk-taking, dangerous behaviour occurred in the clinical room and the second when Billy was able to let me know that he was afraid and what it was that made him fearful.

DANGEROUS BEHAVIOUR IN THE ROOM

When Mrs Heath talked to me, Billy began to climb on the top of the doll's house, putting himself in danger. I linked Billy's dangerous behaviour to him feeling angry and left out when mummy and I were talking and he got down, but he soon repeated this. Mrs Heath told Billy angrily, 'You'll get hurt! And what will happen then? You'll have to go to hospital'. This approach seemed to egg Billy on. Billy argued back saying, 'I'm not hurt!' It was very difficult to find a way of intervening that did not undermine Mrs Heath. She decided to make Billy sit on her knee where she eventually extracted a promise that he would not misbehave. When he got down he clearly wanted to break the promise and tried to do this slyly. I said it was hard for him to keep to his promise. Billy continued to be challenging and Mrs Heath told him that 'Mrs Anderson had thought him a clever boy and now she would not'. Billy made aeroplanes which he threw at me. I encouraged Mrs Heath to change the way she spoke to Billy when he was starting to behave in a dangerous way, telling him that 'it's not safe', rather than trying to engender fear in him. Billy became more cooperative.

THE FINAL SESSION: 'I'M SCARED'

When Billy put himself into danger in this session, Mrs Heath spoke to him saying it was not safe and for the first time in my presence he drew back from danger and resumed symbolic play.

Billy held a cow and fingered the horns, looking at me meaningfully, apprehensive and said 'I'm scared . . .' He said something that Mrs Heath recognized as the name of the killer whale in the film of Pinocchio. He drew the whale. He was frightened of this but he said he would 'punch it on the nose'. I asked him what frightened him about the whale and he said 'it might eat me up . . .'

The scene from the film is one in which Pinocchio seeks his father who has been consumed by the killer whale 'Monstro'. His kind, gentle father is no longer available and he must confront the fear of death in order to reach his good father through the ferocious teeth of the killer, representing the angry dangerous father.

DISCUSSION

Mrs Heath had not wanted Billy on two counts. She did not want a baby, still less did she want a boy. Although the relationship between mother and son had developed some warmth over the three years, Billy was not at all sure that he had a welcome in his mother's mind. In the first vignette, Billy began to behave in a dangerous way when he felt excluded from the couple formed while Mrs Heath and I conversed, and this dangerous behaviour was amplified when Mrs Heath attempted to discipline Billy by trying to make him fearful. When Mrs Heath told Billy that 'Mrs Anderson had thought him a clever boy and now she would not', she inverted the containment I had been offering to Billy, which had been so valuable: 'You like children, don't you?' I am represented as a person who cannot think well of Billy if his behaviour is difficult. Whatever safety had been provided by my thinking about all his feelings had been eliminated by these words. Billy was angry with me and showed this by throwing aeroplanes at me. Mrs Heath had created a gang-type couple with me by an intrusive identification (Meltzer 1992 p. 71), whose specific purpose was to expose Billy to a feeling of exclusion. Her abuse of my mind revealed the powerful and cruel way in which she could expel Billy and wreck his containment. Not only would she not contain his feelings, nobody would, not even the person who had shown that this was their function. This may explain why Billy might often attack a couple, if he felt that the purpose of the formation of this couple had been specifically to exclude him. Billy's choice of a place for the danger was the top of the doll's house, and this seemed to illustrate both his experience of the peril of being excluded from his mother's mind and the dangers within it.

In the second vignette, Billy was able to let us know that he was afraid. He feared being consumed by Monstro. Billy had identified himself with Pinocchio, who tried to be reunited with his good father by facing the ferocious creature that had engulfed his father. In order to do this Pinocchio, like Billy, needed to confront the fury of the angry parent, overcome this and find the good parent. If this is to be done, fear must be denied and danger approached. Mrs Heath tried to discipline Billy by attempting to make him fearful and this attempt was repudiated by him, first, because he repudiated fear, and second, because what she said had not happened: he was not hurt. He angrily tried to prove his mother wrong. When Mrs Heath ceased to try to stir up fear to discipline Billy, he was more cooperative.

If Billy achieved the heroic task of becoming reunited with a more kindly parental figure, then he might at times find that he was also involved in a gang of two. This was an illusory-haven, a seemingly special position that was unstable. The perilous-haven configuration is characterized by the child being in a double jeopardy, either being expelled and trying to confront an angry parent in order to find a sympathetic parent or fearing the loss of a fragile intimacy by being expelled.

Being with mother and son provided me with some difficult situations. I found that I was imperiled by trying to attend to the needs of both parties and threatened with a dangerous consequence from either if I failed to satisfy them. It was clear that Oedipal issues were fundamental to this situation; it seemed very difficult to create a triangular, three-way relationship; there was always the potential for three separate individuals to be reduced to two opposing sides by the use of intrusive identification. In spite of these significant difficulties Mrs Heath was able to try different approaches in handling Billy with a satisfactory outcome, as she did when she ceased to frighten him and told him simply 'it's not safe'.

Further and final thoughts

The most prominent findings of qualitative clinical research into risk-taking, dangerous behaviour in childhood have been presented. The central issue for children and families where there is risk-taking, dangerous behaviour is the hostility from the parent or parental couple to the child and how this is managed. External factors, such as poverty, or internal factors, such as the absence of an established Oedipal triangle, which decrease the parents' capacity to contain emotions and increase their hostility towards their child, create a situation in which feelings are uncontainable, leading to emotions being configured in one of the three configurations described: no-haven, illusory-haven or perilous-haven. Oedipal theory provides a structure in which the known risk factors associated with externalizing behaviour and the actual behaviour enacted by the child are accorded meaning. The outcome of the research has been to bring Oedipal theory into a central place in understanding risk-taking, dangerous behaviour and has led to the development of clinical concepts, the three havens, each of which has different implications both for prognosis and clinical strategies.

References

Anderson, J. (2006) Well-suited partners: Psychoanalytic research and grounded theory. *Journal of Child Psychotherapy*, *32*(3): 329–348.
Bion, W.R. (1961) *Experiences in groups*. London: Tavistock.
Bion, W.R. (1962) *Learning from experience*. London: Heinemann.
Collodi, C. (pen name Lorenzini Carlo) (1883) *The adventures of Pinocchio*. reprinted

by Oxford University Press (2000) entitled *Pinocchio*; also Walt Disney film *Pinocchio* (1943).

Freud, S. (1905) Three essays on sexuality. *Standard edition*, Vol. 7, pp. 125–245.

Freud, S. (1926) Inhibitions, symptoms and anxiety. *Standard edition* Vol. 20, pp. 77–175.

Glaser, B.G., Strauss, A.L. (1967) *The discovery of grounded theory*. Chicago: Aldine.

Harris, M., Meltzer, D. (1986) Family patterns and educability. In *Studies in extended metapsychology*. Perthshire: Clunie Press.

Meltzer, D. (1992) *The claustrum*. Perthshire: Clunie Press.

Sophocles (1942) Oedipus Rex, trans Grene, D. In *Sophocles 1; The Complete Greek Tragedies*. Chicago: Chicago University Press.

Chapter 13

Narratives in assessment and research on the development of attachments in maltreated children

Jill Hodges, Miriam Steele, Jeanne Kaniuk, Saul Hillman and Kay Asquith

Major physical or sexual abuse, and gross neglect, leave physical effects that are visible on examination or can be made visible via X-rays, scans, etc. However, the accompanying psychological and emotional trauma, and chronic emotional abuse and neglect itself, can have equally shattering effects. These are effects not upon flesh and bone, but upon children's understanding and expectations of attachments and family relationships, their capacities for the regulation and recognition of emotion, and hence their emotional and behavioural development.

How to make 'visible' these effects of maltreatment upon a child's mental representations has been a problem in the assessment of young children. Parental report, the mainstay of much clinical practice with children, has obvious limitations when the parents themselves may be the source of harm, especially when the assessment may concern the parents' future care of the child. The limited self-reflective and autobiographical memory capacities of younger children restrict the usefulness of direct interviews or questionnaires. Children may be silenced, or unwilling to reveal abuse for other reasons such as loyalty, self-blame, or fear of loss.

The Story Stem Assessment Profile (SSAP) was originally developed for the assessment of young children where there was concern about abuse or neglect, to assist long-term planning for the child's future. It was devised to provide detailed systematic information about the child's expectations and perceptions of family relationships, in a way that was relatively brief, non-intrusive, and made use of the child's own natural modes of self-expression. Rather than structuring the child's response itself, as questionnaires and similar measures do, the structure is provided by the rating system, allowing the child to respond freely. The detailed SSAP ratings can further be used to derive attachment construct scores for security, insecurity, disorganization and defensive avoidance, as well as other constructs such as positive and negative child and adult representations.

The child is given a series of 'narrative stems' – brief beginnings of stories, played out with doll and sometimes animal figures and simultaneously spoken, dramatized so as to engage the child emotionally in the scenario presented and activate the attachment system – and then the child is invited to 'show me and tell me what happens next'. The child's narratives are examined via a manualized, validated rating system, which allows comparison with other children of the same age (Hodges, Hillman, Steele & Henderson 2007). Both verbal and non-verbal aspects of the narrative are rated, allowing information to be gained from displayed behaviour, which may reveal implicit expectations, and making 'visible' the representations of attachment and family relationships that the child envisages in the story situation.

The SSAP includes story stems devised on the basis of clinical experience in the assessment of abused children, together with stems selected from the MacArthur Story Stem Battery (MSSB; Bretherton & Oppenheim 2003), which was devised for much wider research uses, and has been employed primarily with non-clinical populations. The stems are always administered in the same order, using a standard doll 'family', and also animal figures in two stories (Hodges, Steele, Hillman & Henderson 2003a, Hodges, Steele, Hillman, Henderson & Kaniuk 2003b). Interviews are video- and audio-taped and the transcripts, containing both the verbal and non-verbal narratives, are then rated in accordance with a manual. Each of the child's thirteen stories is rated for the presence of specified themes, covering representations of parents, representations of children, aggressive manifestations, indicators of engagement or avoidance, aspects of positive adaptation and indicators of disorganization. The rating manual provides detailed criteria and benchmark examples; raters trained on this system for research purposes achieved good levels of reliability on a three-point rating, percentage agreement overall being 87 per cent.

Individual children's narratives give a vivid picture of individual differences in expectations of parents and interactions, and efforts at defence and emotional regulation, as illustrated by the three short examples below. An assessment would not, of course, be based upon one stem, but takes all thirteen stories into account.

SSAP story 4

Picture from school

The child is at school, while the rest of the family are at home. While s/he is at school, the child makes a picture. S/he says 'This is really good, this picture I made! I like this picture! I'm going to take it home when I go home from school'. S/he takes it home after school and knocks at the door . . . Show me and tell me what happens now.

Irene (7 years old)

Irene showed the girl immediately climbing onto the parents' laps, saying 'Mum! Dad! I got a picture for you'. The mother responds 'Wow' in a tone of admiration. Irene said that the child sat 'on her Daddy's lap' and the story ended with the child watching TV with the parents.

Irene's narrative shows the child approaching the parents directly, expecting and receiving a straightforward positive response. She also displays some positive everyday family life. Some of her other story completions displayed much more difficulty and negative expectations. This range of representations reflected her experiences; she suffered many adverse experiences in her first years of life, including the breakdown of two planned permanent placements. However, at the point of assessment she had lived for well over a year in a foster placement. It was evident from her foster parents' descriptions and from observation that she was developing an attachment relationship with them, despite other difficult behaviour, and her narrative reflects the availability of this representation of responsive, positive relationships with parents, a hopeful prognostic indicator.

Jane (5½ years old)

In Jane's story completion, no-one answers the door. The girl comes in and puts the picture on the Mum's' lap, saying 'there'. Jane does not show any response or comment from the parents. The girl sits by her sister and they watch TV. Prompted with the question of whether the Mum or Dad said anything about the picture, Jane showed them saying 'It's a very good picture, well done'. Jane's tone as she gave these words was flat and affectless.

Jane's background was one of physical, and in particular emotional, neglect, by parents who were not actively abusive or aggressive but were very often insensible and unavailable to her because of drug misuse. She had remained in their care, with considerable input from her grandmother, until placement in a foster home several months before this assessment. In her narrative, Jane does not display negative affect or actively negative themes, but rather a lack of affect or responsiveness from the parents, and also little effort by the child to engage them, besides a lack of any positive praise or affection. Jane's response to the prompt suggests that she knows the desirable 'script' for the parents' response, but lacks conviction or expectation based on experience that this response will be forthcoming. Her other narratives were broadly consistent with this example.

Steven (just 8 years)

In Steven's narrative, the dad answers the door and asks 'What's that stupid picture?', then throws it away. The child figure runs away. The dad 'rips up his picture'. When prompted, Steven said that no-one else said anything about the picture, or noticed it. The rest of the family goes on a picnic, leaving the boy behind. They hide from the boy, who looks for them but cannot find them. He goes to his room at the top of the house and throws himself out – he 'cracked his head'. The Dad is very angry with him, calling him 'stupid' and locking him in the room. The boy then calls the police who say 'stupid kid'.

Steven's narrative, like others in his assessment, is strikingly undefended in its many aggressive and negative representations, which include active rejection by the parent and other (potentially helpful) adults. Steven had been exposed to domestic violence and maternal mental health problems, as well as emotional abuse, neglect and disruptions in care. Unlike many maltreated children (who may also show very aggressive and catastrophic material in their narratives), Steven showed very little defensive avoidance, such as reluctance to engage in the task, efforts to cut short his narratives avoiding elaboration or avoidance of anxiety-provoking themes given within the narrative stem.

Child psychotherapists are accustomed to children's individual clinical material providing such vivid and meaningful pictures, and children's narrative responses certainly generate such material in abundance. Over and above this, however, the rating system means that information can be derived from the child's narratives that is systematic, evidence-based in that the child's responses can be compared with reference groups of other children (see Clinical Assessment below), and designed for empirical research as well as clinical use. It is replicable, lends itself to standardization, and is transparent, in that it makes evident the basis on which judgements about the child are made.

What do children's story completions represent?

Children's narrative responses, across an array of different story-stem scenarios, reflect what they can imagine happening in these hypothetical situations. They are not, generally, autobiographical reports, but they are systematically related both to children's experiences and to how they as individuals deal with and can portray with those experiences (Hodges et al., 2003a). We see them as one 'window' into children's underlying basic scripts for human relationships; the examples above illustrate how different these scripts may be. The story stems allow a wide range of possible completions; if a child's narratives tend repeatedly to evidence the same kinds of themes, this points towards the existence of a particular underlying set of expectations, or mental representations.

Broadly, we take children's mental representations of relationships as equivalent to what Bowlby, in formulating attachment theory, referred to as 'internal working models'. From infancy onward, the child mentally organizes reality experience, constructing generalized representations of expectable interactions of self and others (Bowlby 1971, Stern 1985). These models come to guide the child's perception and understanding of current experience, and expectation of new interactions, and as they develop and stabilize they tend to become automatic, operating increasingly outside conscious awareness (Bretherton 1985). These models combine different forms of registration of experiences. They include non-verbal and non-conscious forms of memory, such as sensorimotor and 'habit' or 'procedural' memory – ('rules' governing behaviour and interaction with the world, which are not necessarily represented in consciousness). They also include generalized memories that can be verbally recalled as expectable 'scripts' for experience, and specific autobiographical memories; and it is these sorts of verbally based memory that are capable of being repressed into the unconscious as a result of anxiety and conflict. Although verbal and non-verbal forms of registration of experience may be congruent, this is not necessarily the case. An important feature of the narrative task and of the rating system is that it gives equal weight to children's verbal and non-verbal narrative responses, potentially allowing access to these different aspects of the representation. Crittenden (1994) notes that if children routinely experience abuse, these abusive experiences may no longer be represented as occasion-specific episodes but instead become a part of the child's 'unscrutinized, taken-for-granted understanding of the nature of relationships'. When a previously abused child enters a new adoptive family, his or her models for understanding the world may greatly distort that child's perceptions and responses to his or her new parents.

Importantly, representations of self and attachment figures are not homogeneous. Children can establish different attachment relationships with different caregivers, and also have the capacity to explore in imagination many counterfactual possibilities, which also form part of their mental representations; hence the importance of play as a version of thinking – an 'experimental kind of acting' (Freud 1911). Representations displayed in children's narratives may reflect imagined possibilities, as well as other defensive and emotional aspects; although structured by the child's earlier experiences, they do not simply mirror them. However, they are all available as part of the child's possible repertoire of internal representations. This can be an important indicator for future development. An abused child, who none the less possesses some mental representation of what can be expected from a good-enough parent, may be better able to recognize and use good-enough parenting in a new family than a child for whom such a representation is lacking or based tenuously on idealization, undercut by representations based on actual negative everyday experiences.

The natural history of change in attachments after adoption placement

An increasing number of studies have used narrative techniques to make assessments of children's mental representations of attachment relationships in their own families (e.g. Bretherton, Ridgeway & Cassidy 1990, Oppenheim, Emde & Warren 1997) including children in families where the parent has maltreated the child (e.g. Buchsbaum et al. 1992, McFie et al. 1999, McCrone et al. 1994, Toth et al. 2000; see Warren 2003 for a review of findings in risk and clinical populations). Clinically, we have used narrative assessments to examine mental representations of family life in children recently removed from maltreating families into foster care (Hodges & Steele 2000); thus studying the persisting effects of abuse and neglect.

We have also used the SSAP in research to track the emotional recovery of such previously maltreated children once placed in new families, and to demonstrate for the first time the 'natural history' of this process of slow and uneven recovery of the child's mental representations of attachment and family relationships (Hodges et al. 2003b, 2005). The SSAP technique has allowed us to go beyond existing studies of the progress of attachments in older adopted children, which has relied on parental report and observation in the absence of a means of examining the child's mental representations.

Such children are likely to be already showing difficulties as they leave care and enter their adoptive homes. In terms of reported and observed behaviour, differences between children adopted *in infancy* and those growing up in their birth families are generally small, compared to differences accounted for by demographic variables (Brodzinsky, Smith & Brodzinsky 1998, Hodges 2003). This is not the case for older children adopted from care, because of their prior experiences of abuse, and discontinuities of care prior to and within the care system. Children in Local Authority care have significantly more mental health difficulties than even the most socio-economically disadvantaged children living in private households (Ford, Vostanis, Meltzer & Goodman 2007), and children leaving care for adoption are a particularly high-risk group compared with those leaving care for other reasons (Performance and Innovation Unit (PIU) 2000). It was a group of such children whom we set out to study.

The attachment and adoption study

This research took the form of a prospective longitudinal study, carried out as a collaboration between Great Ormond Street Hospital, the Anna Freud Centre and the Coram Family Adoption Service.[1] We studied two groups of adopted children: one group had suffered major abuse and neglect, and multiple changes of caregivers, before being placed for adoption between the ages of four and eight years old. We carried out assessments, including the Adult Attachment Interview (AAI), with the adoptive parents prior to placement. As soon as practicable after placement, video-taped narrative assessments and other assessments were carried out with the child. At the same time, the parents were interviewed and other data were collected via questionnaire from the parents. We repeated these assessments one year and two years later. We compared these children with an age-matched group of children who were

1 We are grateful for the support of the Sainsbury Family Trusts, the Glasshouse Foundation and the Tedworth Charitable Trust; and the help and goodwill of the adoption agencies, adoptive families and children, who together made this research possible.

also adopted but had joined their families in infancy. They had not experienced the abuse and discontinuities of care that characterized the earlier lives of the late-adopted group, and had lived with their adoptive families for all but the first few months of their lives. We saw them at the same age as the late-placed group, and followed them up similarly after one year and two years. A follow-up study of both groups in early adolescence is now under way.[2]

In total, we studied 111 children, but a small number were lost to follow-up by the third assessment, and a few were found to have significant learning difficulties and/or autistic spectrum disorder. We excluded these from the analysis, so in what follows we report on a total of fifty-eight maltreated and forty-four early-adopted children. Both groups contained approximately half boys and half girls, and the great majority of children in both groups were white British.

The fifty-eight previously maltreated children were placed in thirty-nine different families. They had experienced an average of five different placements (ranging from two to eighteen) before entering their adoptive families. Most had been subjected to multiple forms of abuse. Our first assessment took place as soon as possible after they entered their new families, to examine the impact of their earlier maltreatment. In practice this was three to four months into placement.

We compared these late-adopted maltreated children with a group of children who were also adopted, but had been placed in their adoptive families below the age of twelve months. The mean age at placement was 3.73 months, ranging from a birth to eleven months. The mean age at first assessment was five years nine months, and the children were followed up for two years, exactly as for the previously maltreated group.

The child brings into the new adoptive family, by way of mental representations, harsh lessons learned from earlier experience about the unavailability, rejectingness or abusiveness of attachment figures, the powerlessness and vulnerability of the child, and the defensive behaviours, cognitions and emotional attitudes needed for survival. The hope is that the child will discover the new and positive possibilities of relationships with his or her adoptive parents. But the child's existing set of attachment representations governs not only expectation and prediction, but also the perception of current experience, so at times the child will inevitably perceive the adopters' behaviour as repeating past experiences with abusing or rejecting attachment figures, thus confirming the child's existing model. Further, this can be self-reinforcing: misperceiving others, children may react in ways that elicit responses that further confirm the existing models.

In setting out to study the course of change in internal representations, we therefore expected to find that some areas changed more, or more rapidly,

---

2 We are grateful to the Big Lottery Fund for supporting this research, and to the young people and families for their continuing willingness to participate.

than others. So in examining the attachment representations of the maltreated children as they enter their new adoptive families, it is not particularly useful merely to establish the child's global attachment category – maltreated children are unlikely to show 'secure' attachment organization, and likely to show attachment disorganization (Carlson, Cicchetti, Barnett & Braunwald 1989). Of greater interest is the fine-grained picture, the component elements subsumed under the general construct of a 'secure' or other attachment organization. For example, a secure organization suggests that there is a representation of parents as providing help and comfort, being responsive to the child's need, being aware when the child may be distressed and recognizing that children have a reasonable sense of self-efficacy and self-esteem. A securely attached child will be able to provide a relatively coherent story, without their response either being inhibited by anxiety or becoming extremely aggressive (Main, Kaplan & Cassidy 1985). Conversely, an insecure organization of attachment implies expectations that parents would not be consistently responsive in providing help or comfort, and could be aggressive or actively rejecting. Attachment disorganization is characteristic, in particular of abuse, reflecting the insoluble dilemma of a child whose attachment figure, needed as a source of protection, is simultaneously a source of threat. These children's narratives characteristically display catastrophic fantasy or extreme aggression unrelated to the story stem, or great constriction and avoidance of engaging in the narrative, often alternating between these characteristics (Solomon & George 1999).

Similarly, in examining changes in attachment during placement, we did not expect simply to find that children shifted from an 'insecure' category of attachment organization to a 'secure' one. This would be too gross a categorization to be useful; developmental recovery in maltreated children can take a very long time and it is likely that some of the effects of their earlier experiences will remain with them permanently or at least well into adulthood.

Rather, we aimed to find a way of examining subtler changes in the components of a child's attachment organization. Would some negative representations alter more readily than others, and were there discernible patterns in how children's attachment representations changed as they settled into adoptive families? Our approach here has some similarities to the technique used by Lush, Boston and Grainger (1991) to study internal change during psychotherapy in foster children. We examined changes in the individual ratings, the 'component elements' described above, so that we could see, for example, whether children became more likely to represent adults as offering help, or less likely to show them as rejecting. We also examined theoretically meaningful aggregate scores, so that we could see, for example, whether the construct of 'security', outlined above, increased over the course of placement.

Adoption study findings

Initial differences

At the first assessment after the late-adopted children joined their families, they differed markedly from the early-adopted group. Their mean construct score for security was significantly lower, and those for insecurity, defensive avoidance and active indicators of disorganization were higher. Many individual themes differed significantly; for instance, the narratives of the previously maltreated children were more likely to show adults unaware when children were distressed or in difficulty, and less likely to show adults as helpful to children. Detailed findings are given elsewhere (Hodges, Steele, Hillman, Henderson & Kaniuk 2005). The story stem findings related in meaningful ways to the Strengths and Difficulties Questionnaire (SDQ) total difficulties and subscale scores. Even at this early stage, a few months into the placement, it appeared that there were some parental effects upon the children's narratives, in particular that unresolved attachment organization in the adoptive mother, as assessed pre-placement on the AAI, was associated with more aggressive and disorganized story completions in the children (Steele, Hodges, Kaniuk, Hillman & Henderson 2003). These children's pre-placement histories were not especially adverse, and are unlikely to account for the finding, which recalls the way in which much younger infants rapidly reorganize their behaviour in concordance with the attachment organization of their foster carers (Dozier, Chase-Stovall, Albus & Bates 2001).

Changes over time in attachment representations

Two years into placement, the previously maltreated children's narratives showed a significant increase in the 'security' construct, as well as in many individual ratings. These ratings included themes of adults providing emotional comfort as well as practical help, being aware when children were in need of help, being affectionate and setting non-punitive limits. Correspondingly, as the children began to see adults as responsive to them, there was a significant increase in how often they showed children seeking help from adults, and a corresponding decrease in themes of magic or omnipotence to resolve difficulties, and of denial of distress.

Along side this increased expectation that attachment needs would be met, there was also a significant decrease in 'defensive avoidance' in its various forms; children became more able to elaborate their responses, both negative and positive, within the safety of a play narrative, suggesting improved affect regulation. They thus seem more able to use representational means to explore new forms of understanding of relationships between the self and attachment figures. In the Strange Situation, it is securely attached infants who have the freedom to engage in *physical* exploration of their surroundings (Ainsworth, Blehar, Waters & Wall 1978). As these older children develop an increasing sense of a secure base, they may become more able to use this *representational* form of exploration of emotional and attachment relationships, further assisting developmental recovery.

Along side these positive developments, however, mean scores on the constructs of Insecurity and Disorganization, for the whole previously maltreated group, did not decrease significantly. However, some children did show significant decreases, mainly those children placed with parents at least one of whom had been rated Secure-autonomous on the AAI (Steele, Hodges, Kaniuk, Steele, Hillman & Asquith, 2008).

In summary, our findings demonstrate that the children showed major progress (in which the attachment organization of the adopters played a significant part) but also that, two years on, the previously maltreated children still showed evidence of their earlier negative representations, and major differences remained between them and the comparison group.

Adoption interventions

Being able to chart children's expectations using the SSAP can provide valuable information for new adoptive parents. In clinical work we have found that narrative assessments early in placement can be used to guide both parents and professionals in understanding children's particular areas of vulnerability, planning appropriate management of difficulties and thus assisting the parents' handling of behaviour and the children's developmental recovery (Hodges 2007).

Clinical assessment

Individual clinical assessment can be benchmarked against the appropriate age group in the datasets now available. These comparisons are useful in assessing whether an individual child does lie within the expectable range, and providing a systematic comparison with those of other children.

As an example, take the following narrative completion for the 'Picture from school' story, by a severely emotionally abused boy aged seven:

> Child ('C') shows boy figure saying 'I'm going to take it home and show everyone'. Father answers the door, says 'Hello – oh, sorry', knocking boy over. C says that dad thought it was some post, and it wasn't really work from school, but something the boy made. The boy runs away. C says 'it *was* some post that he brang, and inside it was a bomb'. The bomb blows up, the people were 'just a little bit hurt'. The boy is nearly blown off a bridge by the wind, holds on but then is hit by the TV as the bomb blows the house up, and falls in the water hurt. Parents, brother

and the sofa all jump in the water to save him; 'For the end, he never done that again, the postman brang that, and they went to the police and the postman got arrested'.

Representations in C's narratives were relatively consistent across the thirteen story completions. His aggregated scores on the constructs of security, insecurity, defensive avoidance and disorganization (Fig. 13.1) can be compared with those from the first assessment of the research study cohorts. This makes it clear that even compared to the previously maltreated group, he showed very high scores on Insecurity and Disorganization, a very low score on the Security construct, and rather little defensive avoidance.

We can also compare *individual* ratings in a child's stories with other children in the same age group, again providing a benchmark for responses. For example, 'C' showed an *adult actively rejecting the child* in two story completions. Comparing this with other six- to eight-year-old children, we find that approximately 90 per cent of non-maltreated infancy-adopted six- to eight-year-olds, and 65 per cent of previously maltreated six- to eight-year-olds show this theme less often, suggesting that although it appears in only two of his narratives, it is nonetheless significant, especially in comparison with non-maltreated children.

Clinical series

Using the SSAP as a standard assessment tool has allowed us to begin a programme of systematic exploration of the impact of particular kinds of

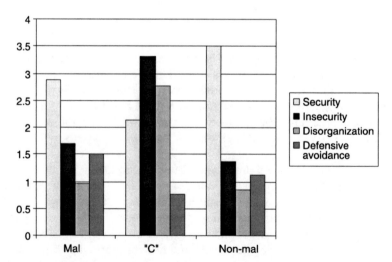

Figure 13.1 Aggregated Story Stem Assessment Profile (SSAP) scores from child C, maltreated (mal) and non-maltreated (non-mal) cohorts.

maltreatment upon children's internal working models, although this is complicated because maltreated children are commonly subject to more than one type of abuse. Varischio (2003) explored the impact of sexual abuse, Wilkinson (2004) examined fabricated or induced illness ('Munchausen's by proxy') and a number of other studies have examined forms of emotional abuse.

Standardization and comparison samples

At present, comparisons can be made with the non-abused, early-adopted children from the adoption research study, as well as between children subject to different types of abuse. Currently, this early-adopted sample represents our best low-risk comparison group, but even children adopted in infancy are at slightly greater risk than non-adopted children (Brodzinsky et al. 1988). Comparisons between this group and individual assessments or clinical series are therefore likely to err on the side of indicating fewer rather than more difficulties. A standardization study is in progress, which will provide a dataset on a sample of children who have always lived with at least one biological parent, and are not known to have experienced abuse or neglect. This will provide a 'normal' group for comparison, and allow further exploration of the psychometric properties of the SSAP.

References

Ainsworth, M., Blehar, M., Waters, E., Wall, S. (1978) Patterns of attachment: A psychological study of the strange situation. Hillsdale, NJ: Lawrence Erlbaum Associates.

Bowlby, J. (1971) *Attachment.* Harmondsworth: Penguin Books.

Bretherton, I. (1985) Attachment theory: Retrospect and prospect. In Bretherton, I. and Waters, E. (Eds) (1985) Growing Points of Attachment Theory and Research. *Monographs of the Society for Research in Child Development, 50* (1–2, no.209) 3–35.

Bretherton, I., Oppenheim, D. (2003) The MacArthur Story Stem Battery: Development, Administration, Reliability, Validity and Reflections about Meaning. In Emde, R.N., Wolf, D.P., Oppenheim, D. (eds) (2003) *Revealing the Inner Worlds of Young Children; the MacArthur Story Stem Battery and Parent Child Narratives.* New York, Oxford University Press 55–80.

Brodzinsky, D.M., Smith, D.W., Brodzinsky, A.B. (1998) *Children's Adjustment to Adoption; developmental and clinical issues.* Thousand Oaks, CA: Sage.

Carlson, V., Cicchetti, D., Barnett, D., Braunwald, K. (1989) Disorganised/disoriented attachment relationships in maltreated infants. *Developmental Psychology* 25, 525–531.

Crittenden, P.M. (1994) Peering into the black box: An exploratory treatise on the development of self in young children. In Cicchetti, D., and Toth, S., (eds) *Rochester Symposium on Developmental Psychopathology, Vol 5. The self and its disorders.* Rochester, NY: University of Rochester Press 79–148.

Dozier, M., Chase-Stovall, K., Albus, K., Bates, B. (2001) Attachment for Infants in Foster Care: The role of Caregiver State of Mind. *Child Development*. 72, 1467–1477.

Ford, T., Vostanis, P., Meltzer, H., Goodman, R. (2007) Psychiatric Disorder among British children looked after by local authorities: comparison with children living in private households. *British Journal of Psychiatry* 190, 319–325.

Freud, S. (1911) Formulations on the Two Principles of Mental Functioning. SE12, 221.

Hodges, J., Hillman, S., Steele, M., Henderson, K. (2007) *Story Stem Assessment Profile (SSAP) Coding Manual, GOS/AFC/Coram study, 2007 revision*. Unpublished manuscript, The Anna Freud Centre, London.

Hodges, J. (2003) Adoption and Fostering. In Skuse D. H. (Ed.), *Child Psychology and Psychiatry. An Introduction*. Abingdon: The Medicine Publishing Company.

Hodges, J. (2007) Understanding the child's development: using story stems to understand the legacy of past family experiences. British Agencies for Adoption and Fostering, Conference on the Assessment Framework, 19 March 2007.

Hodges, J., Steele, M., Hillman, S., Henderson, K. (2003a) Mental representations and defences in severely maltreated children: a story stem battery and rating system for clinical assessment and research applications. In Emde, R.N., Wolf, D.P., Oppenheim D., (eds) (2003) *Revealing the Inner Worlds of Young Children; the MacArthur Story Stem Battery and Parent-Child Narratives*, New York: Oxford University Press 240–267.

Hodges, J., Steele, M. (2000) Effects of abuse on attachment representations; narrative assessments of abused children. *Journal of Child Psychotherapy*, 26, 433–455.

Hodges, J., Steele, M., Hillman, S., Henderson, K., Kaniuk, J. (2003b) Changes in attachment representations over the first year of adoptive placement; narratives of maltreated children. *Journal of Clinical Child Psychology and Psychiatry*, 8, 3 July 2003, 351–367.

Hodges, J., Steele, M., Hillman, S., Henderson, K., Kaniuk, J. (2005) Change and continuity in mental representations of attachment after adoption. In Brodzinsky, D.M., Palacios, J. (eds), *Psychological issues in adoption. Research and practice*. Wesport, CT: Praeger.

Hodges, J., Steele, M., with Hillman, S., Henderson, K. and Neil, M. (2000) Effects of abuse on attachment representations; narrative assessments of abused children. *Journal of Child Psychotherapy* 26, 3, 433–455.

Kaniuk, J., Steele, M., Hodges, J. (2004) Report on a longitudinal research project, exploring the development of attachments between older, hard-to-place children and their adopters over the first two years of placement. *Adoption and Fostering*, 2, pp 61–75, BAAF, London.

Lush, D., Boston, M., Grainger, E. (1991) Evaluation of psychoanalytic psychotherapy with children: Therapists' assessments and predictions. *Psychoanalytic Psychotherapy* 5, 3, 191–234.

Main, M., Kaplan, N., Cassidy, J. (1985) Security in infancy, childhood, and adulthood: A move to the level of representation. In Bretherton, I., Waters, E. (eds.), Growing Points in Attachment Theory and Research. *Monographs of the Society for Research in Child Development*, 50 (1–2, no.209) 66–104.

Performance and Innovation Unit (PIU) (2000). *Prime Minister's Review of Adoption*.

Solomon, J., George, C. (1999) The place of Disorganisation in Attachment Theory;

linking classic observations with contemporary findings. In Solomon, J. and George, C. (eds) *Attachment Disorganisation* New York: The Guilford Press 3–32.

Steele, M., Hodges, J., Kaniuk, J., Hillman, S., Henderson, K. (2003) Attachment Representations and Adoption: Associations between maternal states of mind and emotion narratives in previously maltreated children. *Journal of Child Psychotherapy* 29, 2, 187–205.

Steele, M., Hodges, J., Kaniuk, J., Steele, H., Hillman, S., Asquith, K. (2008) Forecasting outcomes in previously maltreated children: The use of the AAI in a longitudinal adoption study. In Steele, H., Steele, M. (eds) (2008) *Clinical Applications of the Adult Attachment Interview*. New York: Guilford Press.

Stern, D.N. (1985) *The Interpersonal World of the Infant*. New York: Basic Books.

Varischio, L. (2003) LP Story stem battery nell'interpretazione del bambino maltrattato. Tesi di Laurea, Universita' degli Studi di Trieste, Facolta' di Psicologia.

Wilkinson, O.M. (2004) The effect of fabricated or induced illness on children's narrative representations. Thesis, MSc in Psychoanalytic Developmental Psychology, The Anna Freud Centre and University College London.

Chapter 14

Social neuroscience and theories of therapeutic action: Some implications for child psychotherapy

Linda C. Mayes and Prakash K. Thomas

A number of recent advances in social neuroscience potentially offer a new interface with relationship-based therapies and may, in particular, offer new insights into the mechanisms of therapeutic action for such therapies. While traditionally seen as very different domains of discourse with little to no common ground, in the last decade, many cognitive neuroscientists have turned to complex questions formerly considered outside the purview of experimental modelling. Empathy, affiliation, desire, remembering and memory are among the more complex states of mind that are being considered and modelled using contemporary neuroscience methods.

This chapter explores recent work in social neuroscience on the mirror neuron system, and ask how this emerging literature may inform the theory of therapeutic action in mental-health interventions with children. We also consider how potentially they may make an important contribution to psychoanalytic child psychotherapy. We focus on studies on the mirror neuron system, which has been shown to have considerable implications for the rapidity and universality of non-verbal human social discourse, especially for the process of empathy and understanding the minds of others. We stress that this is only one selection among a number of possibilities from contemporary social neuroscience that have relevance for psychodynamic interventions (see also Kandel 1999). In using this example, we make no claim for either a one-to-one correspondence in theory or mechanism. Rather, we propose that the suggested analogies point to shared themes and concerns between clinical work with children and social neuroscience that should be amenable to more careful study.

Mirror neurons and embodied action

Among the apparently unique characteristics of being human is the specially complex and fluid capacity to recognize oneself as a mental agent and to attribute mental states to others even when such states contradict one's own (Gopnik & Meltzoff 1994). Among these mental states are feelings, desires, beliefs and intentions, each the mental substrate of past, current, or not yet executed behaviours. Further, social relationships and social behaviour appear at the core of human behaviour, even from the first moments of interaction between a parent and a newborn. So central is social interaction to all aspects of human functioning that some have suggested social development as the primary nidus of evolutionary change and adaptation in humans (Tomasello 1999). How is it that these complex social abilities arise in humans? Are these abilities a specialized subset of more general cognitive information-processing capacities, or have these abilities emerged as specifically dedicated to social interaction (Blakemore, Winston & Frith 2004)? Even the simplest social interaction poses complex cognitive demands that are not necessarily generally required in most non-social, day-to-day activities (Baron-Cohen 1995). First, we need to recognize the other person as a mental agent with internal mental states similar to our own, at least in ability if not content. Then we rapidly intuit feelings, motivations and beliefs that are guiding the individual's behaviour, while simultaneously understanding that more stable personal characteristics also play a role in the other person's behaviour. At the same time, we decide, consciously or not, how our response may impact the other person, so as to respond both socially appropriately and perhaps to change or manipulate the other person's mental states and, hence, behaviour. These very complex transactions provide cause for suggesting that there may be a distinct set of social cognitive mental processes, and that the efficiency of these processes may in part be based on the mirror neuron system, a very specialized set of neurons first discovered in the early 1990s.

Mirror neurons and motor activity

Mirror neurons were first discovered in the macaque monkey's premotor cortex (Gallese, Fadiga, Fogassi & Rizzolatti 1996), in an area called F5, which is associated with hand and mouth movements. Expectedly, neurons in this region fire when the macaque reaches for an object, but less expectedly, these same neurons fire when the macaque simply sees an experimenter or another monkey performing the same action. These same neurons do not fire when, for example, the monkey observes a grasping motion with no object as a goal (Gallese et al. 1996). Similarly behaving neurons were subsequently discovered in the inferior parietal lobule and the superior temporal sulcus (Gallese 2000). The parietal cortex is reciprocally connected with both superior temporal sulcus and F5.

This special class of neuron was termed 'mirror neurons' because they seem active either when the subject is engaged in an action or when watching a similar action 'mirrored' in another's behaviour (Gallese et al. 1996). Fundamentally, then, mirror neurons seem essential to imitation – the ability to mimic an action that one has not ever seen before as in the classic experiments by Meltzoff and colleagues on newborns' ability to imitate the facial expressions of adults (Meltzoff & Moore 1977). Mirror neurons are a part of action understanding (Gallese 2001). Rizzolatti and colleagues suggest that action understanding precedes imitation, that is, the ability to understand another individual's action and the ability to do the same action are necessary for imitation to occur. Indeed, mirror neurons are not simply a response to the visual characteristics of the action with the goal detected by regions higher than the premotor cortex. Rather, mirror neurons seem to code the goal, and by interpretation, the intention of a given motor act (Rizzolatti & Craighero 2004).

For example, if the macaque has seen the object but then his line of vision is obscured from seeing the experimenter complete the reaching action, these same neurons in the F5 region of the premotor cortex still fire. Conversely, if the macaque does not see any object behind the screen, the neurons do not fire even if the experimenter makes a reaching motion (Umilta et al. 2001). The mirror neurons are apparently coding for the intention of the action rather than the action itself.

Thus, mirror neurons seem to code for a goal, such as grasping an object, regardless of the movements required to accomplish that act (Umilta et al. unpublished data) and findings such as those regarding similar action with different outcome suggest that mirror neurons may be a part of understanding the intentions of another's actions. For example, macaques grasping a piece of food are taught either to bring it to their mouth or put it in a container. Inferior parietal neurons discharge differently depending on the goal of the action – and more strongly for the food-to-mouth action. Further, a similar pattern occurs when the monkey watches an experimenter doing each of the same actions: mirror neurons discharge more strongly to the grasp-to-eat action compared to the grasp-to-place in the instance of food (Fogassi, Ferrari, Gesierich, Rozzi, Chersi & Rizzolatti 2005). Importantly, the neurons discharge before the monkey observes the completed action (either bringing the food to mouth or placing it in a cup). In this way, it appears the neurons code not only the observed motor action but also predict the other's next action, that is, the other's intentions (Gallese, Eagle & Migone 2007). How this prediction of the most likely intention occurs is not clear, but it may be based on the accumulated experience of observing which actions most often follow other actions. Different populations of motor neurons may be chained together to code the observed initial motor act, and the act that usually follows, in a given context.

Mirror neurons in humans

A mirror system similar to that found in the macaque monkey has also been identified in humans (Grafton, Arbib, Fadiga & Rizzolatti 1996) using a number of imaging techniques (Iacoboni, Woods, Brass, Bekkering, Mazziotta & Rizzolatti 1999). In early experiments, volunteers observed an experimenter grasping objects or performing meaningless arm gestures. In both conditions, there was increased neural activation in hand and arm muscles (Fadiga, Fogassi, Pavesi & Rizzolatti 1995). More recently, another study showed that, when observing another person's hand actions, there is modulation of motor evoked potentials from the hand muscles of the observers in temporal synchrony with the observed action, thus suggesting that the motor neuron system representationally matches the observed action in the observer in both the muscles involved and the temporal progress of the action (Gangitano, Mottaghy & Pascual-Leone 2001).

However, these and other experiments do not fully sort-out either specific regions of the brain or the relation to action plans or goals and intentions. In studies using positron emission tomography (PET), volunteers observed grasping actions and, as a control, looked at stationary objects. In these situations, seeing actions performed by another individual activated three main cortical regions – the superior temporal sulcus, the inferior parietal lobe and inferior frontal gyrus, including Broca's area (Buccino et al. 2001), the latter being a homologue to the macaque F5 area. Human mirror neuron systems are activated by both observation and execution of mouth-, hand- and foot-related actions, as well as in the imitation of simple finger movements (Iacoboni et al. 1999).

Human mirror neuron systems respond differently depending on the species observed. For example, in a functional imaging study, subjects were asked to observe communicative, but silent, mouth actions by a human, a monkey and a dog. Observation of human silent speech activated the left inferior frontal gyrus, a part of Broca's area, and observation of monkey lip-smacking activated a smaller part of the same area bilaterally. But observation of the silent but barking dog activates only the visual cortical areas. Thus, actions belonging to the repertoire of the species, that is, talking or lip-smacking, are mapped onto the human observer's motor system but actions not in the species motor repertoire are categorized on their visual properties only (Buccino et al. 2004).

Human mirror neuron systems appear as well to contribute to discerning intentionality of a not-yet completed motor action. Iacoboni and colleagues (2005) asked subjects to watch three kinds of stimuli in a functional imaging setting. The three stimuli were grasping hand actions without a context, a scene containing objects such as plates and cutlery (context only) and grasping hand actions embedded in a context. In the last condition, the context suggested the intention linked to grasping – either drinking or cleaning up. The question was whether the mirror neuron system would distinguish between grasping a cup to drink, as suggested by the context, and grasping the cup to put it away, as suggested by the cleaning-up context. The actions embedded in the context yielded a greater signal increase in the posterior inferior frontal gyrus and adjacent premotor cortex where hand actions are encoded. Further, mirror neuron activity was stronger in both situations in which the context suggested the end goal of the motor action in contrast to observing either the hand grasping a cup without a context or when looking at the context only. As with studies of non-human primates, these findings suggest that the mirror neuron system links basic motor acts to a larger 'motor semantic' network, which makes possible the rapid comprehension of others' behaviours.

Mirror neurons and emotional cues

Emotions also provide important contextual cues for understanding the intentions of motor actions. For example, in the macaque, neurons in the lateral area of F5 respond specifically to mouth actions such as grasping an object to eat, licking and biting. A percentage of these same neurons discharge while observing communicative facial actions performed by an experimenter. These so-called 'communicative mirror' neurons are recruited in the service of social communication (Ferrari, Gallese, Rizzolatti & Fogassi 2003). Further, like actions, humans likely understand emotions in more than one way (Rizzolatti, Fogassi & Gallese 2006). One pathway is through accumulated experience, that is, observing another person experiencing a specific emotion such as sadness may elicit a cognitive cascade processing the sensory information that produces a conclusion of what the other person is feeling (and through memory of personal experience, what the feeling may be like). Ekman has shown that simulation of another's facial expression is accompanied by the experience of the emotion being simulated (Ekman & Davidson 1994). Another pathway may be through a correspondence between the sensory and motor structures that would produce the experience of that emotion in the observer, such as the facial muscles for smiling or anger, as well as tightened fists with anger. The latter pathway is surely faster and may elicit at an experiential, embodied level the same feeling in the observer. There are emerging data suggesting this second pathway is related to the mirror neuron system. For example, feeling disgust activates a similar brain region (anterior insula) whether subjects experience the emotion while smelling an unpleasant odour or when watching a film of someone else looking disgusted (Wicker, Keysers, Plailly, Royet, Gallese & Rizzolatti 2003).

Parallels to the observation of motor actions occur when a subject is observing pictures of emotional face expressions. Their face muscles show muscle activity that corresponds to the facial muscles involved in the observed facial expression (Lundqvist & Dimberg 1995). Further, empathic individuals exhibit non-conscious mimicry of the postures, mannerisms and facial expressions of others (the chameleon effect) more than non-empathic individuals (Chartrand & Bargh 1999). In a study that relied on this effect (Carr, Iacoboni, Dubeau, Mazziotta & Lenzi 2003), participants were asked to observe and imitate emotional facial expressions. Findings from these experiments indicate that humans empathize with others through both observation and imitation of emotional facial expressions. Overlapping networks were activated by both observation and imitation of facial emotional expressions, including inferior frontal and superior termporal cortex as well as insula and amygdala. Moreover, the observation of emotional expressions robustly activated premotor areas. Fronto-temporal areas relevant to action representation, the amygdala and the anterior insula had significant signal increase during imitation compared with observation of facial emotional expression. The insula serves to connect the mirror neuron system to the limbic system. A modulation of the action representation circuit onto limbic areas via the insula should predict, as was observed, greater activity during imitation. In fact, mirror areas should be more active during imitation because of the simultaneous encoding of sensory input and planning of motor output; and the relay role of the insula should also be more prominent. Carr and colleagues suggest that the findings point to an embodied model of empathy. We understand the feelings of others by an empathic resonance grounded in experiencing actions and feelings associated with specific body movements. In other words, empathy invokes the representation of actions associated with the observed emotions. It is the link between mirror neuron, action representation systems and the limbic system via the insula.

Emotions are also conveyed through motor modalities other than facial expression. Touch conveys the wish to be close, and is often used as an expression of concern or of friendship. The experience of being touched on one's body activates the same neural pathways, the primary somatosensory cortex, as observing someone else being touched (Keysers, Wickers, Gazzola, Anton, Fogassi & Gallese 2004). These findings support a shared circuitry dealing with both first-person and third-person experience of touch, that is, when we observe someone being touched, we do not just see the touch and cognitively remember past experiences of being touched. Instead, we understand the touch through an automatic and rapid link with our sensory representation of how it feels to be touched in that specific manner.

Mirror neurons and language

Given the homology between the monkey's premotor area F5 and Broca's region, which is recognized as a key region in the understanding of language, several neuroscientists have suggested that the mirror neuron system represents the neural substrate from which human language evolved (Rizzolatti & Arbib 1998), a speculation that also speaks to the centrality of language in human social communication (Tomasello, Carpenter, Call, Behne & Moll 2005). That Broca's area contains mirror neurons also raises the question of how language might depend on the capacity for early imitation (Iacoboni et al. 1999). Studies not directly related to work on mirror neuron activity suggest a link between action and sentence comprehension. For example, Glenberg and Kaschak (2002) asked subjects to indicate whether a read sentence was nonsense or sensible by moving their hand toward a button (and away from the body) in one condition or toward the body in a second condition. Half of the sensible sentences described an action toward the subject and half described action away. Subjects responded faster to sentences describing movement that was congruent with the required response movement, that is, if the required response was to move away from the body and the sentence described such an action such as throwing, then the subject response was faster. Similar results are also found with sentences describing not action but transfer of information such as 'she told you about the game' versus 'you told her about the game'. In these examples, again response time is faster if the response movement is congruent with the implied movement of the sentence, that is, 'she told you . . .' would be congruent with a subject's arms moving toward their body and vice versa (Glenberg & Kaschak 2002).

Findings such as these lend support to the hypothesis of language as embodied, that is, for language describing action, the neural systems that execute an action are involved in understanding the semantic content of the same action described verbally (Lakoff & Johnson 1980). Such an embodiment hypothesis suggests that the mirror neuron system should be activated on listening to action-related sentences. Further evidence linking language and motor action comes from functional imaging studies. For example, silent reading of words, or listening to sentences referring to arm, leg or face actions, leads to activation of areas in the premotor–motor areas congruent with the meaning of the action words (Hauk, Johnsrude & Pulvermuller 2004). Listening to sentences expressing actions performed with the mouth, the hand and the foot produces activation of different sectors of the premotor cortex, depending on the muscle group used in the passively processed action-related sentences (Tettamanti et al. 2005). Similar findings also pertain both to other muscle groups and to sounds. Watkins and colleagues showed that listening to and viewing speech gestures increased the amplitude of motor potentials recorded from lip muscles (Watkins, Strafella & Paus 2003). Further, in an fMRI study, Wilson showed an activation of motor areas devoted to speech production while subjects passively listened to speech phonemes (Wilson, Saygin, Sereno & Iacoboni 2004). Fadiga and colleagues showed that listening to phonemes induced an increase in motor potentials recorded from tongue muscles that would be involved in the execution of such speech sounds (Fadiga, Craighero et al. 2002).

Embodied simulation

How do children understand the other's perspective and empathically relate to another's feelings? According to one theory, a child (or adult) adopts another's perspective, imagines mental states, such as feelings, beliefs, and desires that might be consonant with the other's perspective and, from these imagined mental states, infers the mental state of the other. By this theory, one understands or represents the mental activities of another person by a simulation process, that is, by imaginatively putting oneself in the position of the other and using one's mental processes to generate mental states and behaviours that can be attributed to the other person (Gordon & Cruz 2004).

But the findings from the various mirror neuron studies call aspects of this simulation theory into question. Gallese (2001) proposes a model of shared neurocircuitry, identifying brain structures that are active during both first- and third-person observation (Blakemore & Decety 2001). According to this 'shared manifold hypothesis', analogous neural networks generate analogous emotional experience that permits humans to understand and experience the emotions and sensations that others experience. And this ability is key to the human capacity to attribute minds to other persons and to intersubjectivity. In this embodied simulation theory (Gallese et al. 2007), understanding others' minds and intentions is not a deliberate, conscious effort but a non-conscious, near-reflexive mechanism in which neural circuits are similarly activated in response to another's behaviour. Because of the complex inter-connectivity between the mirror neuron system and other cortical regions, activation of these 'embodied circuits' also generates representational content about what the other person feels, believes and desires. The other person's emotion is experienced physically by the observer and thus directly under-stood almost as a shared body state. Observing the other's behaviour reflex-ively activates in the observer the same motor programme related to the observed behaviour and, in so doing, makes a direct experiential line between the observer and the observed. Activating similar neural circuits in both the observer and the observed enables 'experienced' or embodied understanding even before full conscious awareness. This attuned state makes possible empathic connections to other persons that do not replace or supersede more conscious, sensory or attributional descriptions of what is observed but do place the observer in a physical state approximate to performing a similar action or experiencing a similar feeling.

Implications of mirror neuron systems

Importantly, the work on the mirror neuron system is just beginning and has not yet addressed questions of special relevance to clinicians, and especially to those working with children. These are questions regarding developmental change and sources of individual differences in the mirror neuron system. When might we expect, for example, full elaboration of the mirror neuron system in children? Early work on imitation in newborns and very young infants suggests that at least some components of the system are in place from very early on (Meltzoff & Moore 1977) but how early might the more elaborated aspects of embodied language be active? Might such language be a key part of early parent–infant interaction, and when such interactions are altered, as in instances of parental depression or illness, how might this impact the relationship between language and the mirror neuron system? Related to individual differences, how might this impact on conditions such as depression affect parents' embodied response to their infant? Given the connections between limbic and mirror neuron systems, how does stress impact these embodied responses? Does early stress, as in abuse and/or neglect, impact the development and/or functioning of the mirror neuron system?

Despite these, and many other questions yet to be studied, there are several ways that this work may influence how clinicians think about child development and therapeutic work with very young children. For example, in Winnicott's early concept of the mirroring role of a mother in her response to her infant, he considers how the infant's sense of self differentiates from the mother's consistent mirroring of the infant's feelings and needs (Winnicott 1965). Other developmentalists, including Stern (1985), draw attention to an intersubjective process between parents and infants that involves often coordinated, synchronized movement, voice, prosody of speech and facial expressions. Developmental theorists have assumed that an infant's sense of self and awareness of mental states is constructed from these many accumulated interactive moments. What has always been unstated in these theories is how this construction occurs. Mirror neuron systems may provide one such mechanism, with the automatic mirroring of action patterns that are, in turn, a part of complex mental states. That embodied simulation is made possible through mirror neuron systems and results in a capacity to understand the mental states of others is key to the speculated relevance of mirror neuron models to psychotherapy. Furthermore, to understand more about functions of mirror neurons, clinical work may be particularly useful in enabling us to ask the right questions of neuroscience research as Fonagy (see Chapter 1) suggests.

Relation to therapeutic work with children

The mechanism(s) by which the mirror neuron system may facilitate empathy and understanding of other minds has implications for ways of knowing in the course of a therapeutic relationship. This is especially true for work with children in which so much of the therapeutic transaction is non-verbal and sometimes very physical (such as when a very young child crawls into a therapist's lap for comfort or reaches out to take a therapist's hand as they walk to the consulting room). Surely all work to date on mirror neuron systems and the relation to 'embodied simulation' (Gallese et al. 2007) is based on directly observable behaviours, such as actions, speech or emotional expressions, whereas much therapeutic work with children may be concerned with unconscious mental states as reflected by the child's play, non-verbal actions and verbalizations.

Granted, then, that the mirror neuron model of empathy as an embodiment of the experience of the other may not fully account for the conscious or top-down processing of the therapist at work – or the therapist reflecting on his or her work with the child – how might these new findings inform ideas about the therapeutic action of relationship-based work with children and families? A number of theorists, including especially Kohut (1984), have spoken about the potential for psychic repair in the face of the therapist's empathic understanding. Similar processes are spoken about in the relation to children, although in this case repair is less the emphasis and more how the therapist's empathic responding helps the child experience him- or herself as better regulated emotionally and as an effective agent that, in turn, may restore adaptive development. In either case, the mechanism of how empathic understanding by a therapist facilitates patient recovery and/or resumed development is still a black box. What we might consider in this case is how both the child and the therapist respond to each other's actions in terms of language, facial expressions and motor behaviour and how, if the mirror neuron model applies, each is responding quickly and non-consciously to the embodied action of the other. A child responds non-verbally to the therap- ist's quiet, gentle stroking of the 'injured' teddy bear and reaches out to stroke the bear him- or herself or may gently touch the therapist's hand. Although the therapist may comment on how hurt or lonely the bear is, much of the communication in this act is non-verbal. In this moment, the child 'mirrors' the therapist's action and by the assumptions of the mirror neuron model or embodied imitation, we might say the child is experiencing the therapist's 'touch' upon his or her own body as well as the therapist's calm (and calming) facial expression. In this way, the therapist's non-verbal actions convey meaning in a directly experienced, bodily sense and the child's embodied simulation of the therapist's actions may clarify the child's own feelings and sense of self-efficacy. Or, considering what Fonagy and col- leagues (2002) have suggested about adult patients in similar instances, the therapist is attuned to the child through his or her embodied simulation of the child's emotional expressions (such as fear or sadness), which in turn is experienced in the child as a simulation of the therapist's response. This continual, congruent, attuned feedback process helps the child 'see' him- or herself in the therapist's actions and experience the containment of his or her feelings. In the language of mentalization (Fonagy & Target 1996), the child experiences him- or herself as having a place or as being represented in the therapist's mind, which helps the child understand him- or herself and see him- or herself through the mind of another helping adult. We might hypoth- esize that, over time, these kinds of embodied experience in the course of a therapeutic relationship are 'learned' as strategies for more adaptive emo- tional and behavioural regulation.

It is important to note that in these instances of communication between a child and therapist, literal mirroring of the child's emotional expression or behaviour is not likely to be therapeutic because of its repetitive nature. It does not provide the child with an embodied response that helps the child learn about his or her own emotional experiences and ways to regulate them.

Such speculation is analogous to Fonagy and colleagues' models (Fonagy & Target 1996) examining how parents mirror their infants, although caution is advised in making too close an analogy between the therapeutic and parenting relationship. The former actively seeks to understand a child's mental world and conveys that understanding to the child through verbal and non-verbal communications. The therapist conveys to the child not a simple copy of the child's experience but one transformed by the therapist's own embodied response and top-down processing of the meaning of both the child's behaviour and the therapist's experience of that behaviour.

It is, of course, critical that these kinds of extrapolations from mirror neuron models are studied in the laboratory. For example, do children show activation of mirror neuron systems when the therapist manipulates a toy, that is, to an action not toward the child but in displacement? Are there important differences in impact between verbal and non-verbal interventions? Do these models imply necessary change in technique or simply a greater appreciation of the potential impact of non-verbal action responses and emotional expressions in the therapeutic relationship? Importantly, these notions of embodied simulation arising from the work on mirror neurons do not replace or diminish how essential it is for therapists to consciously strive to build an understanding of individual patients and the very necessary role of conscious insight into, and reflection on, an individual patient's psychic organization.

Summary

Therapy is not simply imitation and repetition of emotion and behaviour but an intellectual perceiving of emotion and intentionality. The theory of embodied simulation does not preclude the conscious effort of minding emotions and intentions observed in the patient and reflected within the therapist. The challenge appears to lie in integrating conscious and verbally mediated perception with the largely non-verbal, somatic and intersubjective understanding that mirror neural networks provide. Only with such integration can therapeutic technique be influenced and further refined.

References

Baron-Cohen, S. (1995) Mindblindness: An essay on autism and theory of mind. Cambridge, MA: MIT Press.

Blakemore, S., Decety, J. (2001) From the perception of action to the understanding of intention. *Nature Reviews Neuroscience, 2*, 561–567.

Blakemore, S. J., Winston, J., Frith, U. (2004) Social cognitive neuroscience: Where are we heading? *Trends in Cognitive Sciences, 8*, 216–222.

Buccino, G., Binkofski, F., Fink, G. R., Fadiga, L., Fogassi, L., Gallese, V., Seitz, R. J., Zilles, K., Rizzolatti, G., Freund, H. J. (2001) Action observation activities premotor and parietal areas in a somatotopic manner: An fMRI study. *European Journal of Neuroscience, 13*, 400–404.

Buccino, G., Lui, F., Canessa, N., Patteri, I., Lagravinese, G., Benuzzi, F., Porro, C. A., Rizzolatti, G. (2004) Neural circuits involved in the recognition of actions performed by nonconspecifics: An fMRI study. *Journal of Cognitive Neuroscience, 16*, 114–126.

Carr, L., Iacoboni, M., Dubeau, M. C., Mazziotta, J. C., Lenzi, G. L. (2003) Neural mechanisms of empathy in humans: A relay from neural systems for imitation to limbic areas. *Procedures of the National Academy of Science, 100*, 5497–5502.

Chartrand, T. L., Bargh, J. A. (1999) The chameleon effect: The perception-behavior link and social interaction. *Journal of Personality and Social Psychology, 76*, 893–910.

Ekman, P., Davidson, R. (1994) *The nature of emotions: Fundamental questions.* New York: Oxford University Press.

Fadiga, L., Craighero, L., Buccino, G., Rizzolatti, G. (2002) Speech listening modulates the excitablity of tongue muscles: a TMS study. *European Journal of Neuroscience, 15*, 399–402.

Fadiga, L., Fogassi, L., Pavesi, G., Rizzolatti, G. (1995) Motor facilitation during action observation: A magnetic stimulation study. *Journal of Neurophysiology, 73*, 2608–2611.

Ferrari, P., Gallese, V., Rizzolatti, G., Fogassi, L. (2003) Mirror neurons responding to the observation of ingestive and communicative mouth actions in the monkey ventral premotro cortex. *European Journal of Neuroscience, 17*, 703–1714.

Fogassi, L., Ferrari, P. F., Gesierich, B., Rozzi, S., Chersi, F., Rizzolatti, G. (2005) Parietal lobe: From action organization to intention understanding. *Science, 302*, 662–667.

Fonagy, P., Gergeley, G., Jurist, E. L., Target, M. (2002) *Affect regulation mentalization, and development of the self.* New York: Other Press.

Fonagy, P., Target, M. (1996) Playing with reality: I. Theory of mind and the normal development of psychic reality. *International Journal of Psychoanalysis, 77*, 217–233.

Gallese, V. (2000) The acting subject: Towards the neural basis of social cognition. In: Metzinger, T. (ed.) *Neural correlates of consciousness: Empirical and conceptual questions* (pp. 325–333). Cambridge, MA: MIT Press.

Gallese, V. (2001) The 'shared manifold' hypothesis: From mirror neurons to empathy. *Journal of Consciousness Studies, 8*, 33–50.

Gallese, V., Eagle, M. N., Migone, P. (2007) Intentional attunement: Mirror neurons and the neural underpinnings of interpersonal relations. *Journal of the American Psychoanalytic Association, 55*, 131–176.

Gallese, V., Fadiga, L., Fogassi, L., Rizzolatti, G. (1996) Action recognition in the premotor cortex. *Brain, 119*, 593–609.

Gangitano, M., Mottaghy, F. M., Pascual-Leone, A. (2001) Phase-specific modulation of cortical motor output during the movement observation. *NeuroReport, 12*, 1489–1492.

Glenberg, A. M., Kaschak, M. P. (2002) Grounding language in action. *Psychonomic Bulletin and Review, 9*, 558–565.

Gopnik, A., Meltzoff, A. N. (1994) Minds, bodies, and persons: Young children's understanding of the self and others as reflected in imitation and theory of mind research. In: Parker, S. T. et al. (eds) *Self-awareness in animals and humans: Developmental perspectives* (pp. 166–186). New York: Cambridge University Press.

Gordon, R., Cruz, G. (2004) Simulation theory. In: Nadel, L. (ed.) *Encyclopedia of cognitive science*. London: Nature Publishing Group.

Grafton, S. T., Arbib, M. A., Fadiga, L., Rizzolatti, G. (1996) Localization of grasp representations in humans by positron emission tomography. *Experimental Brain Research, 112*, 103–111.

Hauk, O., Johnsrude, I., Pulvermuller, F. (2004) Somatotopic representation of action words in human motor premotor cortex. *Neuron, 41*, 301–307.

Iacoboni, M., Molnar-Szakacs, I., Gallese, V., Buccino, G., Mazziotta, J., Rizzolatti, G. (2005) Grasping the intentions of others with one's own mirror neuron system. *PLOS Biology, 3*, 529–535.

Iacoboni, M., Woods, R. P., Brass, M., Bekkering, H., Mazziotta, J. C., Rizzolatti, G. (1999) Cortical mechanisms of human imitation. *Science, 286*, 2526–2528.

Kandel, E. (1999) Biology and the future of psychoanalysis: A new intellectual framework for psychiatry revisited. *American Journal of Psychiatry, 156*, 505–524.

Keysers, C., Wickers, B., Gazzola, V., Anton, J. L., Fogassi, L., Gallese, V. (2004) A touching sight: SlI/PV activation during the observation and experience of touch. *Neuron, 42*, 1–20.

Kohut, H. (1984) *How does analysis cure?* Chicago: University of Chicago Press.

Lakoff, G., Johnson, M. (1980) *Metaphors we live by*. Chicago: University of Chicago Press.

Lundqvist, L., Dimberg, U. (1995) Facial expressions are contagious. *Journal of Psychophysiology, 9*, 203–211.

Meltzoff, A. N., Moore, M. K. (1977) Imitation of facial and manual gestures by human neonates. *Science, 198*, 75–78.

Rizzolatti, G., Arbib, M. (1998) Language within our grasp. *Trends in Neurosciences, 21*, 188–194.

Rizzolatti, G., Craighero, L. (2004) The mirror neuron system. *Annual Reviews of Neuroscience, 27*, 169–192.

Rizzolatti, G., Fogassi, L., Gallese, V. (2006) Mirrors in the mind. *Scientific American, November*, 30–37.

Stern, D. N. (1985) *The interpersonal world of the infant: A view from psychoanalysis and developmental psychology*. London: Basic Books.

Tettamanti, M., Buccino, G., Saccuman, M. C., Gallese, V., Danna, M., Scifo, P., Fazio, F., Rizzolatti, G., Cappa, S. F., Perani, D. (2005) Listening to action-related sentences activates fronto-parietal motor circuits. *Journal of Cognitive Neuroscience, 17*, 273–281.

Tomasello, M. (1999) *The cultural origins of human cognition*. Cambridge, MA: Harvard University Press.

Tomasello, M., Carpenter, M., Call, J., Behne, T., Moll, H. (2005) Understanding and sharing intentions: The origins of cultural cognition. *Behavioral & Brain Science, 28*, 675–691.

Umilta, M. A., Kohler, E., Gallese, V., Fogassi, L., Fadiga, L., Keysers, C., Rizzolatti, G. (2001) 'I know what you are doing': A neurophysiological study. *Neuron, 31*, 155–165.

Watkins, K. E., Strafella, A. P., Paus, T. (2003) Seen and hearing speech excites the motor system involved in speech production. *Neuropsychologia, 41*, 989–994.

Wicker, B., Keysers, C., Plailly, J., Royet, J. P., Gallese, V., Rizzolatti, G. (2003) Both of us disgusted in my insula: The common neural basis of seeing and feeling disgust. *Neuron, 40*, 655–664.

Wilson, S. M., Saygin, A. P., Sereno, M. I., Iacoboni, M. (2004) Listening to speech activates motor areas involved in speech production. *Nature Neuroscience, 7*, 701–702.

Winnicott, D. W. (1965) Ego distortion in terms of true or false self. *The maturational processes and the facilitating environment* (pp. 140–152). New York: International Universities Press.

Index